Technology,
Reading, and
Language Arts

Technology, Reading, and Language Arts

Jerry W. Willis
University of Houston

Elizabeth C. Stephens
University of Houston Clear Lake

Kathryn I. Matthew
Louisiana Tech University

Allyn and Bacon

Boston • London • Toronto • Sydney • Tokyo • Singapore

Vice President, Education: Nancy Forsyth
Editorial Assistant: Kate Wagstaffe
Senior Marketing Manager: Kathy Hunter
Production Administrator: Rob Lawson
Cover Administrator: Linda Knowles
Manufacturing Buyer: Megan Cochran
Composition Buyer: Linda Cox
Editorial-Production Service: Electronic Publishing Services Inc.

Copyright © 1996 by Allyn & Bacon
A Simon & Schuster Company
Needham Heights, Massachusetts 02194

Library of Congress Cataloging-in-Publication Data

Willis, Jerry.
    Technology, reading, and language arts / Jerry W. Willis,
Elizabeth C. Stephens, Kathryn I. Matthew.
        p. cm.
    Includes bibliographical references and index.
    ISBN 0–205–16286–X
    1. Reading—Computer-assisted instruction. 2. Language arts—
Computer-assisted instruction. 3. Educational technology.
I. Stephens, Elizabeth C. II. Matthew, Kathryn I. III. Title.
LB1050.37.W45   1995
428.4'0285—dc20
                                                     95–35546
                                                      CIP

Printed in the United States of America

10 9 8 7 6 5 4 3 2 1   99 98 97 96 95

We dedicate this book to:

The HIT Group - which is short for Houston Instructional Technology Group. HIT is an active, energetic group of faculty in the College of Education at the University of Houston who are involved in the creation, use, and diffusion of instructional technologies.

and

The outstanding group of graduate students in the UH College of Education who have selected an aspect of instructional technology as their focus for research, practice, and development work.

Contents

CHAPTER 3

Cognitive Constructivist Approaches   45

C H A P T E R 4

Skills-Based Direct Instruction and Technology   67

C H A P T E R   5

Just-in-Time Direct Instruction   95

C H A P T E R   6

Cognitive Skills Direct Instruction   117

APPENDIX

Preface

We had two broad goals in mind when we wrote this book. The first was to inspire. In our own work we find information technologies such as computers and telecommunications to be very useful in many aspects of literacy instruction. This book introduces teacher education students to many of those uses. However, it is not a "how to" book with detailed "press this key" passages. Nor is it a compilation of lesson plans that teacher education students can use to "teach with technology" during their field placements and student teaching, nor a collection of educational software reviews. Instead we have attempted to present a series of conceptual frameworks for thinking about how technology can support instruction—frameworks that will help teachers effectively integrate technology into their own teaching. Naturally, students will need to do much more than read chapters in this book, but a primary purpose for writing this book was to create visions of what information technologies can do that would inspire students to take those additional steps. Thus we have tried to write the book between the level of vague generalities that are difficult to translate into practice and the how-to-do-it specifics that belong in the user manuals of specific programs.

The second major goal in writing this book was to relate theory to practice. Far too many papers, and books, on the use of computers in reading, language arts, English, and literacy instruction take one of two extremes. The first extreme presents one way of using technology (and one theory of instruction) as if it were The Only Way. That presents an impoverished and limited view of technology in education, as if the technological garden has only one family of flowers. In reality, the technology garden is a rich collection of multicolored blossoms that cannot be understood and appreciated by examining just one flower. (We hope you will forgive our flower analogies, but the Bluebonnets and Indian Paintbrush are blooming in Texas as we write this.)

The second extreme involves presenting a range of ways technology can be used but without connecting them to the rich variety of theories, instructional strategies, and models of instruction that populate today's literacy landscape. That approach does not reflect the context of either research or professional practice. A teacher using a language experience approach, or the reading/writing workshop approach, is not likely to be enthusiastic about a new drill and practice program on proper use of commas and semicolons. On the other hand, a teacher who spends most of his or her time teaching phonics skills is not likely to be interested in collaborative writing software that is designed to be used in a language experience classroom. In this book we have tried to relate different ways of using technology to the different theories and traditions in literacy instruction. Collaborative writing software, for example, is covered in a chapter that also introduces other constructivist approaches. Drill and practice software is discussed in a chapter on behavioral approaches to direct instruction. We believe this approach, which places technology in the background and the models or theories of instruction in the foreground, is the best way to help students situate the use of technology within their own frames of reference.

We designed this book for several types of courses. It is short enough to be used as a supplemental or secondary text in "educational computing" or "technology for teachers" courses that are commonly taught in the second or third year of an undergraduate teacher education program (and in many graduate programs that prepare teachers). It also fits well in methods courses, both graduate and undergraduate, especially when the main textbook includes very little on the use of technology in the classroom.

A growing number of programs are adding separate courses on topics like "Technology and the Literacy Classroom" and "Computers, Reading, and Language Arts." This book can be used as a primary text in such courses. A separate course provides the time to go beyond inspiration and conceptual frameworks and explore the growing body of scholarly and professional literature. In many areas visits (actual or electronic) to technology-rich classrooms are possible. A separate course would provide much more time for activities that translate the concepts into practice—creating lesson plans, teaching lessons in real or simulated classes, and engaging in microteaching activities such as those suggested at the end of most chapters in this book.

While there is a great deal of information in this book, we believe students must do more than read the information to become technology-using teachers. They need to try out ideas and to experiment. With that in mind we have selected a disk of software and instructional materials that can be used with this book. The "disk" is actually available over the Internet in a variety of formats. Send an e-mail message to jwillis@jetson.uh.edu and ask for current information on where you can download the disk. It contains demos of commercial software relevant to each chapter in the book as well as shareware and public domain programs that can be used to complete many of the microteaching activities at the end of chapters.

For every book a professor writes there are probably at least a thousand books he or she thinks about writing. For seven years this book was one of those we thought about but didn't write. The reasons were many—lack of time; annual rumors that a "great textbook on computers and literacy education will be out in the fall," or spring, or summer; a concern that it would be difficult to write a text that did not concentrate on one area, such as initial literacy instruction or high school composition. This last concern was removed when we began working together at the University of Houston. Kathy Matthew has extensive experience with the use of technology in elementary literacy instruction and has won awards for software she developed for use in preservice teacher education. Her dissertation involved an analysis of the use of electronic children's books in the classroom. Elizabeth Stephens has taught composition, journalism, and reading in the middle grades and high school. Her dissertation involved the creation of a computer-controlled laserdisk of classroom "minicases" about the use of the reading/writing workshop approach. The minicases currently are used in a number of teacher education programs. Jerry Willis has written many textbooks on the use of technology in education and is editor of the *Journal of Technology and Teacher Education* as well as associate editor for issues and innovations for the journal *Computers in the Schools*. Individually, writing this book would have been a daunting task. Together, the task was still daunting, but we believe we created a much better book through the collaboration. We would welcome comments, suggestions, and critiques. Feel free to send them via e-mail to: jwillis@jetson.uh.edu.

The authors thank the following reviewers for their helpful suggestions: Cathy Gunn, Margaret Moore, and Thomas Drezdowski. The authors also thank the staff at Allyn & Bacon for their help in keeping this book on track.

Technology, Reading, and Language Arts

CHAPTER ONE

Contexts and Content: Approaches to Literacy Education

Every teacher in our schools is a main character in the story of American education. As literacy teachers, we are especially important characters because we are charged with the preservation of our traditions. We teach at least two very basic skills—reading and writing—and we bring the world's literacy into the classroom. In a sense, then, we are the filter through which the world's views are passed on to students. What we choose to teach, and how we choose to teach, is critical. We must continuously make decisions about both the what and the how of teaching.

Beverly, a middle school language arts teacher, for example, had an enlightening encounter with her teaching methods—one that gave her a little more insight into her role as a filter.

Beverly's Story

The halls were quiet. Most of the kids had climbed on their buses or walked home, and Hillside Middle School seemed almost too quiet to Beverly. She'd finished grading the last set of student performance printouts from the adjective usage exercises and sat at her desk thumbing through the teacher's edition of the 7th-grade basal to prepare lesson plans for the next week. As she turned to the front of the guide, her manila folder of printouts slid off her desk and the papers spilled out across the floor. Patiently, she leaned down from her chair to gather them. When they were neatly collected once again, she sat erect on her chair. She did not notice the man sitting in the last desk of the first row until she stretched across her desk to place the folder on top of the pile she would take home with her today. Startled, Beverly dropped the folder too close to the edge of the desk and printouts scattered on the floor again.

"They credit me for those, you know," he said calmly.

Still stunned by his presence, Beverly said nothing. When did he come into her room? Why hadn't she noticed? Why is he wearing old-fashioned clothes? What does he want? Is he a parent? Is she in danger? Who is he? Her mind was filled with questions.

"I'm sorry I startled you," the man said as he stood up and started walking toward her desk. He was a soft-spoken slender man, not very tall. He wore a gray suit with a very thin tie and rather baggy pants. He walked with an air of confidence and authority. His gray hair was very short and it had thinned considerably at the top of his head. He had a large forehead, thin lips, and a pointed chin. From behind his black-plastic frame glasses, his eyes, deep-set and gentle, gazed intently at the spilled printouts on the floor. He reached down and swiftly gathered the papers. Before placing them in the folder, he stared at the top paper as if studying it.

"Humph," he said softly. As he stood, he placed the papers in the folder and the folder on the corner of Beverly's desk.

"I should have introduced myself," he said. He stepped back and sat in the first student's desk of the row directly in front of her desk. "You probably have never heard of me. I'm very much a part of you, though—that is, a part of what you do in this classroom."

Beverly was now more confused, and although she sensed from the gentleness of the man that she was not in any kind of danger, she remained cautious. She leaned back in her chair and crossed her arms slowly. "I'm not sure I understand what you mean, sir, but, uhm, is there something I can do for you?" she asked.

"Perhaps not," he said. He placed both elbows on the desktop, wove his fingers together, and rested his chin on them. "Perhaps I can help you. You see, it's all a matter of my theory of operant conditioning."

"What kind of conditioning?"

"Operant conditioning. You might be more familiar with the term stimulus-response or positive reinforcement," he said with a half-smile.

Thinking it likely that he was a representative of a textbook publisher, Beverly decided to humor him until he was through with his sales pitch, then take his card, tell him she'd consider his product, and escort him out. She thought it was strange, though, that he carried no wide briefcase or stack of books.

"Uh, yes, I think I remember that—from college—it's been a couple of years now. That's you? I mean, that's your theory, you say? I'm sorry I don't quite remember it."

"I thought you might recollect—perhaps parts of it. You may not be aware of it, but you've practiced operant conditioning or something close to it nearly every day in this classroom—as have thousands of other teachers." He still had his chin resting on his hands.

"Practiced it? I have? I mean, we have?" He couldn't be a sales representative; he seemed too calm, too unrehearsed. Perhaps he's an administrator, or someone visiting from the district office. She tried to replay his introduction in her mind to hear his name again. Unfolding her arms and leaning forward on her desk now, Beverly was more intrigued than unnerved by her unannounced visitor.

"For instance," he said, leaning back and placing both hands flat on the desk top, "those forms." He pointed to the folder of printouts.

Beverly placed her hand softly on the folder. "These?"

"Yes, and that basal reader and those objectives in your lesson plans, and the drill and practice program in your teaching machines—I mean, your microcomputers—it's there."

Bewildered, Beverly just stared at her visitor once again, and for the next hour he talked and talked. He told her about his research in psychology, about his life-long interest in how people learn. He described his experiments with pigeons, rats, and chickens and how they demonstrated the effects of shaping, chaining, and schedules of reinforcement. He said he and several other scientists were "behaviorists" because they theorized that humans are conditioned to behave as they do, that is, people respond to stimuli in the environment. Therefore, children in school can be conditioned to learn by teachers.

He talked extensively about the law of effect that a behaviorist before him had formulated and how influential that concept became in his own research. The other psychologist's name was E. L. Thorndike, a researcher now considered the "father of educational psychology."

"Thorndike, in 1913 I believe, made the observation that responses that have rewarding consequences are strengthened or learned, and responses that have negative or aversive consequences are weakened or extinguished. He said, in other words, that a person's behavior can be controlled through reward and punishment." He stopped for a moment as if pondering that idea of the stimulus-response model for the first time.

Beverly sat almost motionless as her visitor continued. He described Thorndike's experiments on animals and how he concluded from those experiments that learning could be studied scientifically. Like Thorndike's stimulus-response theory, he said, his own theory of operant conditioning is based on the assumption that instruction can be designed so that learning can be controlled and measured. Laws of learning can be used by teachers to manage the learning environment.

"Our behaviorist model of learning, then," the man said, sounding as if he were giving a lecture to a gathering, "has translated to classroom practice in this way: Teachers efficiently organize and directly transmit information to students and strengthen the transmission through repetition and positive reinforcement, or rewards. Students master the information, and then teachers use objective tests to measure how successfully the information was learned by the students and whether they are ready to advance to the next set of skills."

"That's part of the basal reader approach. I understand, now," Beverly said. "The individual reading skills that are learned through repetition, the mastery tests, are positive reinforcement for those students who select the right answer. And positive reinforcement for me."

"For you?" he asked.

"Yes, obviously. The teacher's guidebooks that come with the basal readers give us day-to-day and week-to-week instructions on how to break down complex skills into simpler skills, how to present and teach the skills, and how to test to determine how well the kids master the skills. I receive a positive response if my students learn the skills and get higher scores on the tests that come with the basal."

"Of course."

"What did you say your name is?"

"Skinner."

"Of course, Dr. B. F. Skinner."

They were both quiet for a few moments, but the silence was interrupted by the laughter of a man and a woman in the hall. Beverly instantly recognized the voices of Ken and Ginger, two 7th-grade language arts colleagues. Signaling Dr. Skinner to stay where he was, she left the classroom and intercepted the other teachers as they walked down the hall.

"Hey, Ken! Hi, Ginger! I want you to meet someone. He's in my room. You'll never believe it—he says his name is Dr. B. F. Skinner. He just popped up in my room about an hour ago and—well, you just have to meet him." Beverly walked expectantly ahead of the pair, but when she entered her room, he was gone and the folder of printouts was on the floor, the printouts spread in an orderly fashion.

"Where is he?" she said.

Ken and Ginger exchanged looks. Both remembered that B. F. Skinner had died several years before. Ken softly whistled the tune to The Twilight Zone. They laughed and teased Beverly as they helped her to gather the printouts.

"Hey, these are from that CD-ROM, Mastering English Grammar," Ginger said. "I've used Skills Bank II and Sentence Fun. They're great. I need to try this program, too. The state skills test is just five weeks away, and my kids are weak in subject-verb agreement and capitalization. Their scores are lower than I'd like for them to be. I bet this program would really help get them to practice those skills. Looks like your scores are pretty impressive. Got any wisdom to share?"

"Operant conditioning," Beverly said, looking toward the desk where Dr. Skinner had sat for the last hour.

"Huh?"

Beverly slowly stuffed the folder of printouts in her totebag, picked up her purse, and looked at Ken and Ginger. "I promise. He sat right there."

"Who?" Ken asked.

Beverly paused. "Never mind. Do you remember reading about stimulus-response in college? Remember Skinner? Ken, you should—you just graduated."

Ken nodded. "Yeah, I remember that—yeah, the Skinner box—something about pigeons and, uhm, reinforcement, I think. Give me a minute; it'll come back to me. I spent long nights memorizing all those notes in Dr. Wright's psychology class."

The three walked out of Beverly's classroom, their voices fading into the hall's silence.

Beverly, like many literacy teachers, knew well what she wanted her students to do in her classroom and how she would achieve her goal. It is all in the teacher's guide for the basal reader series the district uses and in the manuals for the computer programs on basic skills. What she didn't know was why. Why use a drill and skill computer program and not another type of program? Why use a basal reader and not teacher- or student-selected literature? Why objective tests instead of other forms of assessing and evaluating? As her visitor pointed out, Beverly was acting on the basis of one theory about how humans learn, the behavioral theory of learning. There are other theories of learning, and other literacy teachers whose choices about what and how to teach are quite different from Beverly's. Consider Carl, for example, a 6th-grade teacher.

Carl's Story

He could hear the low hum of middle schoolers shuffling between and around the tall shelves of books, whispering, giggling, flipping through an array of books jacketed in enticing pictures of romance, adventure, mystery, and horror. The noise didn't bother Carl. He was so captured by the computer program he was previewing that he was almost unaware of the library activity.

Knowing that he was the only one scheduled to be in the tiny "preview room" today, he had spread out his choice selections of CD-ROMS, laserdisks, and diskettes so that most of the working space in the room was covered. The two other chairs served as end tables, each topped with a couple of laserdisks. Playing quietly on the TV monitor was The Case of the Missing Mystery Writer, one of Houghton Mifflin's Channel READ (Reading Enters Another Dimension) videodisk series. Carl was absorbed in the mystery when he heard a man ask "Who's Rita?"

"Oh, that's the bookmobile person. She's sort of the kids' headquarters. I really like this. It's literature-based. It gives the kids a problem to solve and at the same time helps them sharpen their critical thinking skills and build vocabulary. And it inspires them to write," Carl said rapidly, as if he needed to clear his mind of his immediate thoughts before he could focus on the fact that someone else was in the room.

"I'm Carl," he said, finally moving his gaze from the TV monitor to the slender, dark-haired man standing behind him. Carl moved the laserdisks from one of the chairs and invited the man to sit.

"Thank you. I'm Lev Vygotsky," the man said in a thick Russian accent. He was not much older than Carl, but he had a scholarly presence that made him seem much older. He wore a pin-striped suit with very short lapels—the kind Jay Gatsby wore in the 1930s.

"Lev, huh? Where you from, Lev? You have an interesting accent," Carl said in his usual matter-of-fact way. "And you've got some cool threads." Carl turned back to the various controls and shuffled through floppy disks and CD-ROMs. He seemed in a rush to preview the assortment he had selected from the storage closet.

"Russia, and thank you," Mr. Vygotsky said, sensing that "cool threads" was a complimentary remark.

"Russia? Neat. I've never met anyone from Russia. Visiting or staying?"

"Staying, I suppose. I like this, this videodisk, as you call it. If used by a group of students or with the guidance of an adult, it can create a zone of next or nearest development nicely."

"A zone of what?"

"Oh, I forgot. When my Russian terms were translated into English the translators used the term zone of proximal development. It is the distance between the actual developmental level as determined by independent problem solving and the level of potential development as determined through problem solving under adult guidance or in collaboration with more capable peers."

"You've lost me, Lev. Aha!" He'd found the disk he was hunting.

"You see, Jean Piaget, a very well-respected Swiss psychologist who studied the natural development of human intelligence, said instruction is most effective if it is presented when the child is most naturally receptive for it. I disagree, to some extent. Yes, learning develops as the child grows towards adulthood, but intellectual development does not necessarily precede learning. Learning precedes development."

Carl placed the floppy in the drive and finally turned to face his Russian visitor.

"Let me get this straight. Piaget—he's the one with the four stages. I remember his name from my college courses and some of the articles I've read in journals. Piaget says that my kids cannot learn something if they aren't ready for it. But you say they can if they are nudged?"

"Quite simple terms—but I suppose that's acceptable." Dr. Vygotsky crossed one leg over the other and held the top knee between his interlocked hands. "The point is that there are things students already know or have mastered. There are other things they just aren't ready for yet—as Piaget said. However, between those two there is the

*zone of proximal development where children can, with help, guidance, encourage-
ment, and support, do things they cannot do independently."*

*"I agree with that," Carl said, nodding. "Last summer I took a two-week workshop on
using the reading/writing workshop approach. I really like it, and it sounds like your zone
of proximal development theory stuff in action. I mean, students choose what they feel
they are interested in and can read. They abandon what doesn't interest them. They
help each other on writing and reading through group conferences. And I help them, or
nudge them, as they work to accomplish the goals they set for themselves at the start
of the term and as they practice the skills they are weak in. It's what is called the process
approach to reading and writing. Their writing is shared, revised, edited and published
here for their peers or sent to magazines or newspapers to be published in a big way."*

"Excellent. Writing should have a purpose."

*"Then you'll like this," Carl said as he reached towards the shelf above the com-
puter for a turquoise box titled The Student Writing Center. "With this program, my kids
write letters to authors of their favorite books, prepare their manuscripts for publishing
in their favorite magazines, publish their writing in their own newsletters and magazines, and make signs for promoting books they think are worth raving about. Yep, they
really get into this program, and they're still getting those sacred essential skills—writing a letter, developing a paragraph, sentence-combining, subject-verb agreement,
punctuation, capitalization, spelling—you name it, they do it."*

"Yes—the sociohistorical theory of learning."

"What theory?"

*"For many years, schools have functioned according to the behaviorist's view of
learning. Most unfortunate. Humans are not animals, you see; therefore, behaviorist
theory, which is built on a foundation of animal experimentation, cannot inform us
about human learning processes. We may develop as animals do, but we have a different way of learning, a constructivist way of learning. We adapt our environment to fit
our goals. Our sign and symbol systems—writing—for example, were developed to
communicate with and to regulate social groups. A better theory is the social constructivist theory of learning."*

*"Social groups. Enter multiculturalism, right?" Carl glanced at the large clock on
the wall and quickly began gathering the materials he had laid out.*

*"Culture is very important—the background of the learner is important. It deter-
mines the tools a child has for learning and how a child learns to view the world. Children raised in different cultures will have different learning styles, diff—" Vygotsky's last
word was drowned by the clang of the bell signaling the end of the period. Carl had
already neatly stacked the materials and in a series of almost rehearsed steps turned
off all the equipment.*

*"It was nice talking to you, Lev. I guess you could call me a social constructivist,
too. Thanks for the theory lesson! See you later." Carl picked up his pad and pen and
ran into Anita Carrera, the librarian, on his way out.*

*"Hey, Madame Carrera," he said teasingly. "I met your Russian assistant. Friendly
comrade—really brainy, too. See you around."*

*"What Russian?" Anita said, but Carl was already past the security turnstile. She
just shook her head.*

Both Beverly and Carl teach within the framework of a particular theory about learning. Beverly, perhaps unknowingly, was practicing within a behaviorist's model. For most of Beverly's life, and probably the lives of her parents and grandparents, the behaviorist theory of

learning had been the dominant one, the one that guided many curriculum designers, teachers, and teacher educators as they sculpted the form of our K–12 schools. Carl, on the other hand, uses a social constructivist approach to his teaching. Although this approach has its roots in the 1920s, it has recently gained the favor of educators. Today some teachers use behaviorism and some use constructivism as they choose what to teach and how to teach it.

In the behaviorist model of learning, teachers directly transmit information to students and reinforce it through repetition, rewards, and feedback. Students master the information, and then teachers use objective tests to measure how successfully the information was learned by the students. As Beverly's visitor explained, this model is built on psychological research—mainly that supporting Thorndike's (1932) stimulus-response theory and Skinner's (1968) theory of operant conditioning. Simply stated, the influence of behaviorism on education has two main thrusts. First, rewards and feedback are critical to effective teaching and learning. Second, complex behaviors can be taught most effectively when they are broken down into smaller, simpler subskills.

The research of Skinner and other behaviorists is evident in the way information is delivered to Beverly's students. She organizes instruction on a topic into units that cover increasingly complex aspects of the topic. For example, she may dedicate six weeks to a unit on "the sentence." The first week's lesson may be on identifying the subject and predicate, and students practice that skill using worksheets with lists of isolated sentences to analyze. Sometimes she uses a drill and practice computer program that resembles the worksheets but, unlike the worksheets, gives immediate reinforcement for correct and incorrect answers. To see if her students have mastered the skill of identifying subjects and predicates, Beverly may give a pretest at the start of the unit and a posttest at the end of the unit. Beverly may not know it, but her choices in lessons, drills, readings, and so forth reflect her application of behaviorism.

Carl, as mentioned earlier, works within the framework of a different theory, constructivism. Rather than seeing information as a thing that can be transmitted to the learner through direct instruction, Carl sees students as independent learners building or creating knowledge for themselves in a learning environment designed to encourage and facilitate just that. Perhaps unknown to him, Carl had internalized the viewpoint of constructivism: direct instruction as practiced by behaviorists confuses students, bores them, and disempowers them because the focus is on the teacher and the "right answer" rather than on the students' natural curiosity and self-regulation. Constructivists believe that knowledge is always constructed by each student's efforts to make sense of the world. Therefore, instruction means providing exploratory and problem-solving situations that allow the student to experiment, to make mistakes, and to work collaboratively with peers to find answers to problems.

Carl's students may each have somewhat different goals in his class, and although they collaborate on projects, they will pursue projects that interest them. For example, some may be working on a persuasive writing piece to send to the city paper or a magazine's writing contest. Others may be reading the most recent Gary Paulsen adventure or Lois Duncan mystery, and still others may be scanning KidsNet, the network for kids on Internet—the electronic information highway. On KidsNet they share stories, distribute papers on local history, and swap e-mail on their likes and dislikes.

Although all are writing, the form and purpose of the writing is determined by the student. Carl may set broad boundaries within which students may work in his class, but the students make many personal decisions and thus commitments. Each student keeps a log of writings, of conferences with the teacher, of conferences with other students, of readings they've done, and of skills that need work. They also keep a reading response journal that is shared with the teacher and other students. At the end of a grading period, Carl determines with each student how close the student came to achieving the goals they had set at the start and what level of quality the student's process of reading, writing, speaking, and listening had been.

A comparison of Beverly's and Carl's approaches juxtaposes the two theories—behaviorism and constructivism—and the implications each theory has for the literacy teacher's role and the role of students. Other theories of learning exist, as do many variations of the two theories discussed in this chapter. The important point is one that has been stated already, but it is worth repeating: knowingly or not, every teacher practices a theory, or theories, about how children and adults learn.

Beverly and Carl were clear about their objectives as teachers but were not aware of the research and scholarship that supports the teaching methods they use. A better understanding of the theoretical foundations of their teaching methods would put those methods in a broader context. Knowledge of theory, however, is not enough to clarify the literacy teacher's roles in the classroom. Basic research and theory building are important, but many factors other than theories of learning determine the day-to-day reality of the classroom. Schools are public institutions that are influenced by a variety of political, social, and cultural forces. Understanding the theoretical foundations will help Beverly and Carl construct the whole story of literacy education. However, they must explore other influences—including a variety of leaders and political events that came before them and left faint but indelible marks on the practice of literacy education.

AN AMERICAN STORY

Let's assume that both Beverly and Carl can trace their family lineage to the Mayflower. If they could time-travel to all of their ancestors' classrooms, they would soon realize that we have been "reforming" education since the first school opened its door.

Beverly's great-great-great grandfather's great-great-great grandfather, who lived in colonial days, learned to read for one primary reason: so that he could memorize the Bible. The *New England Primer* was the predominant text used by children in the mainly agrarian communities of the time. If his family had been wealthy enough and he had been fortunate enough to attend the upper grades of the "fitting schools," he would have learned to read and write Latin and Greek, and he would have studied "oratory" or rhetoric, the art of public speaking. His children and grandchildren lived in a period of growing national identity and unity. Noah Webster identified a need for a common culture to fortify national strength and published *The First Part of a Grammatical Institute of the English Language*, better known as his Blue-Backed Speller (Applebee, 1974). For nearly one hundred years, Webster's Speller taught children the alphabet, syllables, and moral lessons saturated in patriotism. Beverly's ancestors who used the Speller spent much of their time in class memorizing and reciting letters, nonsense syllables, and spelling lists.

By the late 1800s, social attitudes began to change. The standardization of railroad tracks cleared the way for a mobile society; the publication of newspapers and magazines exploded; 14 million immigrants arrived and cities swelled. The adolescent country was simultaneously experiencing the elation of growth and "a profound psychic tension that made people wonder what kind of America was in the making" (Kliebard, 1987, p. 4). Education became a major player in the team that determined the direction the country would go in the century to come. Politicians, business people, and educational leaders turned their focus on schools. Mental discipline, a theory based on the writings of German psychologist Christian Wolff, aligned itself well with the spirit of industrialization. This theory compared the mind to a muscle. Just as exercise improves the power of a muscle, studying particular subjects can improve effectiveness of particular mental faculties like memory, reasoning, and imagination. Grammatical studies of classical languages—Greek and Latin—provided the kind of training the "mind/muscle" needed in the upper grades. In the lower grades younger children relied on William Holmes McGuffey's *Eclectic First Reader for Young Children*, more popularly known as *McGuffey's Reader*, to learn phonics.

Beverly's ancestors may have thought their classroom a boring and uninteresting place because instruction consisted of "monotonous drill, harsh discipline and mindless verbatim recitation" (Kliebard, 1987, p. 6). Schools seemed to resemble the assembly-line of a factory, the Industrial Age icon that symbolized the opportunity for every American to rise, like the gray plume from the smoke stacks, to heights of wealth and success.

Not everyone agreed with the mental discipline approach. Once again, American schools were the arena for heated debates, controversy, and restructuring. Psychologists William James and Edward Thorndike demonstrated through their experimentation that mental discipline was not scientifically sound. In the meantime, Frederick W. Taylor introduced "scientific management" to the factories. Later, proponents would make it an important theory in schools. The heart of scientific management lay in the careful specification of the task to be performed and the ordering of the elements of that task in the most efficient sequence (Kliebard, 1987).

Carl's great-great grandparents, like Beverly's, grew up during World War I. If they were English language arts teachers, they probably heard the jargon of scientific management in conversations about teaching reading, writing, and literature: objective measurement, IQ, minimum essentials, disability/remedial reading, skills development, contract method, and ability grouping.

By the early 1930s, teachers of language arts became disenchanted with the objective and business-like approach of social efficiency, and leaders like Dora V. Smith and Louise Rosenblatt campaigned for what became popularized as the Progressive Education movement. They argued that students should learn to appreciate language and literature, not analyze it, and they called for a consideration of the interest of the child or adolescent to replace the view of the school as a factory and the student as its product (Smith, 1964; Rosenblatt, 1938).

Carl's great-grandmother's junior high school English class during the height of the Progressive Era in the 1930s probably looked much like today's classroom. Teachers were practicing a child-centered method that resembles what today we call whole language. The interests of each student, rather than the value of the subject matter, drove the curriculum.

Teachers emphasized reading for pleasure as well as appreciation and downplayed traditional skills-based, sequential curricula based on phonics rules, grammar instruction, and classical literature. John Dewey, perhaps the most notable of the progressives, was a highly influential philosopher and educator whose "laboratory school" gained notoriety for its child-centered methods. Dewey believed the best way to prepare students to live in a democratic society was to create classroom environments that were themselves democratic and organized to support a child's natural curiosity. Reading and writing, then, were best taught in context—"in the course of building a clubhouse, or cooking, or raising a pair of sheep" (Kliebard, 1987, p. 78). Dewey was particularly opposed to the removal of reading from its natural context. Dewey said, "When the bare process of reading is thus made an end in itself, it is a psychological impossibility for reading to be other than lifeless" (Dewey, 1898, p. 233).

In the late 1930s, when Carl's great-grandmother was in high school, she heard phrases like the unit approach, literature as experience, wide reading, and free reading. Educators like Dora V. Smith introduced and validated literature for the adolescent and preadolescent—what is referred to now as young adult literature (Monseau, 1991). Although many teachers believed in a progressive approach, the economic restraints of the Depression made it difficult for them to acquire the supplies and materials they needed to enrich the literacy classroom. Also, public sentiment was changing. At the cusp of World War II, schools were overflowing with the students who stayed in school because jobs were scarce, and educational leaders began to criticize the progressive method for its "anti-intellectualism" and lack of discipline (Applebee, 1974).

For Beverly's grandfather, who was in school during and after World War II, the common phrases were quite different from the ones his mother heard. He was likely to have taken one or more standardized tests and to have studied reading from basals and literature from the "Great Books." Many of the phrases used in education resembled those used in industry and the military: efficiency, skills, objective measurement, minimum essentials, remediation, contracts, cost-effectiveness.

Growing up in the late 1950s and the 1960s, Carl's and Beverly's parents experienced a classroom that in the early years of their schooling was dramatically different from the classroom in which their grandparents learned reading and writing. The 1957 launching of Sputnik kindled strong nationalistic concerns about education, and the progressives' platform was quickly squelched. A postwar, science-based movement spurred to the foreground a school version of concepts typically applied to industry and the military: students were tracked so that the academically "gifted" received a different education from the "average" and the "low achievers." Once again the focus in literacy classes shifted. The "academic model" highlighted the goals and nature of the subject rather than the needs of the student (Applebee, 1974). Literature, composition and language became the "tripod." "Literature" generally meant the white, Eurocentric, literary collections in basals and anthologies. "Composition" was typically a formulaic exercise by which students were taught to produce syntactically sound, objective, and accurate written products. "Language" encompassed the skills related to parsing. To help the low achievers, reading, grammar, and writing skills were compartmentalized and isolated.

Gifted students were likely to be involved in activities designed to help them appreciate literature. However, the correct interpretations of literature were determined by literary critics. Gone was the reader-response approach advocated by the progressives. Replacing it was the New Criticism—the view that a literary work itself was the object of interpretation and that close reading would avoid distortion of its true meaning (see, for example, Brooks & Warren, 1938). In school, that meant students were expected to "find" what experts had determined to be the correct interpretation of the work.

The 1960s brought winds of change in many areas, including education. Critics of the academic model pointed to its negative social and cultural repercussions. They noted that the practice of tracking marginalized and dehumanized the underprivileged (Applebee, 1974). The pedagogical methods inherent in the academic model were on trial as well; that was evident at the Anglo-American Seminar on the Teaching of English held in Dartmouth in 1966, where conferees called for a more student-oriented approach to teaching reading and, particularly, writing. In what Hairston (1984) describes as a "paradigm shift," the perspective on teaching composition did move away from a product orientation to one that focuses on the process of the act of writing. Although qualitative reports indicate that social and cultural implications of the academic model continue to plague schools (Goodlad, 1984; Kozol, 1992; Brown, 1993), at least one limb of the English/language arts tree—how writing is taught—changed dramatically.

Not as influential as process writing, but still influential, was the philosophy of reader-response theorists. Their rejection of New Criticism and their focus on the process of reading is embodied in this perhaps familiar call by Probst (1986) for modifying the English curriculum and pedagogy:

> However teachers manage to initiate the talk, the purpose is not to reach consensus, to agree upon an interpretation or an assessment of the work. Rather, the purpose is for individuals to work out their own readings, to create out of the text literary works that are appropriate and satisfying for the readers. . . . As they present their own reactions and thoughts and deal with those of their classmates, they are redefining themselves against the background of their society. [p. 37–38]

The English Coalition Conference of 1987 was formed as a 20-year follow-up to the Dartmouth conference. Conferees attempted to define and situate a discipline in a pluralistic landscape of multicultural communities that face economic uncertainty and the demands of information technology and global communication. They brought to the table teacher stories, philosophy, and current research on literacy and learning theory, all of which seemed to support a student-centered learning environment. In addition, they considered the social and political drive for "cultural literacy" (Hirsch, 1988), national standards, and a national curriculum. Consequently, discussions and debates concerned issues such as whose literature constitutes the "canon," what skills should be taught, and what theoretical and ideological assumptions underlie pedagogy (Elbow, 1990).

Although the coalition of researchers and educators agreed not to make a resolute statement about what English/language arts education should be, their elementary, secondary, and college strand reports resonated with the views of the progressives: learning involves the making of meaning and reflecting back on this process of making meaning—not the ingestion of a body of information (Elbow, 1990). Booth (1989) points out that, unlike the age of the progressives, conferees did not subscribe to the polar thinking implied in the "tired formula, 'Teach the child, not the subject. . . . We do not choose between 'the child' and this or that ideal 'subject.' We choose subjects which, by their nature, if taught properly, will lead the child eagerly through increasingly independent steps toward full adult, self-sustained learning" (p. x).

Booth's statement echoes the assumptions of proponents of a teaching approach that has captured the interest of the English/language arts field: the reading/writing workshop approach (Atwell, 1987). Like the progressive movement of the 1930s, it proposes a student-centered classroom environment rather than the traditional teacher-directed curriculum and pedagogy. Unlike the academic model, the workshop approach blends literature, writing, language, and speaking into a literacy event that more closely resembles the activities of society outside of school.

The 1990s education landscape is not monolithic. Despite the popularity of the reading/writing approach in some schools, pedagogy in many schools reflects the academic model. Both approaches are actually modern expressions of traditions that have been with us for many, many decades. The fact is, our two literacy teachers, Beverly and Carl, inherited a legacy that began more than two hundred years ago, even though it has been just over one hundred years since English was first considered worth including in the curriculum of the "common schools." Some of the methods used to teach reading and writing in the 1800s have withstood the forces of time. Some have not. Some have changed only in label. The college entrance literature list that specifies what great works a student must have studied to be admitted to college is gone, but the canon approach remains. Those changes that have occurred over the years are not solely the result of the innovations of teachers, supervisors, or curriculum designers. To a great degree, changes in the classroom are molded and reshaped by forces outside the classroom.

THE PURPOSE OF THIS BOOK

Why the history lesson? The reason is simple. To know where we are going, we need to know where we are and where we've been. Only when we situate ourselves in the story of the teaching of literacy will we know what role we will play as teachers of literacy. How we teach and learn literacy in a technology-enriched classroom may in some respects look the way it did in the structured classroom setting of the early 1800s. Other features of the technology-enriched classroom may resemble characteristics of the progressive classrooms of the 1930s and 1940s. Think of the chapters in this book as lenses through which to see the different ways technology is used in the classroom. Many of the chapters present ways to use the technology within a particular conceptual or theoretical framework. As Chapters 2 through 6 unfold, they will compose an image of a technology-enriched literacy classroom that looks and sounds differently depending on the theory that is in the background. Because the most current direction in classroom instruction reflects the tenets of the constructivist theorists, we will begin there. Chapter 2 provides a lens into the technology-enriched classroom practice that embraces a social constructivist theory. Chapter 3 covers a related approach, that of cognitive constructivism. Chapter 4 explores direct instruction models based on behavioral approaches to integrating technology into literacy instruction. Chapter 5 discusses the role of direct instruction within a constructivist framework, and Chapter 6 considers technology use from a perspective of cognitive information processing theory.

Chapter 7 explores the possibilities when computers are used to support portfolio building, test making and test taking, gradebook management, and more. Chapter 8 serves two purposes. It introduces the ways telecommunications can be used in literacy instruction, and it catalogs some of the electronic and print resources for literacy teachers, such as the World Wide Web, newsgroups, journals, magazines, and organizations that are dedicated to helping educators stay informed about current methods of teaching literacy. Concluding the book is a brief guide to microteaching (Appendix A), which describes how microteaching can be used, as Hawisher and LeBlanc (1992) suggest, to "re-image" the teaching of literacy in the Virtual Age.

This book is an invitation to literacy teachers at all levels of schooling to consider the use of technology as part of an effort to reconceptualize, to explore, to experiment, and to work through failures to success. Knowing what forces are playing on us as we teach helps us to look to the future and feel comfortable with the certainty of change.

REFERENCES

Applebee, A. (1974). *Tradition and reform in the teaching of English: A history*. Urbana, IL: National Council of Teachers of English.

Atwell, N. (1987). *In the middle: Writing, reading, and learning with adolescents*. Portsmouth, NH: Heinemann–Boynton/Cook.

Booth, W. (1989). Foreword. In R. Lloyd-Jones & A. Lunsford (Eds.), *The English Coalition Conference: Democracy through language*. Urbana, IL: National Council of Teachers of English, and New York: Modern Language Association of America.

Brooks, C., & Warren, R. P. (1938). *Understanding poetry*. New York: Henry Holt.

Brown, R. (1993). *Schools of thought*. San Francisco, CA: Jossey-Bass.

Dewey, J. (1898). The primary-education fetish. *The Forum, 25*, 315–328.

Elbow, P. (1990). *What is English?* New York: Modern Language Association of America, and Urbana, IL: National Council of Teachers of English.

Goodlad, J. (1984). *A place called school*. New York: McGraw-Hill.

Hairston, M. (1984). The winds of change: Thomas Kuhn and the revolution in the teaching of writing. *College Composition and Communication, 33*(1), 76–88.

Hawisher, G., & LeBlanc, P. (Eds.). (1992). *Re-imagining computers and composition: Teaching and research in the Virtual Age*. Portsmouth, NH: Heinemann.

Hirsch, E. (1988). *Cultural literacy: What every American needs to know*. New York: Vintage.

Kliebard, H. (1987). *The struggle for the American curriculum 1893–1958*. New York: Routledge.

Kozol, J. (1992). *Savage inequalities: Children in America's schools*. New York: Crown.

Monseau, V. R. (1991). Dora V. Smith: A legacy for the future. In J. Gerlach & V. Monseau (Eds.), *Missing chapters: Ten pioneering women in NCTE and English education*. Urbana, IL: National Council of Teachers of English.

Probst, R. (1986). Mom, Wolfgang, and me: Adolescent literature, critical theory, and the English classroom. *English Journal, 75*(6), 33–39.

Rosenblatt, L. (1938). *Literature as exploration*. New York: Appleton-Century.

Skinner, B. F. (1968). *Technology of teaching*. New York: Appleton.

Smith, D. V. (1964). *Dora V. Smith: Selected essays*. New York: Macmillan.

Thorndike, E. (1932). *The fundamentals of learning*. New York: Teachers College Press.

Vygotsky, L. (1978). In M. Cole, V. John-Steiner, S. Scribner, & E. Souberman (Eds). *Mind in society*. Cambridge, MA: Harvard University Press.

SOFTWARE DISCUSSED IN THIS CHAPTER

Many software companies sell primarily through mail order distributors and retail computer and software stores.

Channel READ (Reading Enters Another Dimension). Houghton Mifflin.

Skills Bank II and Sentence Fun, from Mastering English Grammar, CD-ROM.

The Student Writing Center. The Learning Company. Available from many educational software suppliers, including Educational Resources (800-624-2926).

Note: The definition of zone of proximal development in the Vygotsky narrative and his explanation of it was taken from Vygotsky, 1978.

CHAPTER TWO

The Social Constructivist Perspective

Beverly and Carl knew early in their career planning that they wanted to be teachers. Another teacher, however, reflects a different story. His is a story of change, and what he discovered is that change is the natural condition of life. Peter Tangeman was a practicing dentist who woke up one Thursday morning and decided he had thought about it enough. It was time to follow his true professional calling, teaching in a middle school. On Saturdays he was a volunteer who tutored at-risk middle school students at the YMCA. Those few hours a week gave him more satisfaction than all of his best days leaning over a dental patient. He had been out of high school for 12 years now. Based on articles in magazines like *Time* and *Newsweek* and coverage of education on television, he thought the field surely must have shifted since he was last in school. To check out that hypothesis, he did some research at the local university, spending a couple of weekends in the library. First he leisurely scanned the titles of books and professional journal articles as he strolled between the standing shelves. Titles on book jackets and journal covers published in the late 1960s and the 1970s indicated that "basics" and "skills" were the focus of educators. Classrooms, he surmised, could be expected to reflect the approaches and strategies inspired and directed by the "back to basics" movement—a phrase he barely remembered from TV news and conversations between his uncle and aunt, who were teachers in those years. After thoroughly reading a few articles, he realized how his own schooling very much reflected one approach to teaching.

As he moved into more recent literature, he noticed that by the 1980s computer technology in the classroom emerged as a central issue in articles about curriculum and instruction. He was pleased to know that educators were keeping up with technological advancements. Computers had been used in health care for many years, and he was not

15

surprised to learn they were also popular in education. He was unfamiliar, however, with another issue that seemed to emerge and take center stage along with educational technology. The term *constructivism* increasingly appeared in the titles of educational books and professional journal articles. He found titles of books like the following:

> *Constructivism in the Computer Age* (Forman & Pufall, 1988)
>
> *Constructivism and the Technology of Instruction: A Conversation* (Duffy & Jonassen, 1992)
>
> *In Search of Understanding: The Case for Constructivist Classrooms* (Brooks & Brooks, 1993)
>
> *Constructing the Social* (Sarbin & Kitsuse, 1994)

In the titles of journal articles, he found an array of intriguing verbs and phrases associated with constructivism—anchoring, situating, meaning making, contextualizing, integrating, collaborating, facilitating, and problem solving. These were noticeably prevalent among the articles that called for school reform, and they were in the leading professional journals for educators in all disciplines—math, English, social studies, and science. He then narrowed his investigation and focused just on the journals in the English language arts field, because that is where he hoped to teach. He found that these constructivist approaches and strategies were indeed quite evident in the feature and editorial contents of many journals, including *English Journal, Language Arts, Journal of Reading*, and *The Reading Teacher*.

After his informal search, Peter Tangeman was convinced of three things: teaching is truly the career choice he should have made years ago; now is a challenging and stimulating time to be an educator; he needed to find out more about constructivism.

WHAT IS CONSTRUCTIVISM?

If 50 educators were asked what constructivism is, most likely each would have a different conceptualization of this theory about how we learn. It is much easier to declare that constructivism is a major trend today in literacy education than it is to say what it is. The constructivist theory is one perspective, one lens through which we can view the world. Through this lens, knowledge, or "truth," is constructed by each person individually. Constructivism has two general branches: cognitive and social. The social constructivist theory is most often attributed to a Russian psychologist and philosopher who lived in the 1930s, Lev Vygotsky. His writing has recently been revived and adapted to modern learning environments. This chapter will unpack social constructivist theory. The first part of the chapter will guide you through the roots of the theory. Then you will examine what this perspective looks like in a technology-enriched literacy classroom, and finally, you will learn why it has become so popular. Vignettes of classroom activity will be interspersed to demonstrate the ideas being discussed.

CONSTRUCTING THE MEANING OF SPAGHETTI

How each of us interprets, or makes sense of, what we perceive depends on our own background knowledge and the context in which we assimilate new knowledge. Consider the American interpretation of Italian spaghetti as an example of how individuals construct knowledge. In Italy, pasta is served before the main meal, usually veal or chicken, and spaghetti therefore has no meat in it. In the United States, however, spaghetti is most often served with a meat sauce and is the main meal. There is thus an Italian meaning of spaghetti and an American meaning. They overlap to some extent, but they are different in many ways. Children growing up in Italy will construct a meaning of spaghetti that is different from the one constructed by children growing up in the United States. The idea that knowledge cannot be delivered to students, that they must construct their own meaning, and that that meaning is inextricably linked to their cultural history and the context in which they are learning, is at the heart of constructivism.

Seasoned teachers of literacy perhaps know that constructivism is really not a new idea. In the United States, a constructivist approach was the prominent perspective among public educators in the 1930s and 1940s. (See Chapter 1 for a brief history of language arts education.) Collins (1991) explains this viewpoint and contrasts it with an opposing perspective, a more didactic approach to teaching and learning:

> Two views of education have been at war for centuries: the didactic (for information-transmission) view and the constructivist view. The didactic view prevails among the general public. It holds that teachers should be masters of particular domains of knowledge and that their job is to transmit their expertise about these domains to students through lectures and recitations. Students should memorize the facts and concepts of the domain and practice its skills until they have mastered them, and they should be able to demonstrate that mastery on appropriate tests.
>
>   The constructivist view, which undergirds the work of John Dewey, Lev Vygotsky, and Maria Montessori, holds that teachers should be facilitators who help students construct their own understandings and capabilities in carrying out challenging tasks. This view puts the emphasis on the activity of the student rather than on that of the teacher. [Collins, 1991, p. 30]

Collins goes on to say that although the constructivist view has been for some time the preferred perspective at many of the leading colleges of education, it "has made little headway in penetrating public education in America or, more generally, in the world at large" (p. 30). Collins believes, however, that as technology moves into the classrooms, they may take on a more constructivist perspective as well. In his review of the literature Collins found eight trends in classrooms that use technology. They are listed below. After reading this chapter, return to this list and decide how many of them are constructivist approaches to teaching and learning.

1. A shift from whole-class to small-group instruction.
2. A shift in the teacher's role away from lecture and recitation and towards coaching.

3. A shift from the teacher working primarily with better students to working with weaker students.
4. A shift toward more engaged students.
5. A shift from assessment based on test performance to assessment based on progress, products, and effort.
6. A shift from a competitive to a cooperative social structure.
7. A shift from all students learning the same things to different students learning different things.
8. A shift from the primacy of verbal thinking to the integration of visual and verbal thinking. [Adapted from Collins, 1991, p. 31–36]

THE ROOTS OF SOCIAL CONSTRUCTIVISM: VYGOTSKY'S LEARNING THEORY

Understanding the roots of social constructivism will help you grasp how technology is used in a constructivist environment. The science of psychology has produced a number of learning theories, or theories that explain what occurs in our minds as we learn. These learning theories historically have been the fuel for educational reform. Generally, behind every movement, philosophy, approach, or strategy in literacy education is a learning theory. At the turn of the century, for example, the theory of mental discipline, or what was called faculty psychology, explained the mind as a muscle that improved with exercise. Consequently, reading and reciting classical literature in Latin and Greek was considered an appropriate exercise for sharpening mental faculties.

The most current learning theory guiding education is, ironically, one that was developed some 60 years ago. The writings of Vygotsky only recently have been translated and published in English. In *Mind in Society* (1978) and *Thought and Language* (1962), Vygotsky explains what he calls a sociohistorical theory of learning. Vygotsky, emphasizing the cultural influences and social context of learning, advocated a discovery model of learning. In this model, the teacher plays an active, involved role, but the student's mental abilities develop naturally, through discovery. Three principal assumptions of Vygotsky's sociohistorical learning theory will be presented here. One is that the community plays a central role in the individual's making of meaning. A second is the importance of tools for cognitive development. A third is the assumption that perhaps is most frequently referred to in educational research, the zone of proximal development.

MAKING MEANING

In a Vygotskian classroom, learning is promoted through collaboration—collaboration among students and between students and teacher. Students share background knowledge and learn through the negotiations that take place within this community of meaning makers. People who surround the individual student, and the culture within which that person lives, greatly affect the way he or she makes sense of the world. In today's literacy classroom, where a community of interpreters of literature interacts and negotiates meaning, computer-based technology can provide the forum for sharing, negotiating, and constructing knowledge. Consider the case of Mr. Carr's junior class, where a program designed to support collaborative writing and discussion is being used:

Flying on Daedalus

The students shuffled into the computer lab, taking their spots, turning on the machines until the whole room was a symphony of hums, beeps, and low conversations with neighbors that slowly dissipated. Within minutes, the 18 students were each focusing on a monitor's glowing screen.

Mr. Carr had left his message on the Daedalus interchange as he had promised. Daedalus, a program that supports collaborative writing and idea exchange, was working out better than he had anticipated. This was the third week that he had used this program with his students, and in that time he had noticed that students who are normally quiet in classroom discussions were very vocal on the computer. Also he found that he was not the central guiding force on the screen as he is in classroom discussions. He told another English teacher that using Daedalus seemed to make the students less conscious of his "teacher presence." Students seemed to be more candid, more open, and more responsive to each other.

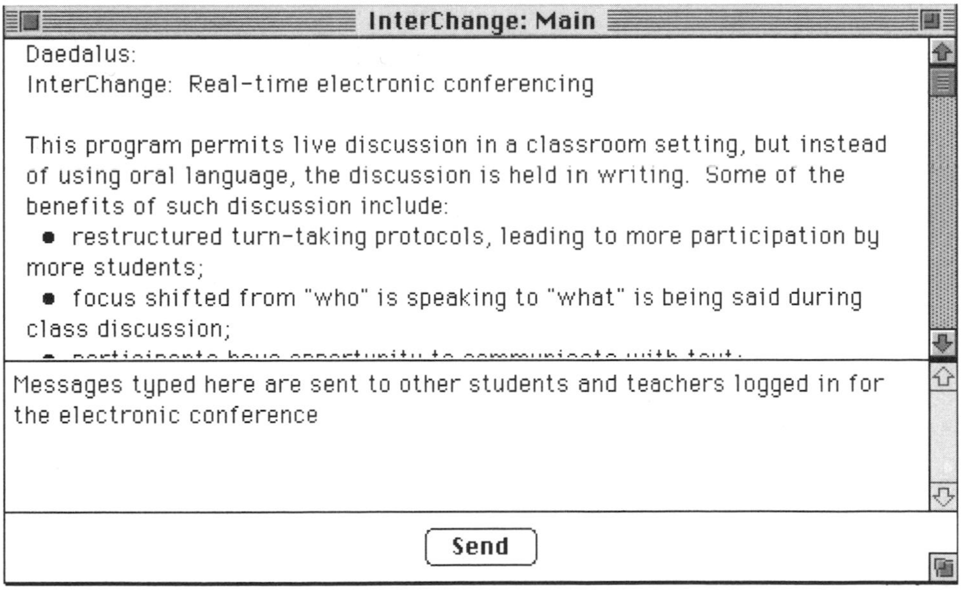

FIGURE 2-1   The Interchange feature of Daedalus lets a teacher present a prompt to students and can be used as the forum for discussion.

He did not have to address the class as their leader. Instead, looking into his screen, he waited to see responses to his message. Today, his message was the following:

```
I found this poem last night. It caught my attention.
Please read it and let me know what meaning you find in it.

    Night Crow

When I saw that clumsy crow
Flap from a wasted tree,
A shape in the mind rose up:
Over the gulfs of dream
Flew a tremendous bird
Further and further away
Into a moonless black,
Deep in the brain, far back.
```

Except for the hum, the lab was quiet. After a few minutes, one student began typing. Eventually, the clicking of the group as they typed filled the room. Soon words appeared on everyone's screen. At the front of the words was the author's name. Some students were still typing, some stared at the wall, thinking, and some read the first message on the screen.

```
Tom: I get the feeling that this poet is saying that we
have reminders in our life about things we'd rather forget—
or try to forget. This last weekend I met a really nice
girl who was wearing a familiar perfume. I remembered that
it was one a girlfriend I had my freshman year wore. I had
a bad experience with that girlfriend, and I think I might
have been uncomfortable with my new friend because of an
old friend's memory.
```

Sally's message appeared on the screen right below Tom's.

```
Sally: It seems that the poet just can't have it all.
Maybe his "clumsy crow" is all he can get, but what he
really wants is that "tremendous bird" that flies into the
black and just seems to disappear. I think this theme is
something we can really relate to in the 90s. We hear so
much about how we will never be as successful as our par-
ents were and how there aren't jobs out there. It's like
our "tremendous bird" is just a dream of making it big
that's flying away and disappearing.
```

More and more messages were sent to the screen. Tom, Sally, Mr. Carr and others who had already sent theirs were now reading and planning their next message.

Seema: I think this has to do with women. Is the poet a woman? I think she sees herself in the "clumsy crow" because she feels unqualified or like she isn't being given credit for what she can do because she's a woman. In her mind, though, she is that tremendous bird. But no one knows because she's not given a chance to show how she can fly. Only she knows.

Mr. Carr participates in the conversation as one of the members of the interpretive community rather than as a director or monitor. However, he makes suggestions, provides information, poses questions, responds to others' interpretations, and offers his own interpretation.

Mr. Carr: Seema, that's a very interesting and intriguing interpretation. I wouldn't have thought of it. Now that you present this interpretation, I can see how a woman could have easily written this. But it was written by a man, Theodore Roethke. He lived in the 1940s and 1950s and won a Pulitzer Prize for poetry in 1954.

Does anyone have a comment on how this poem might relate to the mood of the country in the time that he lived?

For the next 35 minutes, the class and teacher entered responses to the poem, asked questions, and discussed the varied interpretations. They discussed imagery, theme, and symbolism. They chose to have a lengthy exchange on the poet's choice of a crow and not another type of bird. Eventually, a barrage of messages was rapidly being entered, so that it seemed as if several "screen conversations" were occurring. In cases like this, Mr. Carr would take the role of monitor and interrupt so that he could "re-focus" the dialogue.

Mr. Carr: Slow down! It seems we've split into several different strands. Although they are all very interesting and worth pursuing, let's get back to Tom's comment about the crow and what effect this poem would have if the bird had been something other than a crow.

Mr. Carr announced on the screen that there were only five minutes left of the class time and asked them to summarize what they learned from the Daedalus conversation. The students discussed symbolism and how imagery changes the effect of poetry. They talked about how so much can be packed into a few lines, and perhaps most importantly, they talked about how each of them had a different perspective and no one perspective was the correct one. Later Mr. Carr printed out the dialogue and made copies available to the students so they could use the information to begin writing a short essay on "Night Crow" or inspired by "Night Crow"—if they wished—to add to their portfolio. When Mr. Carr asked them how they felt about using the interchange for discussions, the students responded with comments like "love it," "great," "fun and inviting," and "let's do it again."

Mr. Carr's activity using the Interchange feature of *Daedalus* allowed his students to explore their background knowledge, negotiate meaning with other members of the interpretive community, and construct their own interpretations of poetry. Clearly, background knowledge, social and cultural contexts, and the negotiations that occurred in this community of readers and writers were the main ingredients that made this activity a worthwhile and satisfying one for Mr. Carr's students and for Mr. Carr.

What Vygotsky would have to ponder today is what a community is. With a program like *Daedalus*, this discussion could have been conducted from different parts of town. Telecommunications makes possible the grouping of communities with no physical restrictions. Cultural exchange, then, is limitless.

TOOLS FOR COGNITIVE DEVELOPMENT

According to Vygotsky, culture and society give the student the cognitive tools needed for development. The type and quality of those tools determine the pattern and rate of development. Adults such as parents and teachers are conduits for the tools for the culture: a cultural history, a social context, and language. Today's tools also include electronic forms of information access, and the use of these electronic tools has implications for the use of language as we construct and communicate knowledge. Students can construct and present knowledge in a variety of modes. Multimedia tools provide the context for communicating with text, sound, and images—both still and moving images such as animation and video. Literacy, then, is not restricted to ink on paper. Consider the case of Ms. Wallace's 5th-grade class as they explore U.S. history through accessing information, reading, writing, publishing, and producing multimedia presentations.

The Sights and Sounds of the Civil War

Ms. Wallace's 5th-grade students have launched into an intensive study of the Civil War. Rather than rely only on the textbook, Ms. Wallace gathered a collection of books and software to help the students research this period of U.S. history.

The students have formed five groups to work collaboratively on this research project. Each group settled on a topic of interest to them after some preliminary research. Their topics include battles, Confederate Army, Union Army, events leading to the Civil War, and daily life during the war.

Cindy, Shawn, Megan, Brenden, and Alicia are looking for events that lead up to the Civil War. They began their search using the time line in Compton's Multimedia Encyclopedia.

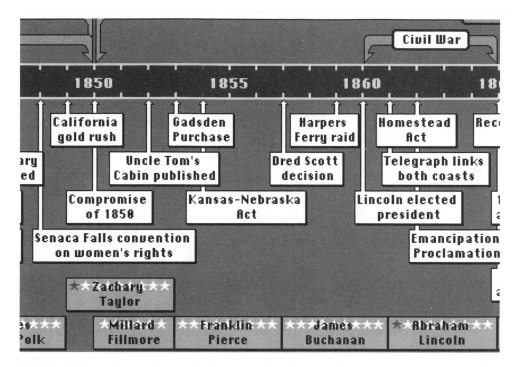

FIGURE 2-2   The time line provides students with a visual representation of some of the events leading up to the Civil War.

"I think we should each pick one of these topics just before the Civil War and do some research on it," says Alicia.

"Good idea. I'll look up information on the Compromise of 1850," volunteers Brenden.

"I want to learn more about the Dred Scott Decision," says Alicia.

"The raid on Harper's Ferry is what I want. We visited there last summer," says Cindy.

"I'll look up the Gadsden Purchase, whatever that is," offers Megan.

"I guess that leaves me with the Kansas-Nebraska Act. I remember seeing something about it in the textbook," says Shawn.

"Let's start searching for information. Remember, if you see something on someone else's topic, be sure to share it with them," Cindy reminds the group.

"I think we should plan to get together and compare notes tomorrow during class. Be sure and check any encyclopedias you have at home," suggests Brenden.

Melissa, Rahim, Ali, Sandra, and Wally are doing research on the Confederate Army. They started up The Civil War Game on the computer, took the role of General Jeb Stuart, and now face decisions about gathering an army.

They are given a choice of four options for raising an army.

"I remember Ms. Wallace saying that there was lots of information available under info in the Menu Bar. Let's look there to find out what conscription means," suggests Melissa.

FIGURE 2-3   Taking on the role of General Jeb Stuart means the students have to make some tough decisions about leading an army into battle.

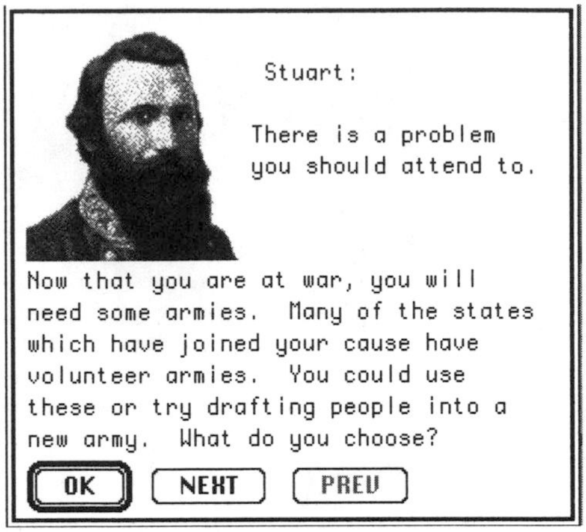

```
                    Stuart:

                    There is a problem
                    you should attend to.

Now that you are at war, you will
need some armies. Many of the states
which have joined your cause have
volunteer armies. You could use
these or try drafting people into a
new army. What do you choose?

  [ OK ]    [ NEXT ]    [ PREV ]
```

A third group of students is gathered around another computer listening to the sounds of the Gettysburg CD-ROM and observing the diagrams and maps. They're busy gathering information about the Union Army.

"Wow, this is going to be easy. Look, there is a whole section on the Union Army," Avelino remarks.

"Remember we have to use more than one source for our information," Matthew reminds the group.

"I know, but this looks like a good place to start," Ross replies.

"Listen to the sounds! We can record some of them to put in our presentation when we finish," exclaims Gwen.

"What presentation?" asks Madelyn.

"The one we have to do for our final project. Remember Ms. Wallace showed us a little about the Multimedia Workshop? That's what we'll use to create our final project," states Gwen.

The group researching the major battles of the Civil War has found an excellent starting place in Compton's Multimedia Encyclopedia.

"I really like looking things up in this encyclopedia. You just have to click to find out all kinds of information," Samuel says.

"I like the fact that we print this stuff out and not have to write it down," says Judith.

"I'm glad we have lots of copies of that encyclopedia because it sure is easier to use than all those books," comments Thuy.

The students are responsible for putting together a weekly newspaper to share their research, and they will put together a multimedia presentation. Both of these projects will be completed using the Multimedia Workshop. Their weekly newspaper and presentations will be put in the library as reference sources for other students.

Ms. Wallace's classroom provides the tools for cognitive development. Students use language to expand their knowledge of the historical content being investigated. The exchange of ideas, too, is an avenue for the exploration of cultural differences as students express their personal interpretations and analyses of the historical events of this country.

THE ZONE OF PROXIMAL DEVELOPMENT

As mentioned earlier, Vygotsky's brand of constructivism is called social constructivism because he emphasized the critical importance of interaction with people—other children, parents, teachers—in cognitive development. If Vygotsky is correct and the child's cognitive development increases in social or group settings, the use of technology to connect rather than separate students from one another would be a very appropriate use within this theory. Much of the collaborative problem solving that is at the center of the *Jasper Woodbury* programs is an example of applied social constructivism. All the lessons in the *Jasper Woodbury* series are related to simulations that put students in real problem situations where they must solve realistic, and hopefully interesting, problems. Through video clips from a videodisk, readings, and teacher-supported discussions, students are introduced to situations Jasper Woodbury finds himself in. He, for example, may propose to his school principal that a dunking booth be part of the next school fair (a teacher falls into a tank of water if the student hits the target with a ball). Jasper must use several types of math to complete a proposal for the dunking booth and write a proposal to get the booth into the fair. Obstacles become in-context tasks that students collaboratively examine and resolve. The *Jasper Woodbury* series provides a setting for social interaction and builds on the best known of Vygotsky's theoretical concepts, the zone of proximal development.

Vygotsky's zone of proximal development emphasizes his belief that learning is fundamentally a socially mediated activity. Thinking and problem solving, according to Vygotsky, can be placed in three categories. Some can be performed independently by the child. Others cannot be performed even with help. Between these two extremes are tasks the child can perform with help from others. Those tasks are in the zone of proximal development. If a child uses these cognitive processes with the help of others such as teachers, parents, and other students, they will become skills and abilities that can be independently practiced. As Vygotsky put it, "What the child is able to do in collaboration today he will be able to do independently tomorrow" (Vygotsky, 1978, p. 211). In reading instruction, the terms independent level, instructional level, and frustration level correspond to Vygotsky's zones, with instructional level being the same as the zone of proximal development.

Electronic books, multimedia, and telecommunications can create the setting for students to work within their zone of proximal development. Consider how Ms. Dean's students become engaged in discovering information about fables, and how she supports and encourages their discovery.

A Fable Festival

Ms. Dean's 3rd-grade class is in the midst of a fable festival. With the help of her students and the librarian, she gathered a collection of fables in both print and electronic versions. The class started their reading with Aesop's fables. Eventually they will examine fables from different lands, and they will culminate their study by writing and publishing their own fables.

Because the students read on different levels and have different writing abilities, they have been formed into teams that contain a mixture of weak and strong readers

and writers. They're working together to make sure that everyone on the team participates and understands what they are reading and writing. The room is filled with the
buzz of active, energized students.

"That's my favorite version of The Tortoise and the Hare," says Linh.

"Mine, too," chimes in Pinky. "Have you read it in Spanish?"

"No," Linh replies. "I don't know Spanish."

"That's OK; I'll tell you what it says," Pinky reassures him.

"OK."

"Now, we have to compare and contrast that version with another one we read,"
says Jacob as he attempts to keep the group on the task. "Which one are we going to
use?"

"Let's use the one in the book with the fox on the front," suggests Diego. "That's my
favorite version of The Tortoise and the Hare."

"You mean the one by Ann McGovern," says Jacob. "Is that okay with everybody?"
The others nod in agreement.

"Let's do what's different first," says Pinky. "The CD-ROM version is longer and has
lots more information."

FIGURE 2-4   The Living Books version of *The Tortoise and the Hare* has colorful
illustrations and lively animation. The language used can be switched between Spanish
and English.

"Yeah, and it's more modern. They're wearing tennis shoes," says Jacob.

"Whose turn is it to be writing this down in our booklet?" asks Linh.

"It's Pinky's turn," says Jacob.

"Okay, I'll write. Think of some more things," responds Pinky.

The children continue comparing and contrasting the two versions of The Tortoise and the Hare.

Another team of children is seated at the computer, flipping through their copies of a fable they downloaded from the Internet via the Project Gutenberg archives. On the computer screen in front of them is Aesopolis.

"We need to see which fables are in both Aesopolis and our collection of fables from Project Gutenberg," says Tina. "Then, we'll have some to compare."

"What about The Peacock and the Crane?" asks Richard.

"No," replies Tony.

"Hey, here's The Tortoise and the Hare. I know it is in both of them," asserts Miguel.

With a quick click of the mouse The Tortoise and the Hare appears on the computer screen. Quickly flipping through the Gutenberg files Tina also finds The Tortoise and the Hare.

"In Aesopolis we can also look at the, uhm, what was his name? Jacob? Joseph Jacob!" says Miguel. "Let's compare all three versions."

THE HARE & THE TORTOISE

The hare was always boasting about how fast he was. Tired of listening to him, the tortoise challenged him to a race. The hare thought she was joking, but the tortoise kept challenging him. A course was finally laid out, and the race began. The hare was so sure of his speed that he stopped in the middle of the race to take a short nap. Meanwhile the tortoise slowly made her way along the race course. When the hare finally woke up, he saw the tortoise nearing the finish line and ran as fast as he could, trying to catch up. But he was too late and lost the race.

Moral: Slow but sure wins the race.

Jacobs | Dictionary | List OF | Next Fable | STOP | AESOPOLI

FIGURE 2-5 *Aesopolis* offers two versions of the fables with on-line help features.

The rest of the group listens intently as Richard reads the fable from the computer screen. Suddenly he stops and faces the group. In almost a whisper he asks, "How are we going to write one of these?"

Trey replies, "I don't know. Let's ask." Ms. Dean has been visiting the different groups. They call her to their group's corner of the room to ask her advice.

"How are we going to know how to write a fable?" Brad asks her. "What do we put in the fable? How are we going to make a book?"

"We know you told us, but we still aren't sure," says Miguel.

"Right now I want you to read as many fables as you can," Ms. Dean advises them. "Fables have certain characteristics and structures. Try to discover those as you read. Next week, we'll talk about what you have discovered. You'll use a program named ClarisWorks to write and illustrate your fables. Remember, the entire group is writing fables. You don't have to write one all alone. Does that help?"

"Yes. We'll keep reading and discussing fables," says Janet. "I think I know one thing about fables, they have animal characters."

"That's right. You'll do fine on this project," Ms. Dean reassures them.

Activities such as this one in Ms. Dean's class provide opportunities for students to help other students and teachers to help students as they explore language and its conventional uses. After the students in Ms. Dean's class discuss the characteristics of the fables they reviewed, they will write an original one. They will bring their background knowledge and their newly acquired knowledge to the composing table. As they write, they will learn about other cultures, other environments, and themselves.

VYGOTSKIAN PRINCIPLES IN A TECHNOLOGY-ENRICHED CLASSROOM

Classrooms where instructional strategies compatible with Vygotsky's approach are used don't necessarily look alike. The activities and the format can vary considerably from room to room. However, four principles would be applied in any Vygotskian classroom:

Learning and development are social, collaborative activities. The interaction children have with adults and other children is critical. This suggests that using technology to enhance communication, contact, and interaction would be beneficial. The interaction should not, however, be one of information delivery. According to constructivists, you cannot really teach anyone anything. Students must construct understanding and knowledge in their own minds. However, that process is facilitated by collaboration and teacher guidance. Programs such as the new workgroup software that support collaborative problem solving and interactive decision making enrich the learning environment.

The zone of proximal development can serve as a guide for curricular and lesson planning. Children don't simply know something or not know it. They may arrive at a particular learning experience without knowing something but be ready to master the task if they have appropriate support. Appropriate support may include everything from thoughtful guidance from the teacher and productive discussion sessions with other students to electronic information resources such as encyclopedias on CD-ROM, software such as grammar checkers that help students identify potential writing weaknesses, and electronic brainstorming software that supports group problem analysis. In addition, the teacher may help students puzzle through a complex concept by simplifying the problem they are dealing with to bring it within the zone of proximal development. Then, as they develop understanding and the zone moves upward, the problem situation can be made more complex.

School learning should occur in a meaningful context. Constructivist instructional models emphasize the need to provide learning experiences within a meaningful context— often the context in which the knowledge is to be applied. Technology can facilitate this in many ways. An elementary class, for example, can exchange letters with a class in Australia while exploring the laserdisk program *From Alice to Ocean*, the story of one woman's trek through the continent on foot. A high school class studying *Macbeth* can take a simulated trip around Scotland and desktop publish a newsletter, complete with scanned photographs and charts, about the country.

Relate out-of-school experiences to the child's school experiences. Technology can help accomplish this in several ways. A 5th-grade class studying family history, for example, could create a multimedia presentation about the stories of their families, enhanced with scanned photographs, audio recordings, old maps, and excerpts from newspaper clippings. They could use telecommunications to research information that would inform their research in genealogy.

CONSTRUCTIVISM IN THE TECHNOLOGY-ENRICHED LANGUAGE ARTS CLASSROOM

What does a social constructivist English language arts classroom look like? In an 8th-grade language arts class taught by a constructivist teacher, students select the novels, stories, nonfiction, plays, and so on that appeal to their interests. The teacher provides guidance and support in the process of selecting and in the process of reading and writing. At times the class may read the same literary piece and discuss it as a group. Or small groups may discuss a literary piece or a written draft. In that case, members of the group are considered an interpretive community or a discourse community, a community of readers and writers—like the group in Mr. Carr's junior class who work in collaboration to make sense of the text.

Suppose the book being discussed is Mark Twain's *The Adventures of Huckleberry Finn*, a book that has become controversial because some consider it a revered American classic while others have succeeded in barring it from use in schools because of racist undercurrents. One teaching approach to *Huck Finn* is to conduct a lesson in a way that ensures students understand the traditionally accepted interpretations of the book. Think of this as something like handing out a recipe for a casserole to the students. If the recipe is followed precisely, we would expect the cooks to produce casseroles with the same flavor and appearance every time they are made—class after class, year after year. From a constructivist viewpoint, that is impossible. Although the text of the recipe may appear unchanging, constructivists believe the recipe itself is not static. It will be varied by the cooks every time it is reproduced. Therefore, the resulting dish may be a little different or even radically different, depending on how the recipe is adapted, and the adaptation has everything to do with the background and experience of the cook, the context (the surroundings and time period) in which it is considered, and the interactions of the cook with others. An interpretation of *Huck Finn* by a student growing up in an area where racial prejudices are a part of the culture may be quite different from one made by a student born and raised in a multicultural environment where racial prejudice is considered unacceptable by most of the community. An interpretation of *Huck Finn* by an 8th-grade discourse community living in Selma, Alabama, may vary considerably from the 1940s to the post-Sputnik 1950s or the civil rights years of the 1960s or in the midst of the multiculturalism awareness movement of the 1990s. The emphasis, then, is not on a recipe for knowing what *Huck Finn* is about. Rather, it is on how the students absorb the information, filter it, and reproduce it in a form that reflects a personal interpretation—an experiencing—a unique version of the casserole.

Computer-based technology supports a constructivist discourse community because it provides ways to access and process information, to experience audio and visual presentations of literature, to publish, and to communicate across distances. The 8th-grade discourse community doing a unit study of *Huck Finn* would look like a workshop in which different activities are taking place. For example, the class may be divided into four small groups who are preparing for a debate to determine if *Huck Finn* should be banned. After researching arguments for and against censorship, each group could collaboratively write a persuasive essay using *Aspects*, a writing program that allows conferences in which two or more students can write a single document from different screens. Once the essays are completed, a debate could be conducted with representatives from each group making up two teams, one for the pro side and one for the con side.

Another small group could conduct a poll on racial equality or censorship through KidsNet, an electronic telecommunications service for students on the Internet (See Chapter 8 for more information), to tap into the opinions of other 8th-grade students in different schools, districts, regions, or states. Still another group might research archives to find information about Mark Twain, racial discrimination in the 1880s, and reactions to Mark Twain's work when it was first published. Those who are intrigued with the issues brought up in the novel—racism, friendship, adventure, abandonment, loyalty, cynicism, morality, and hypocrisy—might respond to the work through writing a poem or a short story. Using a word processing program would allow them to easily draft, revise, and edit as they craft their literary piece. Using a presentation program like *Persuasion* or *PowerPoint*, they can display their creation on a series of screens that have color, sound, and animation.

The culmination of the unit of study could be a newsletter produced using a desktop publishing program like *The Student Writing Center* or *PageMaker*. The newsletter could include informative articles, editorials, poetry, fiction, graphics related to the poll, and pictures scanned from books, magazines, or other sources. It could be distributed to each member of the class, to other classes within the school, to other schools, and to members of the community. Also, articles could be submitted to writing contests. For example, every year, the National Council of Teachers of English recognizes hundreds of students through their Promising Young Writers Program for Eighth Grade Students—a competition that "seeks out students who demonstrate exceptional writing skills and recognizes them for their achievements." Poetry, fiction, nonfiction, or other work could be submitted for publication in national teen magazines that publish student writing, for example, *Merlyn's Pen*, *Kid's Magazine*, *Stone Soup*, or *Scholastic Voice*.

The electronic version of *Huckleberry Finn* by BookWorm is also a good resource. Mark Twain's words come alive with graphics, audio recordings, and movies. In addition, students can read, use references, take notes, and write papers at the same time because the program provides productivity tools that enhance the experience of reading and responding to literature. When the electronic book is explored by a small group, the discussion that results from individual interpretations provides a rich learning experience.

In this 8th-grade constructivist classroom, students use *Huck Finn* as the springboard from which to explore their interests, read and synthesize information, use their background knowledge as they formulate their own interpretations, take risks, share and justify their views, and publish their writing. Their learning environment is a fertile context for learning. Books and writing supplies are abundant. Computer-based technology is easily accessible and always available. Students are encouraged to take ownership of the room, and the teacher provides support, coaching, guidance, and direction.

Perhaps this description of a constructivist classroom resembles a whole language classroom or a reading/writing workshop environment. In fact, methods of teaching language such as whole language and the reading/writing workshop are models of a constructivist perspective applied in practice. These and others (authentic instruction, situated learning, and anchored instruction) will be discussed below. The basic premise of a constructivist classroom is that students learn language in purposeful ways. Because they connect their exploration of reading, writing, and communication to the real world, their learning transcends the classroom. Programs like *Aspects*, Kidsnet, *The Student Writing Center*, *PowerPoint*, and the electronic book version of *The Adventures of Huckleberry Finn* help transport students to that real world.

SOME CONSTRUCTIVIST INSTRUCTIONAL MODELS

When Peter Tangeman, the dentist at the start of this chapter, conducted his research of professional journals, he likely came across articles that contained one or more of these terms in the leads of articles about instructional styles: whole language, reading workshop, writing workshop, situated learning, anchored instruction, and authentic instruction. All of these classify particular methods of teaching and learning. All are rooted in constructivist theoretical ground and consequently overlap. Situated learning and anchored instruction are evident in whole language and the reading/writing workshop. Although the whole language and workshop approaches are nearly identical in their foundation, whole language is more often used to describe elementary school activities and reading/writing workshop is more often used to describe middle and secondary school activities. The explanations provided here are intended to give a brief overview of these concepts and to show how technology can be used to support them.

WHOLE LANGUAGE

Whole language has been described as a philosophy, an approach, or a theory-based instructional practice. Regardless of how whole language is categorized, it can generally be described as "a perspective on learning and teaching based on a number of fundamental theoretical assumptions" (Edelsky, 1992). One of these assumptions, which is certainly in line with Vygotsky's social constructivism, is that learning and literacy are social activities. Whole language advocates stress that using authentic language activities is the most effective way to teach reading and writing. For example, authentic literacy activities may include writing letters to family members or pen pals, reading stories aloud to others in the household, scanning a magazine for articles of interest, writing to order something, to tell a story, to explain something, or to complain about something. Reading is for the appreciation of writing, and writing is done to produce text that will be read by real audiences. Because the teacher is a member of the social community of readers and writers that emerges in the classroom, the teacher is a model who demonstrates literacy by practicing reading and writing along with the children.

Another assumption is that making sense of things is a major part of learning. Therefore, learning is a transactional activity. Each member of the literate community constructs meaning by bringing background knowledge to the task of reading and writing and by discussing the stories read or the pieces written with other members of the community. Such active involvement on the part of the learner means each child responds to literature in a unique way and shares that response with others.

A third assumption of whole language is that learning requires taking risks and experimenting. Students are allowed to make choices related to the activity with which they are involved. For example, they are free to choose the books they would like to read or the writing form—storytelling or poetry, for instance—that they would like to try. Students and teachers negotiate a curriculum, one that taps the students' interests and provides for new and challenging experiences.

Perhaps the most fundamental aspect of taking risks in learning literacy is taking ownership of work. Students are given responsibility for interpreting what they read and for writing what they mean in authentic contexts. One role of the teacher guiding a student's experimentation is to praise strengths so that the student becomes a confident risk-taking contributor to the literate community. Weaknesses are not completely ignored, but they do not drive the teaching strategies or the learning activities.

One assumption of whole language that has incited much public debate in recent years is that written language is learned like oral language. That is, literacy is learned whole to part and back to whole. In this approach, phonics is taught within the activity of reading and writing rather than as a prerequisite for reading and writing, which has been the traditional approach in elementary education. As a result, whole language is considered by some to ignore phonics. This is not the case, however. Phonics know-how is achieved in a whole language environment by immersing children in language. Letter/sound relationships develop as spoken words and written words are connected. Teachers work within the child's zone of proximal development by reading aloud big books, posters, and poems and discussing prominent sound features within the text, thereby reinforcing letter/sound relationships. They play tape recordings of books, poems, and songs and encourage children to listen to tapes and follow printed material.

Many electronic books, such as the *Living Books* series from Broderbund, reinforce letter/sound relationships by highlighting words in the story as they are pronounced in the charming voices of animated characters. In *Grandma and Me*, one of the most popular of the *Living Books*, the child-character tells the story of a trip to the beach with his grandmother. The illustrations on the screen are colorful and attractive, but the most appealing feature is that elements of the scene move and make sounds if the viewer clicks them with the computer's mouse pointer. For example, when the bus coming down the road is clicked, you hear the motor and the squeal of brakes. Just as the student can connect the sound of the bus with the image of the bus, the student can connect the sound of the words with the letters that make up the words of the story. The words are placed at the top of the illustrations, just as is done in many picture books, and each word is highlighted as it is read. In addition, the student can click on any word in the text and hear it pronounced. Electronic books are excellent materials for creating social activities and promoting reading and writing in an authentic and meaningful context.

Perhaps the most debated issue concerning whole language is whether it is effective. Several studies support the argument that the whole language approach is a sound and rational approach to teaching literacy. Ribowsky (1985) for example, compared a code emphasis approach (intensive focus on phonics) with a whole language approach (Shared Book Experience approach; see Holdaway, 1979) on emergent literacy of kindergarten students. The results showed that whole language students did better on tests of letter recognition and knowledge of consonant letter/sound relationships. Whole language children showed significantly greater growth in their concepts about print and various aspects of language and literacy.

A two-year study by Stice and Bertrand (1990) compared 50 at-risk first graders, 25 in five different whole language classrooms and 25 in traditional phonics and skills-based classrooms. Both quantitative and qualitative measures were used. Whole language children showed great gains and better performance on all measures than did the children who attended traditional phonics and skills-based classes. The researchers concluded that the whole language students had a greater awareness of alternative strategies for dealing with reading problems. They also concluded that whole language children appeared more aware that the purpose of reading is to make meaning (rather than merely to call out the words) and that they appeared to be developing greater independence in both reading and writing. An annotated list of research that supports the whole language approach can be found in Stephens (1991).

READING/WRITING WORKSHOP

In the last decade the reading/writing workshop has gained favor and fervor within the educational community. As with most methodological or pedagogical innovations, the workshop has been redefined, realigned, and renamed on its journey towards tradition. It's early predecessor was perhaps the writing workshop (Murray, 1968), popularized by the

various writing projects that began in the late 1970s. Reading workshops grew to complement the writing workshop; they invite students' "active involvement as readers of others'
writing" (Atwell, 1987). Because they encompass reading, writing, speaking, and listening, they are also referred to as literacy workshops (Strickland & Strickland, 1993).

What does a reading/writing workshop classroom look like? Perhaps the most immediately obvious feature is its physical appearance. Unlike the arrangement of a traditional
classroom—rows of desks, a centrally located teacher's desk, and some bookshelves, the
workshop may be divided into several areas with tables for writing, a table for conferencing, rugs and bean-bags for lying on the floor to read, a publishing area with computers and
bookbinding equipment (Atwell, 1987; Rief, 1992). Hundreds of books, a variety of reference materials, and writing supplies (paper, pens, pencils) are available for student use,
and student work is displayed throughout. Most importantly, the teacher rarely takes center stage; instead the teacher moves from student to student, assisting with writing, reading, and publishing—all within the same class period.

Collaboration in the workshop entails sharing responses, ideas, drafts, and finished
written products through conferences with the teacher, conferences with peers, and journal
exchanges with each other, with the teacher, and with members of the nonclassroom community such as parents and siblings. Collaborating to make meaning, rather than surmis-
ing or reiterating teacher-held interpretations, is the function of small-group discussion and
whole-class discussion. The role of the teacher is also that of a learner who, in collaboration with students, constructs meaning through reading, writing, speaking, and listening.

Perhaps this role of the teacher as a collaborator and facilitator is most clearly mani-
fested in the exchange that occurs during a conference. Conferences are typically designed
to help students form and achieve their personal goals. Students make appointments with
the teacher to discuss their writing (Elbow, 1990). Atwell (1987, p. 87) says the teacher in
a conference sits quietly, waits, listens, and gives "time and ownership" so that students
can be helped to know "what it is they want to use time to do." Rief (1992, p. 123)
describes her role in eliciting her student's self-reflection:

> I ask the student to read his or her piece or a portion of it. I jot down what I liked or heard
> or what struck me, write down any questions, and add a suggestion or two after the read-
> ing. I try to keep all my responses focused on the student's response to "How can I help
> you?" That question alone asks the student to evaluate the strengths and weaknesses of the
> piece before a conference even begins.

Students do not start the workshop knowing how to conduct a conference, and Atwell
describes how she "sets the tone for workshop talk" by role playing and by providing
structured guides for establishing productive and positive conferencing techniques. The
merit of conferencing was identified in Atwell's study of her students, which revealed that
whole-group sharing and peer conferencing were integral to their writing environment.

When technology is added to the picture, conferencing takes on new dimensions. As
the case study of Mr. Carr's literature response activity shows, small groups can engage in
prewriting activities such as brainstorming, or they can share responses to each other's
writing using the Interchange feature of *Daedalus*. The advantage of conferencing electronically is that the entire conversation is documented. Each member of the conference

group can get a printout of the comments made by peers. *Aspects* is a similar writing program that offers another advantage. Small groups or whole classes can respond or edit a single document simultaneously. Or they can create a document collaboratively. For example, after one person sets up a conference on screen, others are invited to join and can take turns writing the same document from different computers. By opening a "chat box," students can have an on-screen dialogue about the direction of the piece. All members of the conference have the ability to add or change text on the shared document, or they can change the text's font or other attributes.

Journals, particularly dialogue journals, also serve as forums for discussion. Atwell turned to these on the hunch that "kids' written responses to books would go deeper than their talk" and that "a written exchange between two readers, student and adult expert, would move readers even deeper inside written texts, with the give and take of the dialogue helping them to consider and develop their thoughts." Her hunch was validated by the resulting correspondence, which went "far beyond plot synopses and traditional teacher's manual issues such as genre, theme, and character to give accounts of our processes as readers, to speculate on authors' processes as writers, to suggest revisions in what we've read, to see connections between a published author's work and our own writing, to see connections between books and our own lives, and to engage in some serious, and not so serious literary gossip" (p. 165).

Keeping dialogue journals on a hard drive that is accessible to all members of the class allows students to easily read literature responses written by others and to enter comments into their journals, continuing the ongoing conversation Atwell describes. Such dialogue journals do not have to be restricted to the students and adults within the immediate community of readers and writers, however. Using telecommunications, dialogue can extend beyond the locality of the community to other communities throughout the country, even throughout the world. Using Internet resources, newsgroups can be established for the purpose of evaluating young adult literature, for example. Sharing responses with readers and writers in this manner offers marvelous opportunities for serious and not-so-serious "literary gossip."

Knowledge shared within the reading-writing workshop is collaboratively constructed. As Strickland and Strickland (1993, p. 185) state "Learning is organic, shaped by contradictions, growing with the viewpoints and arguments being offered." It is this process of interpretation of literature or of their own writing that is at least as important as the object itself in determining the direction of literary study (Elbow, 1990; Rief, 1992). Electronic tools not only facilitate but also expand the possibilities for activity that supports a constructive process inherent in the workshop approach.

"At the beginning of the year I immerse all of us in reading and writing experience, so we can begin to find our own voices and so the students can trust me as a learner also," Rief notes (1992, p. 123). Students in a reading/writing workshop are encouraged to bring to their activity the knowledge that they have accumulated as inhabitants of social and cultural communities.

Through workshop activities such as peer conferences, small group discussion, dialogue journals, response journals, and projects that encourage them to investigate people and places in the community and to communicate orally, through writing or other media with audiences beyond the teacher and the classroom, learners are teachers. Rief (1992, p. 3) stresses that, in becoming conscious of the diversity, all players gain knowledge:

We are all different—all bringing our own learning experiences and learning styles into that room. No matter what I present, each student sees it differently and takes his or her own meaning from that experience. It is this diversity that I try to foster in my classroom. I want to hear all the diverse voices of my kids. I want them to hear each other. We are all learners/teachers.

SITUATED LEARNING

Vygotsky's theories, and those of other developmental psychologists, were the foundation for the concept of situated learning (see Brown, Collins, & Duguid, 1989). The articles in the March 1993 and October 1994 issues of *Educational Technology* are dedicated to the topic of situated learning. In her review of situated learning, McLellan (1993, p. 5) explains that the developers, including Brown, Collins, and Duguid, believed that "many teaching practices implicitly assume that conceptual knowledge can be abstracted from the situation in which it is learned and used." Situated learning proponents, however, argue that "knowledge is situated and is partly a product of the activity, context, and culture in which it is used (p. 5).

Thus, it cannot be taught in the abstract. It must be taught in context. Brown, Collins, and Duguid (1989) suggest one form of situated learning, cognitive apprenticeship, the goal of which is to help students construct their own understanding of the topic. Activities to support that include coaching and mentoring, providing a cognitive scaffolding that helps the learner make sense of a topic, serving as a mentor and coach, and helping the student relate the topic to both personal experiences and the context in which that knowledge will be applied. Situated learning proponents also support collaborative problem solving as an instructional strategy.

For the teacher considering adoption of this approach to the classroom:

> . . . the challenge of situated learning theory becomes one of developing methodologies and course content that support cooperative activity, and reflect the complex interaction between what individuals already know and what they are expected to learn, recognizing that ultimately meaning can only be established by and not for the learner. [Harley, 1993]

Seen from this perspective the design and delivery of instruction is not the creation and use of detailed lesson plans that specify exactly what the teacher and student should be doing at various points in the lesson. As Harley (1993, p. 49) puts it, "Prespecified, step by step instruction can no longer be developed on the assumption that the process can control the specifics of meaning constructed by the learner." Instead, it is the creation of an environment in which groups of students explore and analyze, think and reflect, propose and act. Technology supports such environments in many ways—from supplying sources of information such as multimedia materials to providing tools of expression that students can use. Another way is the creation of interesting environments in which to study a topic. One such environment was developed by Bransford and his colleagues at Vanderbilt University (Cognition and Technology Group at Vanderbilt, 1993), who refer to the use of their program as "anchored instruction."

ANCHORED INSTRUCTION

This instructional framework emphasizes "conditionalized knowledge" (Bransford et al., 1990, p. 123), that is, knowledge acquired through use in contextualized problem solving situations rather than through the presentation of isolated facts. These problem solving situations, or "anchors," can generate interest and enable students to identify and define problems and to pay attention to their own perception and comprehension of these problems (p. 123). By anchoring or situating learning in purposeful, problem solving environments, inert facts become conceptual tools that can be readily transferred to new problem solving situations. Reflexive awareness (experiencing changes in perception and understanding of the anchor as the situation is considered from new points of view) as well as contextual relevance are key in the construction of knowledge through anchored instruction.

The Cognition and Technology Group at Vanderbilt (CTGV) (1993) designed situated learning environments anchored in the movies *Young Sherlock Holmes* and *Oliver*.

> Students first watched these videos [from videodisk because they had much more control over viewing] and then explored them from the perspective of a film-maker who might be checking each one for quality and authenticity. How interesting and causally connected were the major plot and subplots? How authentic were the settings and the actions of the characters in the settings? By tracing cause connections, character motives, and goal-oriented behaviors, students were able to learn a great deal about the structure of stories, about the nature of life in turn-of-the-century Victorian England, and about general guidelines for exploring the authenticity of a wide variety of stories and settings. [p. 52]

Regarding the challenges they faced in using anchored instruction and situated learning environments, CTGV comments:

> One of the greatest challenges that anchored curricula pose of teachers derives from the need to change their role from a "provider of information" to a coach and often a fellow learner. . . . In the *Sherlock* program, different students might choose to explore a variety of issues relevant to the Young Sherlock and Oliver anchors—issues such as the Egyptian culture that is mentioned in the movie, the nature of schooling in Victorian England, and so forth. . . . In order to encourage and support student generated learning, teachers must be flexible; they cannot follow a fully scripted lesson plan. In addition, teachers cannot be experts in each topic that students choose to pursue, so they must often become learners along with their students. This can be difficult for many teachers, especially when children are accustomed to classroom cultures in which the teacher normally functions as "expert" rather than a "guide" and "learner." [p. 54]

The Vanderbilt group describes other problems teachers face when using situated learning environments. For example, teachers report it is sometimes difficult to decide when "students really need guidance versus when students are struggling in a constructive way with a problem or issue" (p. 54). Situated learning is not raw "discovery" learning where students are on their own without guidance and support from the teacher. In Vygotskian style, teachers take very active roles in the classroom and they do provide some direct instruction. Direct instruction provider is only one of the many roles the teachers play, however, and it is not the most important.

A TIME FOR THE SOCIAL CONSTRUCTIVIST PERSPECTIVE

Why is social constructivism a popular direction for literacy education? The setting is right for social constructivism. Making meaning of the world is challenged in ways that were not possible before today's computer technology. Social values emphasize cultural diversity as the profile of the nation seems more and more to resemble the global community. Businesses are seeking a workforce with creativity, problem solving skills, and the ability to work collaboratively.

As we approach the new millennium, the rapid changes in computer technology, and the ever-growing use of telecommunications in particular, have given rise to the notion of a single world community. Distance is no longer a barrier. Conversations can occur across oceans almost as easily as they can occur across a conference table. Professionals in all fields are finding that teleconferencing opens doors for collaborative problem solving. Surgeons, for example, share expertise as they collectively diagnose patients whom they never physically meet. Business people located in different areas of the world can hold multi-member business meetings without having to travel. Scientists can collaboratively conduct experiments in a virtual lab—that is, they can simultaneously share in a research process as it unfolds in labs located blocks, miles, cities, or oceans apart. Through the telephone and television, college students can monitor or participate in a class discussion although they are far away from the classroom in which it is actually occurring.

Changes in society's values have helped to make education a fertile ground for social constructivism. A long-brewing dissatisfaction with standardization, particularly in testing, brought social and cultural differences to the forefront of community, state, and national debates. Minority groups in particular argued that they remained disenfranchised because they did not share the same cultural background of the test makers. In her 10-year ethnographic study of a community of the Piedmont, Heath (1983) provided convincing evidence that the literacy of socially disempowered children was no less effective a literacy than that considered appropriate by the city school. The children's literacy suited the needs of their community; it was the mechanism they used successfully for making meaning of their world. However, it did not necessarily suit the needs of the city school community. Therefore, children whose cultural and historical literacy was not valued by the townspeople's community were labeled as learning disabled or remedial.

Multiculturalism—another prevailing concept in educational literature—has brought a nationwide awareness to the differences in cultural history and culture-specific understandings of the world. It's within this circle that debates concerning whose knowledge is "American" continue to unravel perspectives on what counts as "knowledge" in our country. Is it solely that of Western heritage? Or is it found in the melding of African, Native American, Hispanic, Eastern, and other cultural histories into one that is implied in the "melting pot" metaphor? Or is what counts for knowledge dependent on the interactions that occur within a consolidation of individual and diverse discourse communities that do not share a common culture? Hirsch (1988) is perhaps the most identifiable of those who would like this country to have a common "cultural literacy." Many proponents of English education reform prefer a national community within which cultural diversity is the goal. At the 1987 English Coalition Conference, scholars, college educators, and school teachers agreed that the goal of literacy education in schools is to uphold democracy through diversity (Elbow, 1990). The conferees brought to the table teacher stories, philosophy, and current research on literacy and learning theory, all of which seemed to support a student-centered learning environment.

Still another area that has supported the movement towards social constructivism is business. Schools have for decades been regarded as the training ground for future political and business leaders as well as the working citizenry who keep our productivity competitive in an increasingly global economy. Often politicians and business people have taken significant roles in the formulation and reformulation of schools. In the first half of this century, schools resembled the nation's factories. That was an effective and appropriate model because most of the graduates would find employment in factories. Following directions, writing in business conventional form, and working independently, for example, were among the skills that were valued by the business world. Times have changed. Most recently the business community has urged educators to teach future employees to be creative, solve problems, be technologically literate, and collaborate well in teams in order to reach consensus and execute plans.

As Cunningham (1992, p. 36) points out, a social constructivist perspective in education is fitting in a time when collaboration and cooperation are essential social, economic, and cultural processes:

> The role of education in a constructivist view is to show students how to construct knowledge, to promote collaboration with others, to show the multiple perspectives that can be brought to bear on a particular problem, and to arrive at self-chosen positions to which they can commit themselves, while realizing the basis of other views with which they disagree.

SUMMARY

The basic claim of constructivism is, according to Bruner (1990, p. 25):

> simply that knowledge is "right" or "wrong" in light of the perspective we have chosen to assume. Rights and wrongs of this kind—however well we can test them—do not sum to absolute truths and falsities. The best we can hope for is that we be aware of our own perspective and those of others when we make our claims of "rightness" and "wrongness."

A constructivist teacher creates a context for learning in which students can become engaged in the process of their own discoveries. They are guided through problems, adventures, and challenges that are rooted in real life situations, that interest them, and that have self-satisfying outcomes. They are aware of their own strengths and weaknesses and they work towards meaningful goals. Teachers facilitate their growth, as do peers and other members of their community. Technology provides essential tools with which to accomplish the goals of a constructivist classroom:

- Telecommunications tools such as e-mail and the Internet provide a means for dialogue, discussion, and debate—interactivity that leads to the social construction of meaning. Students can talk with other students, teachers, and professionals in places far from their classroom. They can become aware of similarities and differences in modes of interpretation that relate to cultural or social differences.
- Networked writing programs like *Aspects* and *Daedalus* provide a unique platform for collaborative writing. Students can write for real audiences who respond instantly and who participate in a collective writing activity.
- Problem-solving simulations like the *Jasper Woodbury* series make learning meaningful. Students join intellectual forces to solve problems and develop the literacy skills that are needed to solve a particular problem.
- Desktop publishing and presentation programs provide readers and writers access to an authentic purpose for literacy—publishing.
- Interactive electronic books like the *Living Books* provide scaffolding to help students advance within their zone of proximal development. Young readers can associate sounds with letters and images. The captivating visual and audio features of electronic books make them appealing tools that can engage readers in lively social activity.

Peter Tangeman, the dentist intent on becoming a teacher, will find after his search of timely literature that the constructivist approach to literacy education is one that provides students with a learning environment rooted in authentic activities—activities that relate to real-life social interactions. He will find that technology offers endless opportunities to enhance meaningful and purposeful literacy activity that extends beyond the classroom itself. Once in the classroom, he will find that he will be a member of a community or readers and writers, as much a learner as a teacher.

MICROTEACHING ACTIVITIES

1. Take the role of a composition teacher working with a group of three or four students (volunteers from your class) who will be discussing this chapter electronically using *Daedalus* or another similar program. During the class meeting before you will do this microteaching, select your volunteers and let them know they will be participating in this activity. Then reread "Flying on Daedalus" in this chapter and adapt the approach to the task of discussing this chapter.
2. Pose a problem that can be solved by locating and interpreting information available on electronic information resources the class can use. Electronic encyclopedias or CD-ROMs on special topics such as dinosaurs, animals, plants, or ecology might be

useful resources. An example of a problem might be "we can plant a small garden in a plot beside our classroom windows, but we need to know what plants will survive well in our climate, the soil conditions, the plants' fertilizer needs, whether the growing cycle for the plants fits our school year, pests that might attack the plants, and whether our location on the north side of the building will be a problem for the plants. Use the resources available to develop a list of 4 to 8 plants your group thinks would be best for the class garden." Help students spend about 30 minutes on their task in small groups of 4 or 5. Because this activity would normally be spread across several days in a classroom, you may want to provide more help than usual to point students to useful resources and help them learn to use them. If time permits, enter some of the plant lists in one of the computer programs available today that "grow" plants on the screen to see how the garden would look in 2, 4, 8, 12, and 16 weeks.

3. Assume you are the team leader for a group of literacy teachers in your school. Select 3 or 4 other students from your class and assign them roles as other teachers on your team. You are meeting before the beginning of the year to plan 3 social constructivist literacy activities that all the teachers on the team will use in their classrooms. Set the scene by explaining the subject and grade level this team teaches, and lead the group in a brainstorming session that generates 6 or 7 ideas that are not in this text but do fit the constructivist approach. Once you have at least 6 possibilities, work with the group to narrow the list down to 1 or 2 lessons. Then discuss how the lesson would work in the classroom, what materials would be needed (software, computers, books, consumable materials), and how much time would be assigned to the lesson.

REFERENCES

Atwell, N. (1987). *In the middle: Writing, reading, and learning with adolescents.* Portsmouth, NH: Heinemann.

Bransford, J. D., Sherwood, R. D., Hasselbring, T. S., Kinzer, C. K., & Williams, S. M. (1990). Anchored instruction: Why we need it and how technology can help. In D. Nix & R. J. Spiro (Eds.), *Cognition, education, and multimedia: Exploring ideas in high technology* (pp. 115–142). Hillsdale, NJ: Erlbaum.

Brooks, M., & Brooks, L. (1993). *In search of understanding: The case for constructivist classrooms.* Alexandria, VA: Association for Supervision and Curriculum Development.

Brown J., Collins, A., & Duguid, S. (1989). Situated cognition and the culture of learning. *Educational Researcher, 18(1),* 32–42.

Bruner, J. (1990). *Acts of meaning.* Cambridge, MA: Harvard University Press.

Collins, A. (1991). The Role of Computer Technology in Restructuring Schools. *Phi Delta Kappan, 73* (1), 28–36.

Cognition and Technology Group at Vanderbilt. (1993). Anchored instruction and situated cognition revisited. *Educational Technology, 33*(3), 52–70.

Cunningham, D. J. (1992). Assessing constructions and constructing assessments: A dialogue. In Duffy & Jonassen.

Duffy, T. M., & Jonassen, D. H. (1992). *Constructivism and the technology of instruction: A conversation.* Hillsdale, NJ: Erlbaum.

Edelsky, C. (Ed.). (1992). *Language arts topics and educational issues: Information sheets.* Tucson, AZ: Center for the Expansion of Language and Thinking.

Elbow, P. (1990). *What is English?* New York: Modern Language Association of America, and Urbana, IL: National Council of Teachers of English.

Forman, G., & Pufall, P. (1988). *Constructivism in the computer age.* Hillsdale, NJ: Erlbaum.

Harley, S. (1993). Situated learning and classroom instruction. *Educational Technology, 33*(3), 46–51.

Heath, S. B. (1983). *Ways with words: Language, life, and work in communities and classrooms.* New York: Cambridge University Press.

Hirsch, E. D. (1988). *Cultural literacy: What every American needs to know.* New York: Vintage Books.

Holdaway, D. (1979). *Foundations of literacy.* New York: Aston Scholastic.

McLellan, H. (1993). Situated learning in focus. *Educational Technology, 33*(3), 59.

Murray, D. (1968). *A writer teaches writing.* Boston: Houghton Mifflin.

Ribowsky, H. (1985). The effects of a code emphasis approach and a whole language approach upon emergent literacy of kindergarten children. EDRS document, ED 269 720.

Rief, L. (1992). *Seeking diversity: Language arts with adolescents.* Portsmouth, NH: Heinemann.

Sarbin, T., & Kitsuse, J. (1994). *Constructing the social.* Thousand Oaks, CA: Sage Publications.

Stephens, D. (1991). *Research on whole language: Support for a new curriculum.* Katonah, NY: Richard C. Owen.

Stice, C., & Bertrand, N. (1990). *Whole language and the emergent literacy of at-risk children: A two-year comparative study.* Nashville, TN: Center of Excellence, Tennessee State University.

Strickland, J., & Strickland, K. (1993). *Uncovering the curriculum: Whole language in secondary and postsecondary classrooms.* Portsmouth, NH: Boynton/Cook.

Twain, M. (1885). *The adventures of Huckleberry Finn.* Boston: Houghton Mifflin.

Vygotsky, L. (1962). *Thought and language.* Cambridge, MA: MIT Press.

Vygotsky, L. (1978). *Mind in society.* Cambridge, MA: Harvard University Press.

SOFTWARE DISCUSSED IN THIS CHAPTER

Most of the software discussed in this chapter is available at large software centers that carry educational programs or from some of the larger mail order educational software suppliers such as:

Computer Centerline, 1500 Broad Street, Greensburg, PA 15601. Phone: 800-852-5802.

Educational Resources, 1550 Executive Drive, Elgin, Illinois 60123. Phone: 800-624-2926.

In the list below the producer of each program is listed where available, but many software companies sell primarily through mail order distributors and retail computer and software stores.

Aspects. Group Technologies, Inc.

Compton's Multimedia Encyclopedia. Compton's.

Daedalus. Daedalus.

Grandma and Me. Broderbund.

Jasper Woodbury series. Voyager Company.

Living Books series. Broderbund.

Multimedia Center.

PageMaker. Adobe/Aldus.

Student Writing Center. The Learning Company.

The Adventures of Huckleberry Finn. Bookworm Student Library.

The Civil War Game.

The Tortoise and the Hare. Broderbund.

CHAPTER THREE

Cognitive Constructivist Approaches

When Peter Tangeman completed his coursework and was certified to teach, he almost immediately was offered a job teaching 6th grade. On the first inservice day, he arrived early at the school's auditorium, where he found four rows of seats reserved for his group. Several people were there already, and he discovered that one of them was an old friend from high school, Julia Mason, who greeted him with curiosity.

"Peter, how are you?" she said. "I thought you went to medical school."

"Dental school, yes, and I practiced dentistry for a few years, but I decided that wasn't what I really wanted to do. It happens! How long have you been teaching, Julia?"

"This will be my eighth year."

"Eight years—that's great. I'll really depend on you to get me through my first, then. Do you have any secrets? Inside tips? Maybe some advice for the rookies?" he asked as he pulled out a yellow pad from his portfolio.

"Yes, read everything," she said, smiling. "This is a good example." She held up a magazine called *Language Arts*. "Lesson one: this is one of the informative journals in our field. And it's got a great article on constructivist CD-ROMs."

"Oh yes, constructivist. I know about that, about Vygotsky, about Piaget."

"Good," she said. "Then you'll fit in well in our program. We all use the whole language approach to teach reading and writing. Our methods are based on Piaget's constructivism. It's called cognitive constructivism."

"Did you read that in there?" he asked, pointing to the journal.

"As I said, read everything. And—" Before Julia could finish, the school's principal called to her. Promising to return soon, she handed the journal to Peter, then joined the principal near the stage.

Peter flipped through the pages to the table of contents. "Multimedia programs from a cognitive constructivist viewpoint" was the title of the third article listed. He smiled, shook his head slightly, and quietly observed Julia and the principal talking at the foot of the stage.

"Cognitive constructivism. OK. Read everything. OK, I will," Peter thought to himself.

WHAT IS COGNITIVE CONSTRUCTIVISM?

In Chapter 1 you learned that there are a variety of theories about how we learn. In Chapter 2 you were introduced to Vygotsky, a psychologist and philosopher whose work is the basis for the social constructivist perspective, a perspective that is becoming more and more evident in current school curricula. In this chapter you will read about another psychologist, Jean Piaget. Like Vygotsky, he proposed a theory of learning that places the child's individual development at the center of instruction. The followers of Vygotsky and Piaget share this basic assumption about learning, but they represent the two facets of the constructivist perspective: social constructivism and cognitive constructivism. Although the perspectives are actually quite similar, there are fundamental distinctions between them.

Remember that social constructivist educators stress the role of cultural history and social structures in the intellectual development of learners. They view language as the tool humans use to make sense of the world and as the tool adults use to guide students to new cognitive abilities. An adult can help a child advance toward higher levels of knowledge and reasoning if the adult works within the child's zone of proximal development. Vygotsky's claims were in fact a response to Piaget's claims. In a sense, social constructivism is an elaboration and modification of cognitive constructivism as it was described by Piaget.

For Piaget, intellectual development cannot be pushed; it unfolds just as physical development does—naturally, at its own pace. All learners advance along stages regardless of cultural or societal differences. As they mature physically, they mature intellectually. Much research has been done on the maturation process along these stages, and the focus of the research has been on the mental processes that occur when people interact with their environment. This is perhaps where the line between social and cognitive constructivism is most clearly defined. Social constructivism spotlights the role of language as a tool used to spur forward intellectual growth; cognitive constructivism explores how language is processed at different stages of natural human development. The Vygotskian theorist would claim that children's intellectual maturation can be prompted and facilitated by adult intervention. A teacher, then, would take the role of a guide, and the classroom would have many opportunities for the teacher to provide scaffolding for the student as meaning is constructed. The Piagetian theorist, on the other hand, views intellectual maturation as a process that advances along its own natural and unique path, at its own genetically determined pace. The teacher neither directs nor urges learning but, instead, takes the role of facilitator, assessing the stage at which the student is functioning and providing a learning environment that coincides with the stage of development of each student. By doing this, the teacher recognizes the students' natural curiosity and challenges their problem solving abilities.

Cognitive constructivist researchers who engage in the study of how we become literate focus primarily on the cognitive *process* of reading and the *process* of writing. What happens in our minds as we read and write? How do we process the information we gather from our environment? Goodman (1994), for example, theorizes that errors readers make in reading are actually miscues. That is, they are produced by the same cues that produce appropriate oral responses to symbols. He sees reading as a process of sense making rather than simply an attempt to accurately decode and pronounce symbols.

Cognitive constructivists explore the natural inner processes that occur when a person reads, writes, or otherwise makes meaning and expresses or communicates thought. Many of the popular writing process techniques (prewriting, writing, revising), for instance, were first identified in the laboratories of researchers who set out to investigate the human process of writing rather than the written product. Perhaps the most well known of these is Emig (1971), who examined the writing behavior of 12th-grade students. Emig asked the young writers to compose aloud, that is, to tell her the thoughts and feelings that came to them as they wrote three short themes. She also asked them to reflect on their writing experiences growing up. She concluded that when young writers are engaged in meaningful writing, they devote much time and energy to planning, prewriting, and revision. Emig described the traditional product-oriented approach to writing as "neurotic" because drilling students on mechanical skills such as spelling and punctuation did not improve student writing and only served to disinterest writers and to disengage them from their natural process of writing. She called for a focus on the writer's inner processes, both mental and emotional, to guide instruction. Her study sparked a series of investigations into the private engagement of the writer in the act of writing.

Various forms of technology can stimulate and challenge the students' natural processes as they engage in literacy activities. Most exciting of these is multimedia. These tools let students explore the environment for a new type of literacy—one that adds visual images, sound, and hypertext capabilities to the child's literary expression and may have effects that are yet to be explored by educational researchers and psychologists.

This chapter will outline the roots of cognitive constructivism, how Piagetian principles come into play in a technology-rich classroom environment, how knowledge is constructed in that classroom, and the connection between Piaget's theory and whole language.

THE ROOTS OF COGNITIVE CONSTRUCTIVISM: PIAGET'S THEORY OF DEVELOPMENT

B. F. Skinner (1968), the best-known American behavioral psychologist, advocated the stimulus-response model to explain how we learn. His theory suggests that the most successful learning occurs when information is broken down into small parts that can be mastered. Learning can be observed as it happens by measuring the behavior of the learner. In the literacy classroom, this stimulus-response learning theory is evident in the skills development methods that are often used to teach reading and writing. Individual skills like letter-sound recognition in reading and capitalization rules in writing are isolated. Teachers use direct instruction, and students, who are drilled on the skills, demonstrate the behaviors that indicate they have mastered the skills and can advance to more complex skills that can then be applied to naturally occurring reading and writing experiences. The application of this bottom-up approach is explained more fully in Chapter 4.

The direction of education shifted when the behavioral theory of learning was challenged by a more child-centered learning theory developed by Swiss psychologist Jean Piaget (1972). Piaget proposed a developmental theory of learning and published more than 60 books on how children think. The premise of his theory is that children construct knowledge about their world through their active involvement in experiences that are meaningful to them and appropriate to their level of cognitive development. Piaget stressed that intelligence is a natural process that is continually unfolding. His genetic theory of cognitive development "above all sees knowledge as a continuous construction" (p. 17). Rather than the bottom-up approach commonly accepted in education, Piaget proposed a holistic approach. Children, he claimed, construct their knowledge at their own pace through reading, listening, exploring, and experiencing their environment.

Piaget's name is perhaps most often associated with the periods or stages of cognitive development: sensorimotor, concrete preoperational thinking, concrete operations, and formal operations.

Sensorimotor: birth to about age 2. In this period the focus is on movement and coordinating actions. Words are associated with objects.

Concrete Preoperational Thought: age 2 to about age 6. Language is used to verbalize mental activity. Children's play imitates their world, and they often make sense of what they see by giving life to inanimate objects. Cartoons, nursery rhymes, big books, and animated computer programs like *KidPix* and *Bailey's Book House* suit the child's natural interest in animism and fantasy.

Concrete Operations: age 7 to about age 11. Thinking moves from a one-dimensional to a multi-dimensional mode. Children can relate one idea or event to a system of interrelated parts; therefore, they are able to comprehend the conventions of a story (setting, plot, conflict resolution). Multimedia programs like *My Own Stories* and *HyperStudio* provide a canvas for the young reader/writer to build stories using text, colorful graphics, sound, and animation.

Formal Operations: age 11 to about age 15. Children can formulate theories, solve problems creatively, and evaluate; they can compose logically and interpret literature based on a broader comprehension of the rules that govern society. BookWorm's CD-ROM version of Mark Twain's *The Adventures of Tom Sawyer* is, for example, a stimulating visual and auditory reading experience that challenges the student to interpret and evaluate the story on different levels.

Cognitive abilities progressively develop through these stages until the child can reason logically. Although Piaget does not address the child's development of literacy skills as much as he does the child's mathematical and scientific reasoning, his stages have provided a basis for rationalizing curriculum for teaching reading and writing. Whole language, some have argued, is grounded in Piaget's genetic development theory. This will be discussed more fully later in this chapter.

Piaget's stages distinguish cognitive abilities temporally. Three processes of cognitive development—assimilation, accommodation, and equilibrium—are the mechanism that advances the learner.

Assimilation: integration of new data with existing cognitive structures, or schemata.

Accommodation: adjustment of cognitive structures to new situations.

Equilibrium: continuing readjustment between assimilation and accommodation.

Piaget recognized in children's cognitive conflicts the processes of knowledge construction in action. In other words, when children's behavior indicates cognitive conflict, such as argumentation, they are attempting to equilibrate or self-regulate. In Piagetian terms, they are attempting to accommodate information that has been assimilated. The result of this conflict is the restructuring of schemata, the knowledge the child had before thinking about the new data and resolving the problem presented in an unfamiliar situation.

PIAGETIAN PRINCIPLES IN A TECHNOLOGY-RICH ENVIRONMENT

Perhaps the most important responsibility of the teacher in a Piagetian classroom is to provide an environment for the spontaneous research of the child. The classroom filled with plenty of authentic activities to challenge students will allow students to construct their own knowledge. Also, students must be given opportunities to discover truths at their own pace and through their own experiences. Technology, particularly multimedia, offers a vast array of such opportunities. Three key Piagetian principles can guide teachers as they plan and create a technology-rich and challenging environment: learning is an active process, learning is a social process, learning is a developmental process.

Learning Is an Active Process

Direct experience, making errors, and looking for solutions are vital for the assimilation and accommodation of information. How information is presented is important. When information is introduced as an aid to problem solving, it functions as a tool rather than an isolated arbitrary fact (Bransford, Sherwood, & Hasselbring, 1988). Houghton Mifflin's *Channel READ* is a laserdisk program that places the student in a problem-solving situation. Young sleuths in the video are faced with a mystery to solve. They consult with Rita, the Bookmobile. Through telecommunications, she links them with real characters who teach them reading and writing strategies that will help solve the mystery. Similarly, the Learning Company's CD-ROM *Super Solvers Midnight Rescue* provides the young reader with hundreds of stimulating readings—short stories, posters, and newsletters—to solve a mystery. Children are challenged to find main ideas, recall key facts, and draw deductive conclusions. In one case, for example, the Master of Mischief has taken over Shady Glen

School, and, disguised as one of his five robots, he and his team plan to paint the place invisible. The student must use comprehension skills and deductive reasoning to interpret the information provided and stop the Master.

Writing using a computer also provides the active learning for cognitive development. Multimedia writing packages in particular stimulate creativity and challenge the writer to formulate thoughts and link them to images, or visual representations, of their world. *My Own Stories* by MECC and *Make-A-Book* by Teacher Support Software provide K–2 children with the opportunity to write, illustrate, and publish their own book with graphics. *MicroWorlds: Language Art* gives students in grades 4–8 the tools to create visual poetry, advertising, haiku, or cinquain in any shape, color, or direction. They can add special effects to their poetry or advertisement, such as sound and animation. Using software like *MicroWorlds*, children learn the conventions of language, book structure, and forms of poetry in a hands-on, creative activity.

Learning Is a Social Process

Group collaboration is perhaps one of the fundamental principles of Piaget's theory of learning. Forman and Cazden (1994) note that "Piaget placed more importance on peer interaction than upon adult-child interaction, so it is not surprising that the bulk of research on collaboration has shared a Piagetian perspective" (p. 172). Collaboration, interaction among a community of learners, small-group activities—these are essential for the real

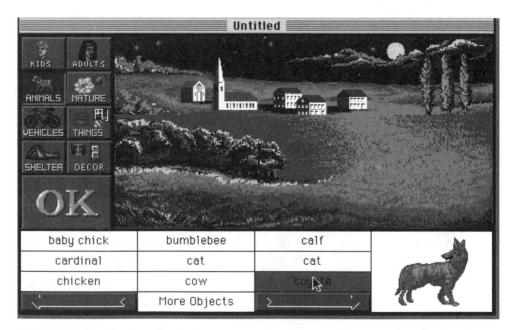

FIGURE 3-1 *My Own Stories* lets young writers use graphics, sound, and animation to design the page where they write their story.

and experimental activities that provide new information to build the child's schemata. The appropriate—almost natural—setting for technology in the classroom is one that invites social interaction. Computer screens are public. Several students can simultaneously view how one student is creating a newsletter with *The Student Writing Center* or reading about and viewing underwater life in Mindscape's *Oceans Below* CD-ROM. Collaborative groups can instantly see what changes occur on the screen as each member inputs information. Technology initiates children into the language and thoughts of others.

Consider the way Ms. Shellhamer's 3rd-grade class becomes involved in social literacy activities as they use the CD-ROM version of *Arthur's Birthday* as the focus of their activities.

Arthur's Birthday Bash

The 3rd-grade students in Ms. Shellhamer's class are buzzing with excitement. As Ms. Shellhamer explains, today is Arthur's birthday party.

"I enjoy reading Marc Brown's Arthur's Birthday with my students. We read other books about birthdays, such as The Secret Birthday Message by Eric Carle and A Birthday Wish by Ed Emberly. We do lots of reading, writing, and sharing about our

FIGURE 3-2 Arthur is busy addressing the invitations to his birthday party.

own birthdays. Because some of my children are from other countries, we always learn from them about how birthdays are celebrated in their homelands. Everyone has a favorite birthday story to share. Our grand finale is a birthday party for Arthur. This year it's different. We have a computer in the room, and we've used it to enhance our reading/writing workshop."

"This year we read the CD-ROM version of Arthur's Birthday. The children like the way CD-ROM books come to life, and they'll click and click to see what else will happen on the page. I also have several paperback versions of the books for the children to take home and read to their parents, or to read in class when they have spare time."

Ms. Shellhamer invites us to wander around the room, visit with the children, and look at their work posted on the walls. Our first stop is at the computer in the front of the room where Daniel and Ryan are reading Arthur's Birthday. They listen to the computer read them a page, then they read the page softly.

"I can't wait! I can't wait!" said Arthur. "Are you sure it's only . . ."

"I always forget what day that is," says Ryan. "Click on it."

Daniel clicks on the next word, it is highlighted, and then the computer says "Tuesday."

"Tuesday," say Daniel and Ryan. They continue reading until the end of the page. Then, they take turns clicking on their favorite hotspots. Daniel clicks on the baby, and

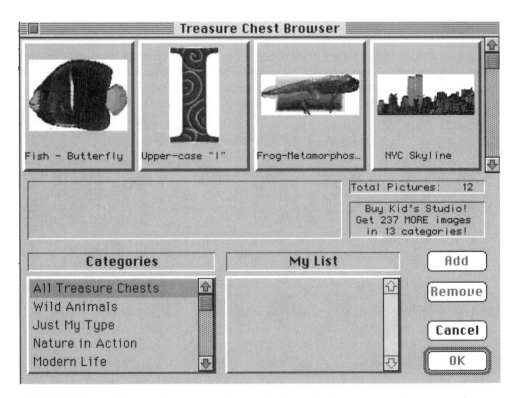

FIGURE 3-3 Kid's Studio comes with a collection of photographs, clip art, comic book characters, and illustrations.

both boys giggle as she throws cereal at D. W. Ryan clicks on Dad's coffee cup, which brings forth another round of giggles as Dad slurps his coffee and his eyes bug out.

We leave Daniel and Ryan and notice a group of students on the floor who are furiously coloring with a variety of colored markers. As we join them, Anita unfolds the banner they are coloring.

"It says 'Happy Birthday, Arthur!' and will go above the chalkboard," offers Sanobar. "We're kinda in a hurry to finish. We made it with Kid's Studio on the computer. I wish we had a color printer."

"Not me," Anita remarks. "I like to color."

Wandering around the room, looking at all the birthday cards and other artwork the students have made for the occasion, we pause in front of an assortment of party invitations.

"That one's mine," a small voice pops up. "I printed two. I took one home to my Mom and she's coming today. This other one Ms. Shellhamer put on the wall."

"Come and see the newspaper I made up about birthdays," says Cindy. We move toward the back of the room where the newspapers are proudly displayed.

"We helped each other write our newspapers. You know, peer editing," explains Cindy. "We had to write something about Arthur's birthday. Then, we got to write something else about our own birthdays. Do you like mine?"

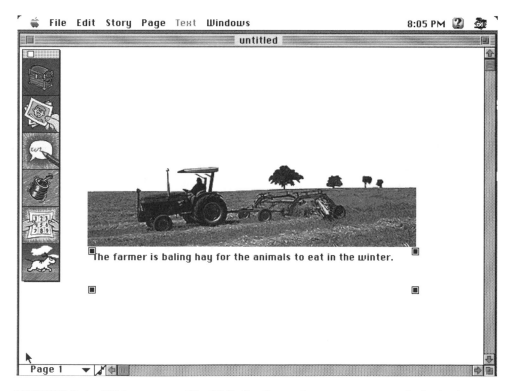

FIGURE 3-4 With programs like Kid's Studio, students can create cards, invitations, and even illustrated storybooks.

Learning Is a Developmental Process

A detailed exploration of the stages of development, schema building, and the construction of knowledge and how these are applied in the teaching of literacy is available in Goodman (1994):

> Piaget (1972) helps us to understand how meaning is constructed. It's easy to assimilate information as we read provided that it fits within our existing schemata. When there is a conflict between what we think we know and what we are learning, then accommodation must occur to rebuild those schemata. Readers must be capable of learning through reading in the sense of assimilating new knowledge to established schemata and also of accommodating existing schemata to new knowledge. But the ability of a reader to comprehend a given text is very much limited by the conceptual and experiential background of the reader, and there are strong limitations on how much new knowledge can be gained from a reading of a given text. [p. 1127]

FIGURE 3-5 The Writing Center makes it easy to create newspapers.

Teachers can provide a learning environment that helps expand the conceptual and experiential background of the reader, however, with technology support such as videodisks and CD-ROMs. These multimedia formats transport students to locations in time and space where they might not go in real life because they are physically or economically unable to. As Bransford, Sherwood, and Hasselbring (1988) note, by using video-technology, teachers can create learning environments that provide the contextual support necessary to make learning more meaningful. They suggest that this should be especially helpful for students who lack the background that is often presupposed in school. Houghton Mifflin's *Channel READ* is a good example of videodisk learning tools. CD-ROM programs that can provide the visual support and informative text to expand the reader's background are plentiful and relatively inexpensive. The ever popular *Carmen Sandiego* series by Broderbund helps students expand their knowledge of geography, history, and technology as they sharpen reading, comprehension, and inferencing skills. Mindscape's *Oceans Below* takes students into the depths of the oceans. Through MECC's *Oregon Trail*, students experience an important episode in U.S. history, and Software Toolworks' *The Animals* transports students to the world-famous San Diego Zoo.

STAGES OR NOT? QUESTIONING PIAGET'S THEORY

Piaget's theory has been challenged by educational researchers who contend that learning does not develop in a distinctive linear progression. They assert that not all children advance in genetically determined stairstep stages of development; one stage does not naturally lead to the next one until the learner has achieved the ability to logically analyze and order her or his environment. Vygotskian supporters argue that adult, peer, older children, and perhaps technological information resources can facilitate and encourage both cognitive and social development. According to Papert, a staunch supporter of Piaget and creator of LOGO (a computer program widely used in elementary schools), technology makes evident that children do progress in these stages, but they do so in different styles:

> In observing children who are programming computers, a substantial number do hold to a path of development that seems in spirit to be like what Piaget . . . would say is the norm. By the time they are 10 and 11, that is to say, just about when Piagetians would expect to see them moving into the formal stage, these children do show a style of programming that fits the model of "the logical." Faced with a problem, they subdivide it, modularize it, deal with the parts one at a time, put them together and make a program that is clearly logically structured.
>
> But other children demonstrate a different style—one in which a program emerges not through planning and subdivision of a problem but through something closer to the way in which a sculptor or painter makes a work of art—a process in which the plan of what is to be made emerges and is refined at the same time as the created object takes form. One might call it more of a negotiation between the creator and the material than an imposition of logical order. [Papert, 1988, p. 12]

Today educators are less confident that Piaget's theory of sequential stages of cognitive development—sensorimotor, concrete preoperational thought, concrete operations, and formal operations—is an accurate depiction of how all children develop cognitively throughout childhood. However, Piaget's analysis of the process by which humans construct meaning—through assimilation, accommodation, and equilibration—is still one of the most widely used frameworks for thinking about thinking. In Piaget's theory, telling children facts is not very helpful; they must experience things for themselves and create their own schema of the world. To do that they need interesting environments to explore that are appropriate to their level of development.

COGNITIVE CONSTRUCTIVISM IN THE TECHNOLOGY-RICH LANGUAGE ARTS CLASSROOM

What does a cognitive constructivist classroom look like? Imagine a 4th-grade language arts class taught by a cognitive constructivist. Opportunities for students to learn reading, writing, and communicating are embedded in thematic units. Within these units, students select novels, stories, nonfiction, comic books, and other reading materials that appeal to their interests. The teacher has created a learning environment filled with an assortment of challenging materials such as books, software, electronic books and encyclopedias on CD-ROMs, laserdisks, magazines, newspapers, games, posters, and audio recordings. Also available is equipment such as a cluster of computers, a printer, laserdisk player, and TV monitor, and supplies like construction paper, scissors, paper, drawing pencils and markers, and bookbinding materials. An LCD (liquid crystal display) panel connected to the computer or laserdisk player and placed on an overhead projector can project a large image of the output from the computer or laserdisk onto one of the blank walls. The image is large enough for all the students in the class to see at once and is often used when collaborative groups of students make reports.

At times the class may read the same book and discuss it as a group. If there are enough computers in the room, all students can together experience one or more programs and discuss them as a group. Or small groups may review a book or set of books, software programs, or a peer's written draft. Three to six people helping each other achieve a goal are often referred to as a cooperative or collaborative group, a peer review group, an interpretive community, or a discourse community. In Piagetian terms, a discourse community could be defined as a community of readers and writers who talk and question each other in order to help each other make sense of the information they are trying to accommodate into their existing schemata.

Suppose the unit of study in this class is animals. The topic is of particular interest because of the students' stage of cognitive development. Some will be in the concrete preoperational thought stage and some will be in the concrete operations stage. Remember that in the concrete preoperational thought stage (age 2 to about age 6), language is used to verbalize mental activity. Children's play imitates their world, and they often make sense of what they see by giving life to inanimate objects. They have a natural interest in animals and fantasy (something that does not go completely away as we develop into adults). In concrete operations (age 7 to about age 11) children can relate one idea or event to a system of interrelated parts. They are able to comprehend the conventions of language such as the elements of a story, the organization of persuasive writing, or the structure of multimedia computer programs.

A unit on animals is particularly challenging and appropriate when many of the earth's animals face extinction. This unit, then, is especially meaningful because it is directly linked to issues outside the school. Students, through reading and writing, can become a part of the issue by using what they produce in class to inform, entertain, or try to persuade others in the broader community with their knowledge. Those in the preoperational stage can engage in imitation or personification of the animals they are studying by writing stories, poetry, or creating multimedia presentations with animation and sound added to text.

Students become engaged in this unit by joining small groups whose task it is to investigate the animals of one "biome," or type of region on earth, such as the tundra, the rainforest, wetlands, or the desert. They then create an "animal friendly" zoo or habitat that will house the animals in large open areas designed to simulate the natural habitat. Each group takes responsibility for the biome they are researching. Multimedia programs greatly enhance and challenge the students as they explore their biome. Through *The Animals*, a CD-ROM from Software Toolworks, students can tour the San Diego Zoo, one of the first to put the visitors in "cages" and create open environments for many animals that are much like their native habitats. Children can read about hundreds of animals, see a colorful map of the zoo, select a biome to explore, or choose a particular animal in that biome to read about and view pictures and video. Students can read a variety of informational reports and persuasive pieces about endangered animal and plant life, and they can read suggestions for things kids can do to make a difference in the effort to protect endangered species. They can read stories and watch video about special characters at the zoo like Dolly, the gorilla, who because of the effects of captivity was not able to respond to her baby as a mother would in the wild. Zoo personnel had to raise the tiny Jim.

Another tool is Davidson's award-winning game, *Zoo Keeper*. The student is placed in the role of a zoo keeper who is in charge of over 50 different animals and faces a band of mischievous troublemakers on the loose. The troublemakers feed animals the wrong food, litter the animal habitats, and cause havoc. To stop troublemakers like "Brain Drain" and "Stir Crazy," the student must travel through oceans, deserts, mountains, and jungles, in hot pursuit. When a troublemaker is caught and the damage is undone, the student is a step closer to sending a zoo animal back to the wild. In order to make the right decisions, the zoo keeper must gather clues by reading about the animals and their habitats.

To complement their investigation of animals, students can read young adult novels such as Jerry Spinelli's *Night of the Whale*, the story of two children who try to save a large

FIGURE 3-6   A screen from Zoo Keeper.

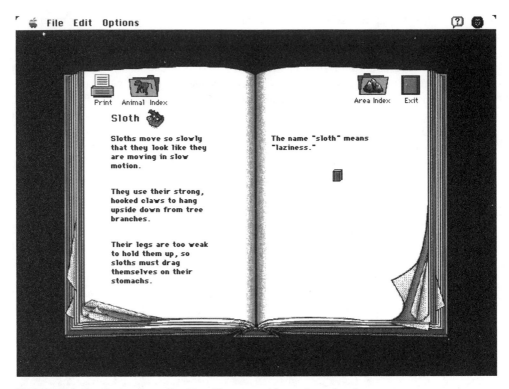

FIGURE 3-7   Pages from the Zoo Keeper guide to the animals.

group of beached whales; Gary Paulsen's story *Dogsong*, about an Eskimo child who jour-neys alone by dogsled into the Alaskan tundra; or Jack London's classic *The Call of the Wild*. There are also mysteries like Peg Kehret's *Terror at the Zoo*, and countless nonfiction books such as *How to Make a Miniature Zoo* (Brown, 1987), *Born Free: A Lioness of Two Worlds* (Adamson, 1987), and *Animals in Their Places: Tales from the Natural World* (Caras, 1987). Children's picture books are great for exploring storytelling and the use of illustration.

To construct their own zoo, students select the animals that will live there and conduct the research needed to create their simulation. For example, they will have to write the informational pieces for visitors at their zoo to read. One obvious resource for information on running a zoo is real zoo keepers. Students can communicate with real zoo keepers through KidsNet, an electronic telecommunications service for students on the Internet. One group of students might tap into the opinions of other 4th-grade students in different schools, districts, areas, or states. Still another group might research archives to find infor-mation about their animal, zoos, and current animal rights issues.

Using a word processing program, students can easily draft, revise, and edit as they craft their informational piece, and also a short story about one or more animals, or a chil-dren's picture book, poem, or letter. The possibilities for literacy activities are unlimited. In addition to their activities creating a simulated world, the students can use their knowledge to impact the real world of animals. They can compose letters to people in public office or in the media who can make decisions with consequences that interest the students.

As the individual biome groups gather and interpret information, view images and video, and read books of their choice, they can begin to plan how they will physically construct their biome and how they will present what they have produced to the others in their class. The teacher keeps track of the individual projects and provides the materials that will spark the students' interest and challenge their ideas.

Multimedia tools greatly enhance the learners' process of assimilation and accommodation within the classroom by allowing students to access people, places, and information easily and quickly. However, teachers must also provide outside-of-the-classroom environments. A field trip to a local zoo would certainly be a desirable addition to this unit, although many zoos today are examples of what not to do instead of models students could learn from. Contact with the real world, however, is very important. As Jon Madian (1994), founder of Humanities Software, says, "When we think we are better served by pixel places than by living creatures in living places, we are dangerously gullible and robbing children of their true heritage—our natural world."

WHOLE LANGUAGE AND SIMILAR COGNITIVE CONSTRUCTIVIST METHODS

The constructivist classroom is, as you have seen, an environment for students to construct their own knowledge. Activities are hands-on. Problem solving is done within cooperative groups, and the tasks are meaningful to the lives of the students. That is the context of a whole language classroom. Proponents of this approach to teaching literacy stress the importance of relating what is new to what is known. That idea translated in Piagetian terms means the student is given opportunities to assimilate and accommodate in a continuing process of achieving equilibrium and building schemata.

One of the most discussed and disputed issues concerning whole language is the method used to teach young children how to read. Some have reduced this argument to a phonics first vs. whole language debate because whole language teachers emphasize learning phonics in context rather than through isolated skills practice. The issue has received such public attention that Goodman (1994) refers to it as the "politics of phonics." (See the beginning of Chapter 8 for an indication of how heated this debate can become.) Perhaps the most fundamental principle of the whole language approach is that written language is learned the way oral language is. Goodman (1994, p. 1093) explains:

> What we've learned from the study of language development, both oral and written, is that language is easy to learn when we deal with the whole of it as we use it functionally to make sense. Little children are understanding and making themselves understood in oral language long before they fully control the sound system. That's because they learn language in the context of its use. Children learn written language in the same way. They may learn the names of letters as they're learning to read, and even have some sense of how they relate to sounds. But they can learn the abstract phonics systems only in the context

of trying to make sense of meaningful print. They're very good at learning language when it's in authentic, meaningful context. They're not very good at learning abstractions out of context.

Encouraging children's development from pre-phonemic to phonemic spelling through independent writing is one strategy of whole language teachers. It is important that the writing focus on the child's personal experience. Many multimedia programs (programs that use text, graphics, animation, video, and sound) based on whole language theory reinforce the letter/sound and picture/word relationships and provide opportunities for writing. *Bailey's Book House*, for pre-Kindergarten through the 2nd grade, presents letters, words, and sentences in meaningful contexts. Children can create greeting cards or stories and then listen to their words spoken by the computer. *KidWorks 2* is similar. It also has a speech component and gives children the tools for writing and illustrating their own stories. For younger children, it provides rebus pictures that can be inserted into their story. *Story Club*, a more comprehensive program that includes a CD-ROM, 10 videodisks, and 10 song cassettes, is based on multicultural folk tales and emphasizes story telling, early literacy, and critical thinking. Children can watch the story "Anansi and His Visitor," for example, on videodisk, then use the CD-ROM version of it and be able to interact with characters. That is, by clicking on Anansi or any of his friends, the crab, the fish, or the eel, children will hear the name and see the word appear on the screen. They can also access a 750-word picture and photo dictionary to find out more about the real-life version of the character they select. As with *Bailey's Book House* and *KidWorks 2*, children can hear the computer read what they write, or they can write and record their own folk tale and hear it played.

A language-rich environment, as Piaget proposed, should provide challenging opportunities for children as their cognitive abilities unfold naturally. The focus is on the development of literacy within the context of students' interests and communicative needs at that moment. A good example of this is electronic books. The Living Books series, which animates popular story books like Mercer Mayer's *Grandma and Me*, guides and encourages children to listen and to follow printed material. The story is read by a delightful critter, Mercer Mayer, and the words on the page are highlighted as they are read. Many of the objects on the screen become active if they are clicked—they dance, sing, spin around, or make humorous comments. Any single word in the text will be read by a critter if it is clicked. Children can read along at their own pace and rehear those words that are challenging to them. Because the books are very appealing, children will spend lengthy periods of time exploring each screen. Immersed in the language of the book, children learn the letter/sound relationship as spoken words and written words are connected.

Although whole language is most often associated with the elementary and middle school level, its constructivist foundation is evident in methods used in secondary school and higher education. The reading/writing workshop, for example, is a whole language approach because it encompasses reading, writing, speaking, and listening in a meaningful context (Foster, 1994; Strickland & Strickland, 1993). This constructivist methodology stretches beyond secondary schools to constructivist perspectives on literary criticism and composition in college English classrooms (Ritchie, 1989). Piaget's constructivism is evident in the reading/writing workshop teacher's interest in student choices. Freedom to choose, as Atwell (1987, p. 43) points out, promotes student empowerment and student agency:

FIGURE 3-8 A screen from *Grandma and Me*.

When they can choose, junior high students will write for all the reasons literate people everywhere engage as writer: to recreate happy times, work through sad times, discover what they know about a subject and learn more, convey and request information, apply for jobs, parody, petition, play, argue, apologize, advise, make money. When they can choose, junior high students will read for all the reasons literate people everywhere engage as readers: to live other lives and learn about their own, to see how other writers have written and to acquire other writers' knowledge, to escape, think, travel, ponder, laugh, cry.

The constructivist classroom's emphasis on student choice informs the curriculum. Because each group of students in a class is different year to year, class to class, the curriculum is continually redrafted. According to Rief (1992, p. 8):

Workbooks don't address the unique learning styles, the extraordinary ideas, the honest thinking, or the prior knowledge each child brings to the classroom. My students are my curriculum. I want to nurture that uniqueness not standardize my classroom so that the students become more and more alike, their only aim to pass minimum competency tests.

In the last six weeks of the year, Rief (1992) requests that her students present a reader/writer project that "proves" their "expertise." The students must present their findings in three different genres (e.g., letter, poem, essay, video, mime) and research a topic three different ways (e.g., writing, interviews, film study). Although her expectations are circumscriptive, the students remain free to choose any topic, to choose the method of their research, and to choose the form of presentation. Rief noted that giving her students choice empowered them not only as readers and writers but as agents of their own learning.

Students in Rief's class could expand their schema of literature, language, and communication through the use of tools such as word processors, presentation programs, telecommunications, and electronic books. Telecommunications, for example, opens new places to explore and real people to meet (see Chapter 8 for more details on using telecommunications in the classroom). Presentation programs like *Persuasion* and *PowerPoint* make presentations of student writing such as poetry or short prose active, attractive, and creative because they allow the student to add images and animation to text (See Chapter 7 for more information on presentation software). Electronic book versions of classics like Shakespeare's *Romeo and Juliet*, Hawthorne's *The Scarlet Letter*, and Shelley's *Frankenstein* support students as they build schema about the writer's craft as well as about historical events and social moods. The animation, sound, video, and story links help students interpret and relate to the text. Finally, several authoring programs like *Authorware Star*, *HyperStudio*, and *SuperCard* can be used to produce video creations that could include TV-like documentaries or commercials. These programs have the capability to allow students to produce movies that are original or interpretations of literature. (See Chapter 7 for more information on authoring programs for both teachers and students.)

The whole language approach is based at least in part on Piaget's theory of cognitive development. Clearly, it is a constructivist environment, and the constructivist perspective evident in the whole language classroom is also evident in upper levels of education. What directs a whole language classroom is a coalition of readers and writers, teachers and learners, all responding to their similarities and differences—all engaged in the assimilation and accommodation processes of making meaning of the world. What is considered the curriculum is more like a charter that unites the teacher and each of the students as they move towards a common goal.

SUMMARY

Cognitive constructivism, like social constructivism, regards learners as agents of their own learning. A social constructivist considers language the avenue through which teachers can inspire or influence cognitive development; however, a cognitive constructivist sees language somewhat differently. Every child's cognitive development is a genetically determined and successive unfolding of stages of meaning-making abilities, and language facilitates that process.

A constructivist teacher creates a context for learning in which students are highly engaged in the process of their own discoveries. The teacher creates an environment that generates problems, adventures, and challenges. Activities are rooted in meaningful situations that interest students and that have self-satisfying outcomes. Students work toward achieving goals meaningful to them and most commonly work in groups. This social inter-action is vital in that it is a setting for cognitive conflict—or discussion, debate, exchange—to occur.

Technology provides essential tools with which to accomplish the goals of a con-structivist classroom:

- Multimedia products such as *The Animals, From Alice to Ocean,* and *Oceans Below* encourage students to travel to far off locations, see some of the world's unique people, animals, and natural and constructed wonders, and listen to unfa-miliar sounds. Through their exploration of multimedia packages, students learn to connect images with text and to pursue their own interests. Therefore, they can engage in activities that will expand their schemata as they naturally seek new information. Electronic encyclopedias such as Microsoft's *Encarta* are rich sources of multimedia information children in all grades can use.
- Problem-solving simulations like *Channel READ* make learning meaningful. Stu-dents join intellectual forces to solve problems, and as they solve problems they develop important literacy skills.
- Interactive electronic books like the *Living Books* help to build students' conceptu-al and experiential background. They immerse young readers in language and pro-vide a setting for them to associate sounds with letters and images. Electronic books for older students provide images and explanations that help to build back-ground knowledge, and they provide a stimulating context for interpretation of often unfamiliar language usage in the classics.
- Games like *Super Midnight Rescue* and *Zoo Keeper* challenge students. Compre-hension and critical thinking skills are stimulated as students read to find main ideas and details in text in order to gather useful clues. They must make inferences in order to solve the case.
- Desktop publishing and presentation programs such as the *Student Writing Center* and *My Own Stories* for younger children provide readers and writers access to an authentic purpose for literacy—publishing. The multimedia programs that allow students to add animation, sound, and images create a rich setting for language use. As students write, draw, paint, animate, and add sound to their interpretation of their world, they construct meaning.
- Telecommunications tools such as Kidsnet provide a means for social interaction via satellite. Students can talk with other students, teachers, and professionals in places far from their classroom.

On the third day of his experience as a teacher, Peter Tangeman was elated, confused, curious, and to some degree, relieved. The elation resulted from his confirmation that his decision was the right one. The 6th-grade students were wonderful—full of energy, curios-ity, and stories of their own. He was confused because there was still as much for him to learn as there was for him to teach. The article in Julia's copy of *Language Arts* about cog-nitive constructivist computer programs had opened new territory for him. Once again Peter headed to a library to do research, only this time it was the school's library where Marie Luna, the school's librarian and media specialist, was delighted to help. Together they reviewed what technology was available through the library and other resources. His curiosity about technology, he found, would lead to weeks, months, years of exploration. So much was available! Could he make good decisions and learn to use the equipment? Marie was very helpful, which was reassuring. Even more reassuring was the help he received from colleagues in his peer conferencing group. Julia was most helpful. Nearly every day, she would place a demo disk, a flyer, a software review article, or just a short note of encouragement in his box. And he read everything.

MICROTEACHING ACTIVITIES

1.   Lead a group of 3 to 7 students in your class who will create a class newsletter. Some articles in the newsletter will report on activities such as microteaching lessons in the class. Others will expand on topics students wanted more information on. Still others will report on the activities of the students in the class—significant events such as new jobs, moves, engagements, births, honors, and accomplishments. Use one of the programs designed for student use and print enough copies of a "special edition" to distribute a copy to each member of the class.

2.   Select one of the computer programs that support several types of writing. With students in the class playing the role of children at the grade level you plan to teach, introduce the software to the students and guide them in a lesson that creates a type of composition they are not likely to have extensive experience with (e.g., a visual poem, haiku, an advertisement). Once you have microtaught the lesson, hand out a sheet listing several skills or cognitive abilities related to the task that are categorized by whether they can be performed independently by the students in the simulated class, are in the zone of proximal development, or cannot be performed by the students even with help. Then lead a discussion of the skills and abilities. Do students agree with your placements on the list? Do they think others are more important?

3.   Create a lesson plan like the one described in this chapter on an activity related to animals, but select a topic appropriate to the subject and level you plan to teach. Distribute copies of the lesson plan to students in your class and microteach one of the segments of the lesson. Then lead the group in a discussion of topics in their teaching fields that would be amenable to this approach. Explore as a group the types of software that would be needed to support the lessons discussed.

REFERENCES

Adamson, J. (1987). *Born free: A lioness of two worlds*. Westminster, MD: Pantheon.

Atwell, N. (1987). *In the middle: Writing, reading, and learning with adolescents*. Portsmouth, NH: Heinemann.

Brown, V. (1987). *How to make a miniature zoo* (3rd ed.). Spring Valley, NY: Dodd, Mead/Teale Books.

Bransford, J., Sherwood, R., Hasselbring, T. (1988). The video revolution and its effects on development: Some initial thoughts. In G. Forman & P. B. Pufall (Eds.), *Constructivism in the computer age* (pp. 173–202). Hillsdale, NJ: Erlbaum.

Caras, R. (1987). *Animals in their places: Tales from the natural world*. Westminster, MD: Sierra Club Books.

Emig, J. (1971). *The composing process of twelfth graders*. Research Report no. 13. Urbana, IL: National Council of Teachers of English.

Forman, E., & Cazden, C. (1994). Exploring Vygotskian perspectives in education: The cognitive value of peer interaction. In R. B. Ruddell, M. R. Ruddell, & H. Singer (Eds.), *Theoretical models and processes of reading* (4th ed.) (pp. 155–178). Newark, DE: International Reading Association.

Foster, H. M. (1994). *Crossing over: Whole language for secondary English teachers*. Orlando, FL: Harcourt Brace Jovanovich.

Goodman, K. S. (1994). Reading, Writing, and Written Texts: A Transactional Sociopsycholinguistic View. In R. B. Ruddell, M. R. Ruddell, & H. Singer (Eds.), *Theoretical models and processes of reading* (4th ed.) (pp. 1093–1130). Newark, DE: International Reading Association.

Kehret, P. (1994). *Terror at the Zoo*. Cobblehill.

London, J. (1987). *The Call of the Wild*. Jefferson City, MO: Scholastic/Apple Classics.

Madian, J. (January, 1994). Technology and writing: An interview with Jon Madian. *Writing Teacher*, 4–8.

Papert, S. (1988). The conservation of Piaget: The computer as grist to the constructivist mill. In G. Forman & P. B. Pufall (Eds.), *Constructivism in the computer age* (pp. 3–13). Hillsdale, NJ: Erlbaum.

Paulsen, G. (1985). *Dogsong*. Riverside, NJ: Bradbury Press.

Piaget, J. (1972). *The principles of genetic epistemology* (W. Mays, Trans.). New York: Basic.

Reif, L. (1992). Seeking diversity: Language arts with adolescents. Portsmouth, NH: Heinemann.

Ritchie, J. (1989). Beginning writers: Diverse voices and individual identity. *College composition and communication, (40)*2, pp. 152–174.

Skinner, B. F. (1968). *The technology of teaching*. New York: Appleton, Century, Crofts.

Spinelli, J. (1985). *Night of the whale*. Waltham, MA: Little, Brown.

Strickland, J., & Strickland, K. (1993). *Uncovering the curriculum: Whole language in secondary and postsecondary classrooms*. Portsmouth, NH: Boynton/Cook.

SOFTWARE DISCUSSED IN THIS CHAPTER

Most of the software discussed in this chapter is available at large software centers that carry educational programs or from some of the larger mail order educational software suppliers such as:

Computer Centerline, 1500 Broad Street, Greensburg, PA 15601. Phone: 800-852-5802.

Educational Resources, 1550 Executive Drive, Elgin, IL 60123. Phone: 800-624-2926.

In the list below the producer of each program is provided, but many software companies sell primarily through mail order distributors and retail computer and software stores.

Arthur's Birthday Party. Broderbund.

Bailey's Book House. Edmark.

Carmen Sandiego series. Broderbund.

Channel READ. Houghton Mifflin.

HyperStudio. Robert Wagner.

KidPix. Broderbund.

Kid's Studio. CyberPuppy Software (716-436-3570).

Living Books Series. Broderbund.

Make-A-Book. Teacher Support Software.

MicroWorlds: Language Arts. LCSI.

My Own Stories. MECC.

Oceans Below. Mindscape.

Oregon Trail. MECC.

Student Writing Center. The Learning Company.

Super Solvers Midnight Rescue. The Learning Company.

The Adventures of Tom Sawyer. Bookworm Student Library.

The Animals. Software Toolworks.

Zoo Keeper. Davidson and Associates.

CHAPTER FOUR

Skills-Based Direct Instruction and Technology

A Skills Bank 3 Lesson

Ms. Anderson's high school composition class has just filed into the computer lab to begin working on Skills Bank 3 writing lessons.

"Thank you for coming into the computer lab quickly and quietly," she greets them. "Please be seated at a computer while I look through this printout to see what you need to be working on." After consulting the printout, Ms. Anderson once again addresses her class. "The following people need to take the writing diagnostic pretest: Shoab, Lu, Honu, Samuel, Marilyn, Jane, and Albert. Shawn, please complete the lessons on language mechanics. Jerome, Harry, and Corinth work on language usage. Salma, Annie, and Jose, try the lessons on sentence structure. Carina, Paul, Sara, and Fred, you need to go to the lessons on clear writing and paragraphs. Please get started."

The students turn on their monitors and computers. Sara accesses the writing section and selects Clear Writing and Paragraphs. She starts with Lesson 1: Misplaced Modifiers. Clicking on Next displays a screen with the definition of modifiers and some examples used in sentences. Sara reads the definition and scans the examples. The next screen contains the definition and a question asking her to identify the modifier.

Sara clicks on the third answer and discovers she made the correct choice. She quickly completes the three sample questions. Now, a definition and examples of misplaced modifiers appear on the screen. Chuckling softly to herself, she reads the first sentence.

Gina returned a sweater to the store that was too small.

Eager to read more silly sentences she moves on through three more sample questions.

"This is fun," she says to Carina, seated at the computer next to her. Once she fin-

ishes with the examples, she discovers ten exercises to complete. Carefully she reads the sentences, noting that in some of them it is difficult to determine which word is the misplaced modifier. Making mistakes is risk free because the computer doesn't beep loudly at her. It simply explains that her choice is not the correct one and tells her to try again. When she is uncertain, she clicks on Hint at the bottom of the screen and gets information specific to that series of sentences.

At the end of the exercises Sara's score is calculated and displayed on the screen. Clicking on Review allows her to go over the ones she missed.

"Hey, I scored 80 percent. I only missed two of them," she announces to Carina, who congratulates her on her success.

"Class, it is time to go," Ms. Anderson tells her students. "I was glad to see you all hard at work. We have so little time in the computer lab. Remember to turn off the computers and push in your chairs."

Sara turns off the computer, and her thoughts turn to lunch as she pushes in her chair.

Reading and language arts teachers are faced with the task of preparing students to read symbols on a page that bear no resemblance to the items they represent. English is not pictographic, as some early written languages were. Nor is it a completely phonic language. The language conglomerate that became English leaves a great deal to be desired in sound-symbol correspondence. Combine these complicating characteristics with the fact that humans have to learn to read without help from innate patterns and predispositions that push spoken language development along, and it is a wonder anyone learns to read English these days.

As noted in Chapter 1, many different approaches are used for reading and language arts instruction. In previous chapters you learned about methods that emphasize teaching reading in meaningful contexts. For example, a 1st-grade teacher using a language experience approach might help children compose a story about their own experiences and then write that story on poster board or on a computer screen. The underlying assumption of this approach is that children will learn to read those odd symbols on a page better if much of the initial instruction is anchored around stories from their own life experiences and involves words from their spoken vocabulary.

Whole language instruction, and several other approaches, were covered in previous chapters. In this chapter, another family of instructional strategies will be introduced. They approach the complex task of learning to read by breaking the process down into component skills and creating lessons that concentrate on those skills. The many strategies of this sort all come under the conceptual umbrella of the *direct instruction* model. Other names associated with this model are active instruction, atomistic instruction, bottom-up instruction, criterion referenced instruction, explicit instruction, part learning (as opposed to whole learning), skills instruction, subskills instruction, skill and drill, teacher-directed instruction, teacher-centered instruction, and behavioral instruction. Gunning's (1992) definition of skills-based direct instruction is succinct:

> In the bottom-up approach, children literally start at the bottom and work their way up.
> First, they learn the names and shapes of the letters of the alphabet. Then they learn con-

sonant sounds, followed by simple and then more complex vowel correspondences. Many basal series and supplementary materials are tied into a subskills approach, as are approaches that employ a management system. [p. 8]

READING BLASTER: ONE EXAMPLE OF COMPUTER-SUPPORTED DIRECT INSTRUCTION

Many direct instruction programs resemble the blue ditto sheets a lot of us spent hours completing during our seatwork periods in Ms. Plemson's 3rd-grade class. The computerized version of seatwork puts the sheets on the screen and lets children enter answers via the keyboard. The one advantage of computerized ditto sheets is that most programs of this type evaluate the student's answer and provide feedback, something Ms. Plemson had to do herself during breaks between oral reading groups. Unfortunately, most of the computerized worksheet programs are almost as boring on the computer screen as they were on paper, and kids don't have the pleasure of being able to paint their hands blue (from the ink on the ditto sheets) with the computer versions and then get into mischief during recess.

Fortunately several software companies read the Tom Sawyer story about whitewashing the fence and have converted those boring worksheets into computer games that have some of the action and appeal of the arcade games children enjoy so much. A good example of this type of direct instruction program is *Reading Blaster* (subtitled *Invasion of the Word Snatchers*), a set of arcade-style games for children ages 7–10. The basic premise of the games, which all have a space theme, is that a sinister character named Illitera has stolen all of the words from Earth and has fled in her spaceship (which from the rear looks a lot like a converted 1957 Desoto automobile). Your job, should you decide to accept it, is to get on board the ship and recover the stolen words. As you go about your dangerous but exciting task, there are all sorts of impediments and problems. Illitera, for example, has taken the ink out of words and put them in splatter pods that must be disposed of carefully before they explode on a planet and cause untold problems. As you play the adventure, a voice from Central Control provides support and directions. Just click the telerecorder for information.

Each *Reading Blaster* game emphasizes a particular prereading or reading skill. For example, *Word Zapper* requires students to grab letters leaking from Illitera's ship. However, any old letter will not do. You must grab the letters that spell the word *de jour*, and Central Control provides hints about what that word is. All sorts of dangers must be avoided while you grab the letters, and fast action is rewarded with a bonus. *Plate Patrol* requires you to alphabetize words on plates that are scattered around a room before you can pass through. Some of the odd creatures wandering around the room are helpful and some are not. Students can read about each creature's personality and learn how to deal with them. In *Spatter Pods*, knowing antonyms and synonyms is required to succeed, as is the help of some aliens who have been imprisoned by Illitera. The telerecorder has information on the special skills of each alien, and the player must read that information and use it to develop a successful strategy.

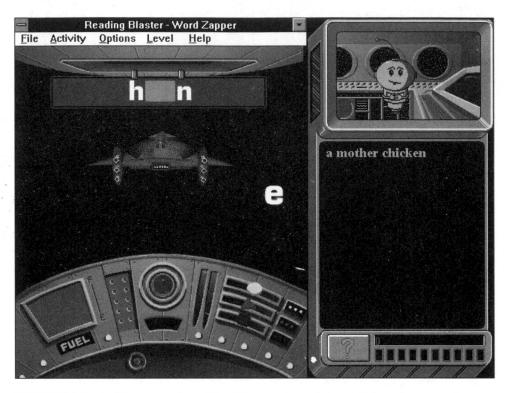

FIGURE 4-1   In this screen from *Word Zapper*, the task is to click on letters as they leak from Illitera's ship, if they are part of the target word.

Reading Blaster is one example of skills-based direct instruction. It is not, however, an ideal piece of direct instruction software. Below are the five steps found in an ideal direct instruction model. How many are found in *Reading Blaster*?

1. Identify the skills that need to be taught (task analysis).
2. Assess the student's level of achievement on the tasks (diagnosis).
3. Teach the skills and subskills, monitor progress, adjust instruction as needed (monitored instruction).
4. Assess the success of instruction (exit tests).
5. Move on to the next skill (or next level of the same skill).

Only a small percentage of direct instruction software includes all five steps. The general idea, however, is to decide precisely what skills the student is lacking and then design instruction to teach them. *Reading Blaster* has no Step 1 or Step 2. It does teach some skills through the games, and it does monitor progress and provide help if a student gets stuck or makes errors (Step 3). It does include Step 4 because it keeps track of progress and will produce individual student reports. Within the limited range of skills it covers, the program does allow students to move on to other skills when they are successful (Step 5). *Reading Blaster* has three levels of difficulty.

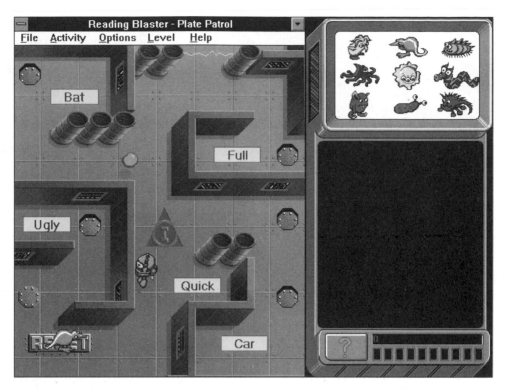

FIGURE 4-2 This screen from *Plate Patrol* shows the interior of the room where the words on plates are scattered.

Thousands of educational software packages support the direct instruction model. Few include all five steps described above. In general, the more included, the better.

THE PLACE OF DIRECT INSTRUCTION IN EDUCATION

The role of direct instruction in literacy is hotly debated. Some experts believe it is a well-established and very successful approach that deserves much wider use.

> We need skills. Teachers need them to systematize instruction and to teach efficiently. Readers need them to approach the complex task of reading efficiently and effectively. [Smith, Otto, & Hansen, 1978, p. 44]

> Our position is that many students will not become successful readers unless teachers identify the essential reading skills, find out what skills students lack, and teach those skills directly. [Carnine, Silbert, & Kameenui, 1990, p. 3]

Others take the opposite view:

There are at least six things that bother us about skill monitoring systems: 1) their psycholinguistic naiveté, 2) their "assembly-line" underpinnings, 3) their concern for skill at the expense of interest, 4) their advocacy of sequencing separable reading skills, 5) the validity of their assessment instruments, and 6) the very notion of mastery itself. [Johnson & Pearson, 1975, p. 758]

Learning to read is not learning to recognize words, it is learning to make sense of texts. In the whole-language program there is no separate phonics instruction. Readers form rules for relating print to speech as they are reading meaningful texts. But these self-developed rules are not over learned and artificial as they would be if they were imposed by a structured phonics program. [Goodman & Goodman, 1982, p. 127]

This direct approach undoubtedly has some value, but there are problems with it. The direct instruction of story grammar (simplified for children) will almost always turn the spotlight on the least important aspects of it: the names of the parts and their usual order. The focus will be on the pieces of structure rather than on the relationships among the pieces because a thorough explanation of every aspect of story grammar is prohibitively difficult and dull. Thus the fluidity of story structure may never be appreciated, and children may never come to use structures creatively. Indirect structures that take advantage of the psychological reality of story grammar are more promising. [Nauman, 1990, p. 62]

Direct instruction is currently the strategy many methods faculty in colleges of education love to hate, in part because it is often based on behavioral learning theories that are now out of favor. Many faculty today advocate whole language instruction that whenever possible avoids the teaching of skills in isolation. However, a sizable body of research supports direct instruction. For example, the follow-up studies (Stallings, 1987) of Follow Through, the federal program that comes after Head Start and is for students in Kindergarten through 3rd grade, found that students in programs based on the direct instruction model had higher achievement in reading and math when compared to students in traditional and Montessori programs. In one of the longest follow-up studies yet conducted, Gersten (1988) found Follow Through students in the direct instruction programs had higher achievement scores, especially in reading, and higher rates of acceptance to college.

Samuels' (1988) review of the research led him to conclude that decoding the symbols of written English is a critical prerequisite for reading that is best learned from direct instruction and extended practice with reading material that is at the child's instructional reading level. On the other hand, Readence (1986) found direct instruction was more effective than other types of instruction when reading comprehension was the objective. Other studies suggest direct instruction methods are superior for teaching vocabulary (Eds & Cockrum, 1985), reading comprehension (Reutzel, 1988; Stevens, 1991), and phonics (Snider, 1990).

The availability of research supporting a particular approach does not prove its validity. Virtually every approach currently advocated has research that supports its use. The availability of research is more an indication that people take it seriously enough to study it carefully.

TYPES OF SKILLS-BASED DIRECT INSTRUCTION

In this chapter, skills-based direct instruction will be explored. Two other types of direct instruction—just-in-time and "cognitive skills"—will be discussed in the following two chapters. Many variations are to be found of skills-based direct instruction, some of which reflect different assumptions about the way children become literate. We have divided skills-based direct instruction approaches into two broad types: out-of-context direct instruction, and preparatory direct instruction. Both of these strategies are efforts to help students master skills considered important in reading and writing. The skill may be some aspect of phonics, the use of context clues, making inferences based on a reading passage, writing topic sentences, composing poetry, or building suspense in a short story. Regardless of the skill involved, direct instruction is used to improve it and thus improve overall reading or writing skills.

Out-of-context direct instruction is based on the assumption that the best way to teach a skill is to isolate it and master it through repeated practice. If you are teaching phonics skills, for example, this approach assumes the best way is to separate the phonics lessons from the act of reading. Teach phonics skills in isolation until they become automatic and then help the student apply them to the process of reading. In grammar instruction, an element such as verbals is removed from its context, practiced through the use of worksheets, and applied to the process of writing.

Preparatory direct instruction assumes that students will need some direct instruction on fundamental reading and language arts skills but proposes that skill training is best accomplished within the framework of meaningful reading and writing. For example, when children begin writing paragraphs, the teacher might offer some instruction on subjects such as writing topic sentences. Preparatory direct instruction is not the primary means of instruction. Instead, it is incorporated into a variety of teaching methods where it plays a supporting role.

In the two sections that follow we will explore in more detail the two types of skills-based direct instruction.

OUT-OF-CONTEXT DIRECT INSTRUCTION

Out-of-context direct instruction (OC-DI) is usually based on behavioral theories of learning. Behaviorism, broadly defined, has been the dominant theory of learning in North America for most of the 20th century. During much of the 1970s and 1980s, when computers were being placed in the classrooms of many schools for the first time, behavioral theories were very popular. An earlier innovation, programmed instruction, which is based on behavioral theories, involved breaking down content into small pieces of information called frames. Several frames from a book on behavioral psychology by Holland and Skinner (1961, p. 41–43) illustrate this type of instruction:

```
A technical term for "reward" is reinforcement. To "reward"
an organism with food is to _____ it with food.
[the answer "reinforce" is provided on the next page]
```

Reinforcement and behavior occur in the temporal order: (1)
_____ (2) _____.

[the answer "(1) behavior, (2) reinforcement" is provided
on the next page]

A reinforcement does not elicit a response; it simply makes
it more _____ that an animal will respond in the same way
again.

[the answer "probable" or "likely" is provided on the next
page]

A programmed instruction textbook might contain several thousand frames of information. Students would read a frame, then answer a question about the frame. Then they would check their answer (get feedback), and proceed to the next frame. During the 1950s and 1960s many programmed instruction books for reading and language arts were produced. Proponents argued that breaking down content into small units (frames) and then testing to be sure the student understood the material had many advantages:

1. *Immediate knowledge of results.* Because students answered questions almost continuously, they were frequently reinforced by positive feedback, and that feedback was immediate.
2. *Individualized learning.* Students could progress through programmed instruction material at their own rate without being held back or left behind by teacher-centered group instruction.
3. *Expert instruction.* Students followed a "coherent sequence" of instruction, that is, a sequence of instruction designed by experts.

Programmed instruction faded into obscurity in the 1970s. One reason for its decline was that many programmed instruction packages were very boring. Also, although programmed instruction individualized the pace of learning, both the content and the sequence of content were essentially identical for all students. The only common variation on content was "branching" for remedial work when a student did not correctly answer a question. Many topics call for much more individualization of content and sequence than is possible with programmed instruction. Another weakness was that breaking down subject matter into small digestible bits of information did not work well for many types of subject matter and many types of learners. Also, learning in isolation is not always the most effective approach. Programmed instruction tends to isolate students, but collaborative group work may be more effective in some situations. Moreover, programmed instruction tends to isolate factual information from its context. Some theories of learning argue that learning occurs best when it is situated within a context that has meaning for the student.

Programmed instruction was essentially dead by 1972, but like the phoenix, it rose from its ashes a few years later. When schools began installing inexpensive personal computers in classrooms in the mid 1970s and the back-to-basics movement became popular, programmed instruction was a handy model for developing educational software. Today tens of thousands of educational software products are based on behavioral models of instruction.

Software for out-of-context direct instruction often uses the programmed instruction model. The case at the beginning of this chapter on the use of Skills Bank 3 illustrates one type of out-of-context software, the tutorial. The two most common forms of out-of-context software in use today are drill and practice (D&P) software and tutorial software. There are many examples of "good" D&P and tutorial programs that meet reasonable design guidelines for this type of software; however, there are more examples of "bad" software in these categories than any other, despite the claims of advertising blurbs on the package. Purchasing decisions should never be made on the basis of advertisements. The program is used in the scenario below illustrates this point.

OC-DI Basic Reading Skills

Ms. Wilson's 1st-grade class has been learning the sounds of letters. She wants them to practice the sounds with the Dinosoft Phonics software installed on the classroom computer. She has set up a schedule so that everyone will get a chance. Jeremy and Josh are just beginning their turn.

"Jeremy and Josh, do you remember how to play Dinosoft Phonics?"

"Uh huh," they reply in unison, as they settle down in two small chairs in front of the computer.

"Today, I want you to work on beginning sounds using small letters. I'll set this up for you. You'll see dinosaurs on every screen. When you finish, you can each print out one to color."

As they watch, Ms. Wilson explains what she is doing. She clicks on Flash Cards and then on Beginning Sounds and then on Small Letters. "What is the first letter in your names?" she asks them.

"J," pipes up Jeremy.

"That's right. Let's look at the first screen. What letter do you see?"

"P," replies Josh.

"Great. Now, look at the three pictures at the bottom of the screen. What do you see?"

"Ham, lantern, and a bird," they reply in unison.

"What kind of bird is that?" she queries.

"A parrot?" offers Jeremy.

"That's right," responds Ms. Wilson. "Now, which one begins with the letter P?"

"Parrot!" pipes up Josh.

"Wonderful! Parrot begins with the letter P. Click on the parrot."

As Jeremy clicks on the parrot, the word parrot appears on the screen in blue just above the picture. At the top of the screen the phrase Nice Job! appears.

"Nice job!" reads Josh from the top of the screen. Both children are pleased with the encouragement.

"Okay, Josh, now click at the bottom of the screen on Next Problem. I'll set the timer. You have 15 minutes to work on the computer before it's Sandy and Sana's turn. Remember to take turns with the mouse," Ms. Wilson reminds them as she turns her

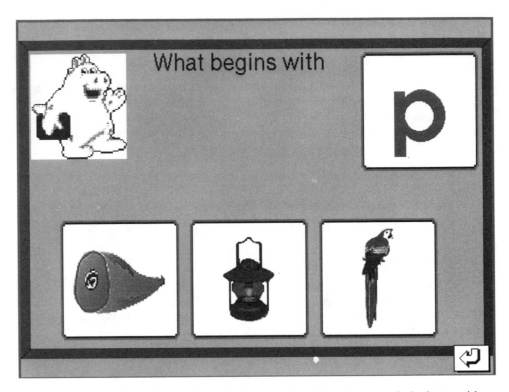

FIGURE 4-3   A screen from *Dinosoft Phonics*. The object is to match the letter with one of the pictures.

attention to the class.

"That's a w," Jeremy says, looking at the screen. "There is a goat, dishes, and a head with hair on top."

"None of those things start with w," Josh says.

"Well, we have to pick one of them."

Josh clicks on the goat. A message appears under the pictures with the words Yes, Need Help, and No.

"Click on Yes," urges Jeremy. Josh clicks on Yes, and the names of the objects appear above them. "Goat, dishes, wig," reads Jeremy. "The hair is a wig, and wig is the correct answer because it is written in blue." They click on Next Problem.

"That letter is a z," states Josh.

"My turn to use the mouse," interjects Jeremy.

Josh slides it toward him. "I know what these are: gum, a blue line, and a car."

"It's a jeep, not a car," corrects Jeremy. "Which one starts with z?"

"I don't know. Click on any one."

Jeremy clicks on the jeep, and the help message appears once again at the bottom of the screen.

"What happens if you click on No?" asks Josh. Jeremy clicks on No, and the names of the objects appear above them: gum, zigzag, and jeep. "Zigzag is in blue, so *that is the correct answer,"* states Josh.

The next screen shows the letter I. "Lightning, fox, and kangaroo," sings out Jeremy as he clicks on the lightning. That's right! appears at the top of the screen.

"What does this bent arrow do?" asks Jeremy as he clicks this icon on the screen.

The words, "You should try this game again soon. Please click to continue," appear on the screen. The children don't understand the directions because they don't yet read well enough.

"Uh oh," says Jeremy. He clicks again and a menu appears—more text the students can't read.

"Click on the last thing," suggests Josh. Jeremy clicks on Choose a Different Activity, which gives him another menu screen. "Now where are we?" asks Josh.

"Let's click on the top one," replies Jeremy. He clicks on Learning Letters and another menu appears.

"Let's try the top one," says Josh.

Jeremy clicks on Small to Capital. A lowercase k appears on the screen, and K, N, D appear in boxes across the top.

"This is baby stuff," Jeremy says as he clicks on the K. "Let's try something else."

Just then the timer rings and Ms. Wilson walks over to the computer. "Boys, that's not where you are supposed to be. Click on the arrow in the corner and go to the main menu, so you can print out a dinosaur to color." At the main menu she has Jeremy click on Coloring Book. The children choose a dinosaur, and soon the printer is printing out a dinosaur for each of them.

"Okay, Josh and Jeremy, go back to your desks and work on your handwriting. I'll bring the dinosaur pictures to you. Sandy and Sana, are you ready to use the computer?"

Dinosoft Phonics has nice color graphics, options for using the mouse or keyboard to control the program, and several types of sound effects. The advertising blurb on the side of the box describes it as an "exciting and innovative program to master pre-reading and early reading skills" which was "developed by a team of leading educators." Unfortunately, the reality of this program is much more down to earth. As the case scenario above illustrates, the program has several weaknesses. If the students could read the instructions at several points in the program, they would not need the training provided by it. In addition, the drills cover only one or two skills, and these are addressed at one level. All children take the same drills, and the program does not use data from responses to decide what should be taught next. In addition, there is no useful remedial guidance or help. Unfortunately, this application is typical of hundreds of drill and practice programs available today. A teacher could easily end up with a cupboard full of inappropriate software if purchase decisions were made on the basis of advertising blurbs on the sides of packages. There are, however, more useful and more effective programs available for classroom use.

Writing Advantage, the program used in the scenario on the next page, is drill and practice software but it is much more useful than *Dinosoft Phonics* because it takes advantage of the computer's data processing power to keep track of student performance and uses that information to decide what to present next.

OC-DI Vocabulary Development

Carol, a high school student, is in the computer lab with her classmates. She is working on Vocabulary Tutor Level 1, a drill activity in Writing Advantage. After she types in her name, the main menu appears on the screen.

Carol chooses Play Game and the words in Group 1 appear on the screen. She reads them silently and chooses to work with the word mistakenly. She presses the Enter key and a sentence appears on the screen: We mistakenly assumed that Joan would come on time, but she was late again.

Next, she reads the prompt at the bottom of the screen, which encourages her to read the sentence for clues to the word's meaning. A second sentence appears: The results can be unpleasant if you choose when playing "Lady or the Tiger."

Following the prompt at the bottom of the screen, she places the cursor between choose and when to indicate where to place the word. Correct, the computer informs her.

Now the computer asks her to type in what she thinks the word means. Quickly Carol types in "to be wrong." The prompts on the screen ask her to use the arrow keys to select the correct part of speech. Not sure, she selects verb. The computer indicates that her answer is wrong but encourages her to continue.

These words appear under the definition: prefix, root, and suffix. Not sure what they mean, she presses the F1 key to get some help.

After reading the help screen, she decides to type in the root of the word. She types in "mistake." Puzzled to discover that is not the correct answer, she next types in "mistaken." Finally, the computer displays the correct answer: tak.

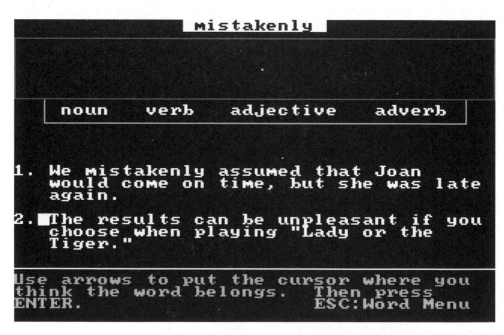

FIGURE 4-4   This program uses student input to decide what to do next.

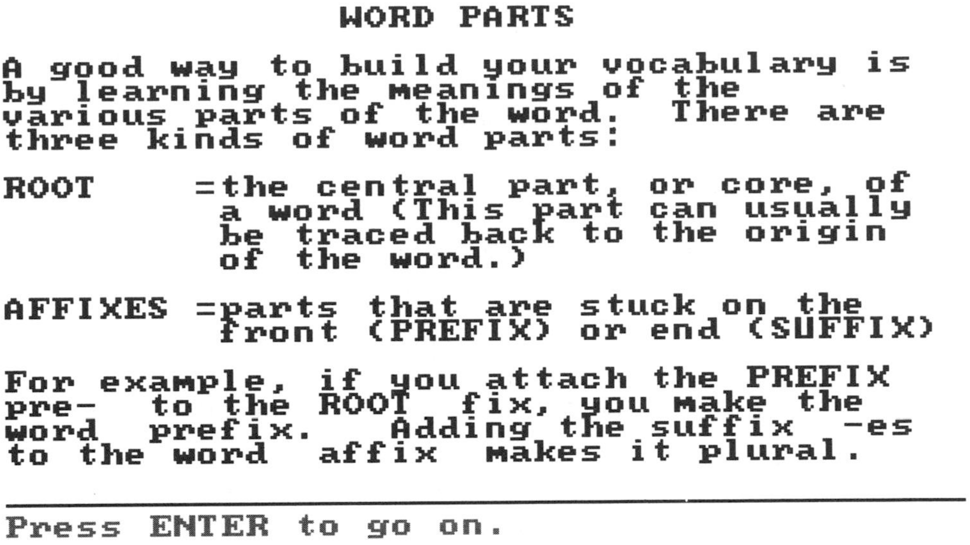

```
WORD PARTS

A good way to build your vocabulary is
by learning the meanings of the
various parts of the word.  There are
three kinds of word parts:

ROOT      =the central part, or core, of
           a word (This part can usually
           be traced back to the origin
           of the word.)

AFFIXES =parts that are stuck on the
          front (PREFIX) or end (SUFFIX)

For example, if you attach the PREFIX
pre-  to the ROOT  fix, you make the
word  prefix.    Adding the suffix  -es
to the word  affix  makes it plural.
```

```
Press ENTER to go on.
```

FIGURE 4-5 Students work with words in the vocabulary lesson in several ways and can get help by pressing the F1 key.

"That's strange," she thinks. "I've never heard of the word tak."

The definitions and parts of speech of "mistake" and "take" appear on the screen. Carol is asked if she wants to change her meaning for the word. She decides not to and goes to the next screen.

Once again she is prompted to choose a word part to study. This time she chooses suffix and types in "enly."

Incorrect, responds the computer, so she types in "ly." Correct!, and two more words, their parts of speech, and definitions appear on the screen. Carol skims over them and when prompted decides not to change the definition of "mistakenly" that she typed in earlier.

She moves on to figure out the prefix of the word and types in mis, which the computer indicates is correct, and the words misjudge and mislead appear on the screen. She reads through their parts of speech and definitions. Once again she responds no to the query about changing her definition of the word.

Now the computer asks her what part of speech "mistakenly" is. She knows they covered that in grammar, and suddenly focuses on the ly at the end of the word. She selects adverb, and the computer informs her that she is correct.

The phonetic spelling and definition of mistakenly appear on the screen. Asked if she wants to test her understanding of the word, she responds yes. At the top of the screen she sees these parts of speech: adjective, noun, and adverb. On the left side of the screen is a list of words. Using the arrow key, she quickly moves the words under their corresponding part of speech. She presses Enter and learns that she has correctly placed only five of the words for a score of 50 percent. Suddenly the words slip into the correct columns. She spends a few minutes studying them, then glances at the clock on the wall. Realizing that it will soon be time to change classes, she shuts down the computer.

As mentioned earlier, this program has several advantages over simplistic drill and practice programs. It uses multiple approaches to teach vocabulary, it adjusts the lesson based on student progress, and it has effective, context-sensitive help. The features of *Writing Advantage* generally should be considered the minimum for usable direct instruction software. Additional features to look for in direct instruction software will be discussed at the end of the chapter.

Writing Advantage is a definite improvement over the phonics program discussed first. The third out-of-context direct instruction program we will explore is even better. *Word Attack 3* is one of several programs distributed by Davidson & Associates that focuses on vocabulary development. The primary purpose of the program is to build the receptive vocabularies of students.

Laura, a middle school student, is exploring Word Attack 3, which has just been installed on the class computer. She has just finished typing in her name.
  "Hello, Laura."
  Surprised, Laura looks at the computer quizzically. She certainly did not expect the computer to speak to her. Quitting the program, she says to Barry, "Come see this." When Barry joins her at the computer, Laura launches Word Attack 3 and types in her name. Once again it responds, "Hello, Laura."

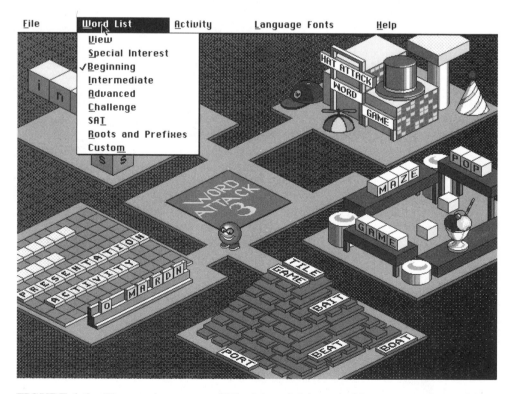

FIGURE 4-6   The opening screen of Word Attack 3 has graphic representations of the five games students can play.

"Hey, that's great," Barry tells Laura. "Let's play a game together."

"Sure. I'll put this on the Challenge level and we'll choose something."

They scan the screen, taking in all the options: Presentation Activity, Tile Game, Crossword Puzzle, Maze Game, and Hat Game.

"Hum, let's play Presentation Activity. It looks like Scrabble and I beat my brother at that last night," says Laura.

"Okay," replies Barry as he clicks the mouse. An options menu appears on the screen.

"Let's study the words first," suggests Laura.

Clicking on the study option causes the definition and sentence boxes to fill in, and scrambled letters appear in a row on the screen. The letters quickly move to the line below and form a word.

"I don't know what that word means. Let's put the level on Beginner and start this game again," decides Laura. They change the level and restart the game. This time the word is mild, and the definition is "gentle, not harsh." The sentence on the screen is "Use a mild soap to wash your face."

Laura presses Enter and a new word, definition, and sentence appear on the screen. They take turns reading through the information for the words keen, dreary, wealthy, and rich. Then timid appears on the screen with the definition "feeling fear; showing shyness."

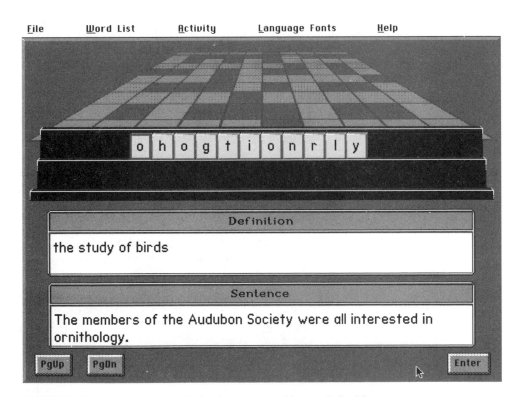

FIGURE 4-7   Students are required to unscramble words in this game.

"Hey look, my name is in the sentence." The text on the screen is "Laura is not timid and loves to meet new people." They work their way through the list, noticing Laura's name throughout the sentences.

Once they complete the list, they return to the menu and chose Solve. Now it is their turn to unscramble the words. The letters imld appear on the screen. Without reading the definition or sentence, Laura clicks and drags the letters down to the next line to spell "mild."

"That was easy," she remarks and clicks on Enter.

"Mild," says the computer.

Clicking on the "Page Down" icon produces causes a new scrambled word: "erctina."

"It's my turn to try this one," says Barry. He reads the definition aloud: "sure; without any doubt." Next, he reads the sentence aloud: "I am certain it will rain today." "The word is certain," he exclaims as he unscrambles the letters.

They quickly move through this activity and on to the next option, Sentence. This activity requires them to figure out the word by reading the definition and a sentence with the scrambled word missing, then unscramble the letters to form the word.

"dimit," reads Barry.

"That's easy," remarks Laura as she reads the sentence supplying the missing word: "Kathy is not timid and loves to meet new people." As they continue the game, they find that the hard part is spelling the words correctly. After two misses, the computer spells the word for them and pronounces it.

When their time on the computer is up, they reluctantly return to their desks. Melissa and Kerry now have their turn. They select the Special Interest category under the word list option in the menu bar and from this choose Computer. Then they move on to select the Crossword Puzzle Game.

Reading the definitions at the bottom of the screen, they quickly type in "boot," "modem," and "dialog box."

"Look at the definition for the word that goes down," says Melissa.

"That's easy," replies Kerry as he types in the word "backup."

Mr. Sheller, their teacher, looks over their shoulders at the screen. "Melissa and Kerry, I know you like doing the crossword puzzle with the computer words, but I'd like you to use the social studies vocabulary words and definitions I put in yesterday afternoon."

"Aw, may we finish this first?" pleads Kerry.

"Yes, if you can do so quickly," responds Mr. Sheller before turning back to the rest of the class.

All the individual programs mentioned thus far are based on behavioral theories of learning. Behavioral theories emphasize tight control of the learning environment, focused instruction, ongoing adjustment of instruction based on the responses a student makes, and regular, detailed assessment of student progress.

One of the most widely used applications of the behavioral approach to educational technology is the *integrated learning system*. Although they vary considerably, most integrated learning systems have these characteristics in common (Maddux and Willis, 1993):

1. Computer-based assessment and diagnosis of student skills.
2. Delivery of instruction via a group of computers that are interconnected, or "networked."

3. Continuous monitoring of student performance and automatic adjustment of instruction where needed.
4. Generation of student and class performance data in a variety of formats for use by teachers and administrators.

Today thousands of students receive much of their basic reading and language arts instruction on computers running any of several integrated learning systems currently being sold to schools. Integrated learning systems generally begin with a computer-administered, diagnostic-prescriptive evaluation of the student's current achievement level. Then the software breaks down the content to be taught into small units, teaches a unit, assesses progress, and moves on to the next unit or provides remedial instruction as indicated. The most popular integrated learning systems cover core content areas such as reading, language arts, and mathematics, but many also include instruction in science and social studies. Integrated learning systems are offered by a number of companies and, because they often include both software and hardware, can cost $100,000 to $700,000 per school if every student in the school is to use the system for at least some instruction each day. Although expensive, they are often touted as the total solution to low-achieving schools, something that can be very appealing to a school board, superintendent, and principal. In fact, they have so much appeal that Bailey (1992, p. 3) wondered "Why do they [integrated learning systems] continue to dominate the school technology market?" when many new forms of technology-supported teaching and learning are available. Using figures from 1989 he concluded that sales of integrated learning systems account for half the money schools spend on educational software.

In their analysis of integrated learning systems, Shore and Johnson (1992) concluded that their strengths lay in three areas:

1. *Lab-based integrated learning systems are less threatening.* Integrated learning systems can be set up in a separate computer lab and maintained by a lab manager. Teachers who use the lab do not have to know as much about technology as they would if computers were put in their classrooms.
2. *Integrated learning systems offer a total curriculum solution to technology.* Selecting and setting up hundreds of individual pieces of educational software can be difficult. Integrated learning systems, on the other hand, involve making one decision rather than many and are the only systems that "have the power to deliver a total curriculum sequence across all grade levels" (p. 38).
3. *Integrated learning systems monitor the progress of all students.* "The entire student population of a school can be monitored across all grade levels and multiple subjects. Students are automatically channeled to the appropriate lessons" (p. 38).

Proponents of some of the theories discussed in this book would probably argue that many of the elements that Shore and Johnson cite as strengths are really weaknesses because they express a factory model of instruction in which students are treated as products who, with quality control, will be shipped from the factory with exactly the same basic knowledge. Critics generally would agree, however, with Shore and Johnson's list of integrated learning systems weaknesses:

1. *Some integrated learning systems are difficult to use.* Integrated learning systems are an outgrowth of old, large computer systems that were designed to be used primarily by computer specialists. Some integrated learning systems reflect that ancestry and are very difficult for anyone without an extensive background in computer science.
2. *Teachers and students may have limited access.* Integrated learning systems are expensive, and it is easy to underestimate how much equipment is needed if all students in a school are to receive instruction in several subject areas via an integrated learning system. The result can be scheduling and access problems.
3. *Some integrated learning systems lack flexibility.* Many integrated learning systems come with predefined curricula. You use the curricula built into the system or you don't use it.
4. *Integrated learning systems are only one type of educational technology.* One reason programmed instruction died out is that most of it was relatively boring. Much of the instructional material on integrated learning systems is also relatively boring. Many other types of educational technology are available—multimedia, hypermedia, telecommunications, satellite-based distance education, cooperative problem solving programs—and many of these other types appear to be much more interesting and appealing to students. Some of these other types are advocated by supporters of the learning theories that oppose behaviorism.

Although integrated learning systems represent one of the most popular ways of delivering out-of-context direct instruction, there are many others. Some involve computers; others do not. Common targets of out-of-context direct instruction in elementary schools are the various aspects of sound-symbol relations—phonics. Below is a brief teacher-directed lesson for beginning readers on vowel correspondence that was developed by Gunning (1992, p. 99–100):

Step 1. Auditory Perception

Hold up a ring, a stick, the numeral six, and a picture of a fish. Have children name each object and listen to see if they can tell which sound can be heard in all the names. As you say each name, emphasize the vowel sound. Then say the vowel sound in isolation. Lead students to see that the words all have the sound /i/.

Step 2. Letter-Sound Integration

Write the words ring, stick, six, and fish on the board, saying each word as you do so. Ask students if they can see what is the same about the words. Show them that all four have an i, which stands for the sound /i/ as in fish and is pronounced /i/. Have students read the words. Discuss other words that have the sound of /i/. If students know the sign words in, is, if, and it, for example, place these on the board and discuss the fact that these have the sound /i/. Have students read the word chorally and individually.

Step 3. Guided Practice

Share a story that contains a number of short i words [the author suggests "Mig the

Pig" for short i sounds]. Pause before the short i words and invite students to read them. Also share songs, rhymes, announcements, and signs that contain short i words.

Step 4. Application

Have students read selections or create experience stories that contain short i.

Steps 1 and 2 are examples of out-of-context direct instruction. Steps 3 and 4, because they involve meaningful text studied in context, are examples of preparatory direct instruction. Hundreds of direct instruction computer programs are available on various aspects of phonics and other reading skills. A sampling of the current generation of programs can be found at the end of the chapter. The list is only a small sample of the direct instruction software available today from educational software distributors. Not all of it meets minimum standards of quality, however, and even "good" software may not fit your instructional objectives. It is therefore critical that you carefully evaluate any program you consider using in your classroom.

Many school districts and regional education service agencies maintain a large library of current software that is available for teacher preview. Where local preview resources are not available, many software companies offer 30- to 45-day review privileges without charge to teachers.

PREPARATORY DIRECT INSTRUCTION

The second type of skills-based direct instruction, preparatory direct instruction, is also based on the assumption that some skills can best be taught independently and then combined for successful reading. However, a number of cognitive theories of learning propose that people learn skills best when they are taught in context. Students therefore should not be taught a skill in isolation that may not be used for months, or years. Preparatory direct instruction occurs at the time of need. Cognitive theories of learning, which emphasize the need to consider how a student is processing, storing, and organizing information, have had an influence on reading and language arts instruction. Constructivist models, as explained in Chapters 2 and 3, have emerged from the work of developmental theorists such as Jerome Bruner, Jean Piaget, and Lev Vygotsky.

It may seem that any discussion of direct instruction is out of place when constructivist approaches to teaching are discussed. Out-of-context direct instruction has been criticized by proponents from many theoretical camps, usually from the perspective that reading is best mastered through active, purposeful exploration of text in situations that are meaningful to the child. From that perspective, reading, like Humpty Dumpty, cannot be broken up and then put back together again. This perspective has led to many different teaching methods that emphasize active involvement with meaningful text. In classrooms today students learn to read through language experience, buddy reading, free reading, and reflective journal writing strategies.

Even if out-of-context direct instruction is rejected as undesirable, there is still the question of whether children need any direct instruction at all. Can they learn to read without any? Some approaches say yes, but in practice most teachers do use some direct instruction. Many teaching strategies use direct instruction to help students begin to master new skills or get beyond blocks or problems. In his discussion of individualized reading plans, Gunning (1992, p. 368–369) had this to say about direct instruction:

> A major criticism of individualized reading was that it lacked a carefully planned program for developing skills. To eliminate this very real weakness, the program should include a period of direct instruction each day. The instruction should be broad in scope and sequential. It should include all the essential strategies and skills that students need: using phonics and context, predicting, summarizing, skimming, monitoring, and so forth. Ideally, the strategy or skill being taught should prepare the students for the pieces they are about to read. It can also address some need that the teacher has detected. For example, students may be having difficulty with words that contain prefixes and suffixes, or perhaps they are not monitoring for meaning and are not aware when a passage doesn't make sense. A series of lessons on affixes or using metacognitive strategies would then be in order.

Gunning goes on to discuss the sequence of instruction that proceeds from a teacher-centered lesson to guided practice and then independent practice. He concludes that "Once the skill or strategy has been taught and practiced under teacher guidance, students can apply it to whatever they are reading" (p. 369). Preparatory direct instruction teaches students an essential skill that is either required for a literacy activity or one that addresses a weakness the teacher has detected.

Several other systems for teaching reading and language arts intersperse direct instruction with another approach. Spiegel, in "Blending Whole Language and Systematic Direct Instruction" (1992), argues that whole language approaches are enhanced and improved by the inclusion of some direct instruction. Bartley (1993) makes a similar point, as does Heymsfield in "Filling the Hole in Whole Language" (1989). Goodman, one of the founders of the whole language movement, wrote a response to Heymsfield titled "Whole Language Is Whole" (1989), which states that the approach does not need to be "patched" with "skills instruction." He argues that teaching discrete skills is incompatible with a whole language approach.

A few research studies address the effectiveness of adding some direct instruction to other approaches such as whole language. For example, Thomson and Miller (1991) studied the effects of adding direct instruction as a "supplement to a literature-based delivery model." Their study added phonics instruction to a whole language approach based on the Houghton-Mifflin Literature Program. Results favored students in the supplemental direct instruction group. In her study of language arts instruction for language-deficient middle school students, Bartley (1993) concluded that adding some direct instruction, oral reading, and class discussion to a whole language approach enhanced reading comprehension.

Another good example of preparatory direct instruction is the work of Idol and Rutledge (1993) with reading disabled children. They believed their students would profit from some direct instruction on phonics. However, instead of providing that instruction out of context, they created material using phonics that prepared the children for the passages they were about to read. The authors created "sound sheets" with rows of sound/letter combinations based on words from passages the children would read after they practiced sounds using the sheets.

Very few pieces of direct instruction software available today were designed specifically for use as preparatory direct instruction. Many, however, can be adapted for that use. For example, *Word Attack 3*, which was discussed earlier in this chapter, includes an Editor that lets teachers create their own lists of words. The games in this program thus can be customized for specific lessons. Many other programs also can be customized by teachers.

AN ADAPTABLE GAME: BEGINNING READING

Computer games are a type of direct instruction program that can be adapted for use as a preparatory activity. Many types of interesting games are available. They generally involve a scenario such as saving a planet or discovering a treasure through knowledge and understanding some skill. For example, *Beginning Reading* is one of a series of educational games from Bright Star Technologies, a subsidiary of a well-known computer game company, Sierra On-Line.

FIGURE 4-8   The opening screen for *Beginning Reading* is a hallway. Children click on a door to choose a game.

FIGURE 4-9   In this game, children must assemble word parts to make the word the monkey speaks.

The opening screen of *Beginning Reading* is a hallway with several doors and two cartoon characters. Through animation and voices that rival the quality of television cartoons, characters tell children how to play the games. Their first task is to pick a door, which will take them to a particular game. Games teach many different beginning reading skills including:

Identifying two-letter consonants and vowel sounds

Recognizing sight words

Using rhyming words

Building complete words from parts of words

Alphabetizing words

Reading a story

Work on any of these skills could be used as preparation for other assignments. The games in *Beginning Reading* are appealing and instructive. For example, in the game of building complete words from parts of words, the monkey might tell students to build the word

FIGURE 4-10   This game requires students to use context to correctly replace the words in the story.

"clock" from parts. Students use the mouse to drag word parts together. If they are unsure about how to pronounce a word part, they can click on it and hear the monkey say it. The monkey's pronunciation is precise and clear.

In the Storybook Room, children listen to a Jack in the Box read the story. Then he pulls words from the story and puts them in a space below the storybook. Children must use their mouse to drag the words back to the correct location in the story.

All the activities in *Beginning Reading* could be used as out-of-context exercises, but they could also serve as preparatory activities.

DESIRABLE CHARACTERISTICS OF
DIRECT INSTRUCTION SOFTWARE

In the early days of educational computing, software selection was easy. You searched for a piece of software on the topic that interested you, and if you found one, you bought it and considered yourself lucky. In the mid 1970s, when personal computers were first appearing in schools, very few educational programs—good or bad—were available. Today the situation has changed dramatically. Thousands of programs support reading, language arts, and composition. Availability is not an issue; appropriateness is. When you consider using computer software for any type of direct instruction, the appropriate software must "fit" in several different ways:

Subject Matter. The program deals with the subject matter at a *level* appropriate to your students and in language that is understandable to them. The subject matter is covered in the *depth* needed and in a *context* appropriate to the cultural and social milieu of your classroom.

Efficiency. For the time invested, the benefits to students are worthwhile.

Approach. The program takes an approach to instruction (drill and practice, tutorial, diagnostic, evaluative, online help, critical with suggestions) that fits the role you want it to play in your curriculum.

Appeal. The program is designed in such a way as to appeal to your students.

Ease of Use. The program is free of bugs, has an intuitive or easy-to-use interface, and has appropriate supplemental materials, such as quick-start guides, understandable student manuals, and comprehensive teacher guides.

Adaptability. The software is capable of adapting to and responding to the range of needs and interests your students are likely to present.

Help and Feedback. The program provides help that advances learning. It does not simply provide the answer when a student asks for help. The feedback is appropriate to the age, developmental level, and context of your students.

Compatibility. The program will operate on the computer and accessories (CD-ROM drive, memory, hard disk storage, color monitor, sound card, music interface) available to your students.

Cost Efficiency. The program is a valuable addition to the curriculum when benefits, and costs (for the software and any equipment required), and effort required to support it are considered.

The ideal program would be rated highly in all these categories. In many cases you will find five or six programs on the appropriate topic, but none will be exactly what you want. You then have to decide whether any of the available software is close enough to your ideal program to be worth using. Often you will be able to adapt the way software is used to fit your needs. Keep in mind, however, that the option of not using technology is always available and in many situations may be the most appropriate choice.

SUMMARY

Skills-based direct instruction is found in classrooms everywhere, no matter what the grade level. It is considered by many to be a necessary form of schooling. It comes in many guises, and it is not always easily discernible. The ideal direct instruction model encompasses five steps, but one direct instruction lesson may have all the steps and another may have only one or two. Both may be appropriate, or inappropriate, depending on the purpose and the perspective of the teacher. As with any other teaching strategy, direct instruction has its proponents and opponents.

In this chapter two forms of skills-based direct instruction were discussed: out of context and preparatory. In the language arts classroom, out-of-context direct instruction focuses on teaching students skills they need to read and write. Students concentrate on learning the skills, often in isolation, through drill and practice, tutorials, and games. Computer-based out-of-context direct instruction is an outgrowth of programmed instruction, which was popular in the 1960s. It is also a major component of many integrated learning systems today.

Preparatory direct instruction plays a supporting role to other types of instruction. The objective of preparatory direct instruction is to teach students fundamental literacy skills they need for reading and writing activities.

As indicated in this chapter, within this category of computer-assisted direct instruction software you can find some of the worst examples of educational software as well as examples of excellent software. Key things to look for include options that allow for customizing the software to meet the students' needs, and options for inputting the teacher's own curriculum.

MICROTEACHING ACTIVITIES

1. Use the editing program in *Word Attack 3* to create lists of difficult words and concepts from one of the courses most students in your teacher education program take. You will need to write up definitions and two sentences using the words or concepts. In a short microteaching activity, divide the class into small groups and direct them to play one or two of the games in *Word Attack 3*. Set the scene by asking students to concentrate on the words and concepts that are still a bit unclear to them. After the activity, decide as a class whether the games are a good way for students to learn all types of vocabulary words. Or are they better suited to some types than others?

2. Select from the collection of direct instruction software available to you one or two programs that could be used as preparatory direct instruction for a student-centered reading activity. Create a lesson plan that includes two or three periods at the computer using the direct instruction programs to teach skills students will need in the next activity. Include in your lesson plan information on the activity the programs will support.

3. Select from the programs available to you a computer game that can be used for direct instruction. In a short microteaching activity, explain the context and purpose of using the software. Then assign some students to play the game individually and some to work in groups of two or three. After they have used the software for 10 minutes or so, lead the class in a discussion of how the software should be used. Is it best when used individually? Is it good for small groups? What are the advantages and disadvantages of group and individual use?

A SAMPLING OF DIRECT INSTRUCTION COMPUTER PROGRAMS

The list below is a sample of some of the thousands of skills-based direct instruction programs available today and their distributors. Addresses for the distributors are provided at the end of the chapter.

Alphabetization and Letter Recognition. Milliken.

Dictionary Skills. Computer Centerline.

Drawing Conclusions. Computer Centerline.

Essential Grammar. Educational Resources.

Essential Punctuation. Educational Resources.

Finding Cause and Effect. Computer Centerline.

Getting the Main Idea. Computer Centerline.

Grammar Mechanics. Educational Resources.

Grammar Problems for Practice. Milliken.

Hugo Hound's Vowel Sounds. Educational Resources.

Learning About Words. Computer Centerline.

Making Inferences. Computer Centerline.

Play and Learn Shapes. Educational Resources.

Practical Grammar. Computer Centerline.

Primary Steps to Comprehension. Educational Resources.

Sentence Combining. Milliken.

Starting with Phonics. Educational Resources.

Steps to Comprehension. Educational Resources.

Stickybear Alphabet. Educational Resources.

The Spelling System. Milliken.

Uncle Clyde's Consonant Slides. Educational Resources.

Using Context Clues. Computer Centerline.

Using Outlining Skills. Computer Centerline.

Victoria: Vocabulary in Context. Computer Centerline.

Winning with Phonics. Educational Resources.

REFERENCES

Bailey, G. (1992). Wanted: A road map for understanding integrated learning systems. *Educational Technology, 32*(9), 3–5.

Bartley, N. (1993). Literature-based integrated language instruction and the language-deficient student. *Reading Research and Instruction, 32*(2), 31–37.

Carnine, D., Silbert, J., & Kameenui, E. (1990). *Direct reading instruction (2nd ed.).* Columbus, OH: Merrill.

Eds, M., & Cockrum, W. (1985). Teaching word meanings by expanding schemata vs. dictionary work vs. reading in context. *Journal of Reading, 28*(6), 492–497.

Gersten, R. (1988). The continued impact of the direct instruction model: Longitudinal studies of follow through students. *Education and Treatment of Children, 11*(4), 318–327.

Goodman, K., & Goodman, Y. (1982). A whole language comprehension centered view of reading development. In L. Reed & S. Ward (Eds.), *Basic Skills: Issues and Choices* (Vol. 2, pp. 125–134). St. Louis: Central Midwestern Regional Laboratories.

Goodman, K. (1989). Whole language is whole: A response to Heymsfield. *Educational Leadership, 46*(6), 69–70.

Gunning, T. (1992). *Creating reading instruction for all children.* Boston: Allyn and Bacon.

Heymsfield, C. (1989). Filling the hole in whole language. *Educational Leadership, 46*(6), 65–68.

Holland, J., and Skinner, B. (1961). *The analysis of behavior.* New York: McGraw Hill.

Idol, L., & Rutledge, M. (1993). Teaching phonics to poor readers: Direct instruction using sound sheets. *Teaching Exceptional Children, 25*(4), 58–61.

Johnson, D., & Pearson, P. (1975). Skills management systems: A critique. *The Reading Teacher, 28*, 757–764.

Maddux, C., and Willis, J. (1993). Integrated learning systems and their alternatives: Problems and cautions. In G. Bailey, (Ed.), *Computer-based integrated learning systems* (pp. 121–136). Englewood Cliffs, NJ: Educational Technology Publications.

Nauman, A. (1990). Structure and perspective in reading and writing. In T. Shanahan (Ed.), *Reading and writing together: New perspectives for the classroom.* Norwood, MA: Christopher-Gordon.

Readence, J. (1986). Direct instruction in processing metaphors. *Journal of Reading Behavior, 18*(4), 325–339.

Reutzel, D. (1988). The effect of a direct instruction paradigm using dictated texts on beginning readers' main idea comprehension. *Reading Research and Instruction, 27*(4), 25–46.

Samuels, S. (1988). Decoding and automaticity: Helping poor readers become automatic at word recognition. *Reading Teacher, 41*(8), 756–760.

Shore, A., & Johnson, M. (1992). Integrated learning systems: A vision for the future. *Educational Technology, 32*(9), 36–39.

Smith, R., Otto, W., & Hansen, L. (1978). *The school reading program.* Boston: Houghton Mifflin.

Snider, V. (1990). Direct instruction reading with average first-graders. *Reading Improvement, 27*(2), 143–148.

Spiegel, D. (1992). Blending whole language and systematic direct instruction. *Reading Teacher, 46*(1), 38–44.

Stallings, J. (1987). *Longitudinal findings for early childhood programs: Focus on direct instruction.* (ERIC Document Reproduction Service No. ED297874)

Stevens, R. (1991). The effects of cooperative learning and direct instruction in reading comprehension strategies on main idea identification. *Journal of Educational Psychology, 83*(1), 8–16.

Thomson, B., & Miller, L. (1991, Winter). *Pilot study of the effectiveness of a direct instructional model as a supplement to a literature-based delivery model; traditional teaching to whole language: A focus on instructional routines.* Florida Educational Research Council Research Bulletin, 23(2). (ERIC Document Reproduction Service No. ED352602)

SOFTWARE DISCUSSED IN THIS CHAPTER

Beginning Reading. BrightStar division of Sierra On-Line, PO Box 600, Coarsegold, CA 93614-0600. Bulletin Board System Number: 209-683-4463.

Dinosoft Phonics. Dinosoft, 9801 Dupont Avenue South, Bloomington, MN 55431.

Reading Blaster. Davidson & Associates, PO Box 2961, Torrance, CA 90509. Phone: 800-545-7677.

Skills Bank 3. Skills Bank Corporation, 15 Governor's Court, Baltimore, MD 21244. Phone: 800-84-SKILL.

Writing Advantage. Innovative Software Corporation, 1800 N. W. 65th Avenue, Plantation, FL 33313.

Word Attack 3. Davidson & Associates, PO Box 2961, Torrance, CA 90509. Phone: 800-545-7677.

SOFTWARE SUPPLIERS AND DEVELOPERS MENTIONED IN THIS CHAPTER

Computer Centerline, 1500 Broad Street, Greensburg, PA 15601. Phone: 800-852-5802.

Educational Resources, 1550 Executive Drive, Elgin, Illinois 60123. Phone: 800-624-2926.

Milliken Publishing Company, 1100 Research Blvd., PO Box 21579, St. Louis, MO 63132-0579.

CHAPTER FIVE

Just-in-Time Direct Instruction

The direct instruction explored discussed in the preceding chapter were all based on a skills or subskills approach to reading and language arts: break the task of reading down into subskills and teach those skills separately. Then help children bring their newly developed skills to bear on the task of reading.

The subskills approach is widely used in reading and language arts instruction. In some methods it is the primary focus of instruction. In many others it plays a support role. However, regardless of the role it plays—primary or support—the focus during skills-based direct instruction is on subcomponents of the overall task. Much, perhaps most, direct instruction uses this model. There are, however, other foundations for direct instruction. One is *just-in-time direct instruction*. Another is *cognitive skills direct instruction*, which will be explored in the next chapter.

Preparatory direct instruction, discussed in Chapter 4, is generally delivered before the student needs the skill, or after the teacher has noted a problem that should respond to some direct teaching. In contrast, just-in-time (JIT) direct instruction puts instruction at the point of need and usually under the control of the student. For example, a child writing a paragraph on a word processor might have a question about punctuation. She might press the Help key, select Punctuation from the menu that appears on the screen, and then select End of Sentence because she is concerned about what punctuation should be used at the end of a particular sentence. In this example, the help would be computer text and graphics on the screen. In just-in-time learning systems for younger children, spoken instruction might be used. The power of information technology such as computers is particularly suited to supporting just-in-time direct instruction.

Just in Time in an English Composition Class

Randy slides into his seat in Mr. Jackson's 9th-grade English composition class just before the tardy bell. "What did we have for homework in here?" he asks.

"Don't you ever do homework?" responds Ben. "We had to finish reading over and revising our drafts of that composition about our family. We're going back to the computer lab to try out Tools for Writers."

"Tools for Writers? What's that?"

"You know, that program he demonstrated that helps you find mistakes in your writing and offers suggestions for corrections," says Ben.

"Oh, yeah. That's the one he said to be sure that we look at the suggestions carefully before we decide to make the changes. It sounds like fun. I'm glad I didn't skip today."

"Pay attention, everyone," Mr. Jackson begins. "Listen up. Be sure you have the corrected drafts of your composition and your computer disk. Let's move down to the computer lab. Once you're working, I'll take roll." Thirty teenagers jostle and shove as they make their way down to the computer lab.

"Quickly find a seat, and listen to my directions," Mr. Jackson tells them, amazed at how much better they listen and work when they're in the computer lab. "As I showed you yesterday, you're going to work with Tools for Writers to help improve your writing. Remember you open Tools for Writers and then open your composition. If you have problems, raise your hand and I'll get to you as soon as I can."

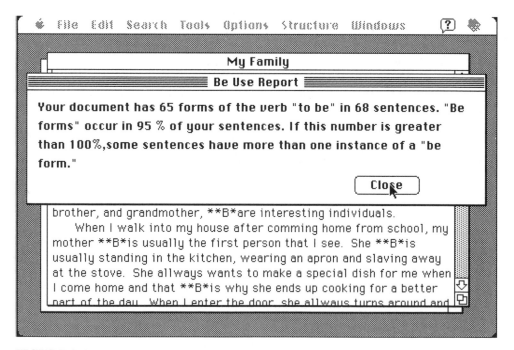

FIGURE 5-1 Feedback on the use of *being* verbs in a paper is one option with *Tools for Writers.*

Randy double clicks on Tools for Writers, slides his disk into the computer's flop-py drive, and opens his file titled "My Family." Scanning the menu bar, he clicks on Tools and slides the cursor down to Be Finder. While the program scans his document, his eyes scan the room to check out what everyone else is doing. Noting that the other students are intently staring at their computer screens, he turns back to his document.

Randy reads through the suggested changes and has the computer make the cor-rections to his paper. He nudges Ben, "Hey, it made some good suggestions about be verbs. Now, what?"

"Have it search for vague words," replies Ben.

Randy finds that option under the Tools menu and selects it. The computer selects a favorite phrase of his: at that point in time. Randy reads his sentence again, then reads the computer's suggested change. "It does sound better that way," he thinks, so he clicks the mouse to tell the computer to make the changes.

"Okay, now what?" he asks Ben again.

Exasperated, Ben says, "Go back to Tools in the menu bar and select each one of those options. Quit bothering me. I want to get this finished."

Once again Randy clicks on the Tools menu to select another option for analyzing his paper.

"Class, let me interrupt you for a minute," says Mr. Jackson. "About 15 minutes before the end of the period, I'd like volunteers to let us work with their papers on the LCD panel. I want you to share corrections you made based on the computer sugges-tions, and also tell us about any suggestions you rejected."

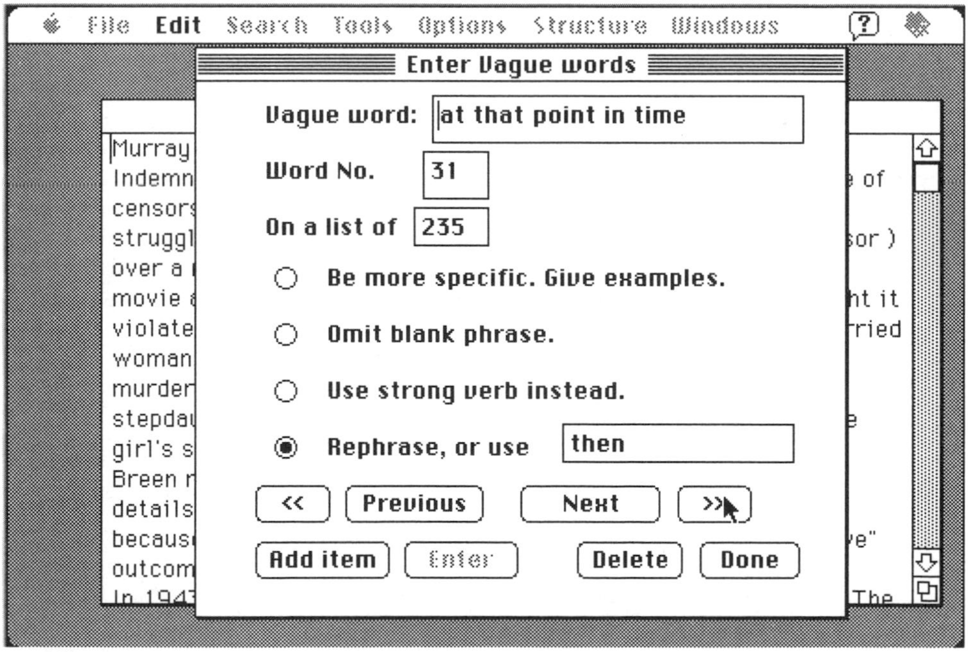

FIGURE 5-2   Searching for vague words, the program finds at that point in time and suggests a change.

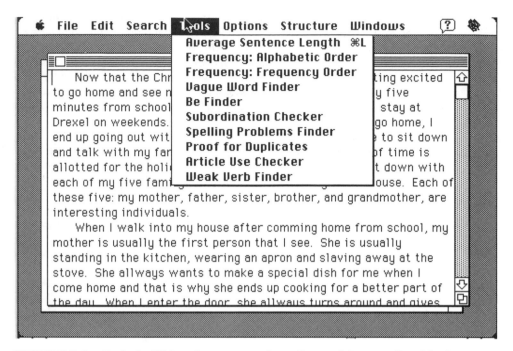

FIGURE 5-3   *Tools for Writers* has many options. Some of them are listed in the Tools menu.

JUST-IN-TIME DIRECT INSTRUCTION: THEORY AND APPLICATION

Like many of the constructivist approaches discussed in other chapters, just-in-time (JIT) direct instruction assumes that children acquire literacy skills best in environments where they are involved in significant meaningful problem solving or exploration. Characteristics of such learning environments include authenticity, situated learning, anchored instruction, and collaboration.

Seen from a constructivist perspective, the design and delivery of instruction is not the creation and use of detailed lesson plans that specify exactly what the teacher and students should be doing at various points in the lesson. As Harley (1994) states, "Prespecified, step by step instruction can no longer be developed on the assumption that the process can control the specifics of meaning constructed by the learner" (p. 49). Instead, instruction relies on the creation of an environment where groups of students can explore and analyze, think and reflect, propose and act.

The assumption behind situated learning or anchored instruction is that children will learn many basic skills on their own in order to solve the problem presented or to explore an interesting text. However, a developing consensus holds that some direct instruction and support may be needed even in many innovative, child-centered activities. The problem is how to develop the observational and professional practice skills needed to make on-the-fly decisions in the classroom about whether a hard-working group of students would profit from some direct instruction or not. In such cases direct instruction is treated as a backup or last-resort strategy that is used when (1) students need a basic skill to solve a current problem and there is little likelihood they can learn it on their own (or the time required to discover and learn the skills is excessive); (2) students seem to be stuck and direct instruction would move them beyond an impasse that would otherwise block their progress or consume too much of the learning time.

The decision to intervene with direct instruction is not a yes or no decision. There are degrees of intervention, and many teachers use a range of interventions—from subtle hints and redirections to outright demonstrations and teacher-centered lessons. One teacher who has wrestled with the question of when and how direct instruction should be used is Nancy Atwell (1987), one of the leaders of the reading/writing workshop approach to teaching composition. This approach focuses on helping students write. In Atwell's class, direct instruction sometimes is provided in the form of mini-lessons, an idea for which Atwell credits Calkins (1986). A mini-lesson is a brief session that addresses an issue raised in previous workshops or in the students' writing.

> It might be an editorial issue—how to punctuate dialogue or set up a business letter. I also use this time to talk about issues of process or technique—the difference between revising and recopying, or how to show rather than tell—and to introduce different modes and genres writers might want to try out for themselves, usually by reading short selections aloud. At the beginning of the year, my mini-lessons deal with procedural issues—how to use the daily writing folder, what resources and materials are available to writers, how to self-edit and where to put writing ready to be teacher-edited, what to do in conference corners. In a mini-lesson on conferences I'll discuss helpful ways of responding, and role-play good and bad conferences with a couple of my kids. At first I lead the discussions, but as the year progresses students share their expertise, too. Mini-lessons generally last between five and ten minutes, just long enough to touch on some timely topic. [Atwell, 1987, p. 77]

Atwell describes her conversion to the writing workshop approach. When she first shifted to that approach, she abandoned whole-group instruction.

> I moved out of the driver's seat and observed as my students sat behind the wheel and took control. I had to stay out of their way for a while and learn from them, another necessary step in my evaluation. But a time came when I felt confident of my new expertise and ready to move back up front, sharing control now with my kids. I learn from them and I share my knowledge when something I've learned will help them. . . . I don't require "mastery" of mini-lesson information; I don't expect every one of my students is going to take to heart every word of the mini-lesson and put it immediately into effect. Even in my old writing assignment days, when I taught pull-out-the-stops, forty-five maxi-lessons, that never happened. [pp. 77–78]

At other times, Atwell teaches skills during individual conferences:

> The editorial issues I teach in individual conferences run the gamut, from syntax to usage to spelling, punctuation, format, and stylistic concerns. There is no one set of editorial concerns, no grade eight skills scope and sequence. There are individual writers with varying

degrees of editorial expertise. By teaching in context, one-to-one, I can go right to the heart of what an individual writer needs. My job as a teacher of skills is to focus on the writing, on the individual piece, and make a judgment about where this writer has come from and where he or she needs to go next. . . .

Since I started explicitly teaching skills in the context of pieces of kids' writing, not only are students more skilled at mechanics, but I'm more knowledgeable about how mechanics work. [pp. 107–111]

Most of Atwell's uses of direct instruction are either preparatory or just-in-time, and her book is rich in detail on how she teaches many different subjects during mini-lessons and conferences. Atwell, however, does not discuss how information technology can support either preparatory or JIT direct instruction. One reading/language arts educator who does is Balajthy (1988), who suggests several ways computers can support child-centered, language experience approaches to reading and language arts. Computer support includes electronic children's books with clickable words that the program will pronounce or define; computer-based methods of providing teacher feedback on student compositions; revision and editing programs that provide feedback on grammar, usage, style, and organization; and writing and publishing software that helps children write and disseminate their work. Balajthy's list includes many JIT direct instruction methods. Some help the teacher provide instruction and support as needed. Others let the computer take the role of aide and guide. We will explore several of these uses of computers in the following sections.

Tools for Writers, the program described at the beginning of this chapter, belongs to a large and growing genre of software: tool software for writing. Spelling and grammar checkers, for example, have been around for many years. All have one thing in common: they analyze original compositions and provide suggestions for improvement. They are excellent examples of JIT direct instruction because they provide feedback as needed during the writing process. Instead of teaching students about punctuation, passive voice, or subject-verb agreement in isolation, they bring students' attention to problems in their own writing that may impede communication, and they offer suggestions about how the problems can be corrected. Programs like *Tools for Writers* are available in many formats, and the particular program that would be most useful in your classroom will depend on many factors. Some programs, like *Tools for Writers*, assume the student has in hand most of the basics for writing well and is now ready to polish. These programs would be inappropriate in the elementary grades or in a beginning English as a second language classroom where the foundations are not yet established. Others concentrate on such elementary issues that, when used with advanced students, they generate too many false hits—potential problems that turn out not to be problems at all.

A helpful exercise is to take one of the programs designed to help novice writers who are at a very basic level and use it to analyze passages from famous novels. The results can be very interesting because the programs often point out problems to be corrected that are actually signature features of a novelist's style. Try running some of Faulkner's sentences through one of the programs to see what it says about sentence length, for example.

THE LITERATURE ON TEXT ANALYSIS PACKAGES

Are grammar checkers useful? Can computer grammar checkers replace teacher feedback? The issue of computerized grammar checkers vs. teacher-generated feedback is much too complex to be boiled down to yes or no answers to broad questions like these. For example, Pennington (1993) argues that text analysis programs, such as grammar checkers, are detrimental rather than helpful in programs for nonproficient students who are studying English as a second language or for students who need help with very basic skills. Too often the writing of students in these categories contains errors that are not appropriately identified by the grammar checkers, and such programs frequently make revision recommendations that are inappropriate for this group. Fischer and Grusin (1993) make a related point on the use of grammar checkers in journalism classes. They caution against using grammar checkers because the programs they evaluated did not identify all the errors journalism students commonly make.

We take a somewhat more positive view of grammar checkers and related programs. Grammar checkers vary considerably in what they check, the types of recommendations they make, and the level of writing proficiency assumed by the software. If any of these conditions do not match your students, then the program may well be inappropriate. On the other hand, appropriately used grammar checkers that fit a student's level of proficiency and type of writing can be very helpful. Standard, commercially available grammar checkers and text analysis programs have been used successfully in the elementary grades (Milone, 1990), with learning disabled students (Dalton, 1990), in high school (Elkins, 1986; Roberts and Mutter, 1991), and college (Hult, 1985). Text analysis programs that fit the students in your class may not always be available on the shelves of local software stores, however. In the future we may see more specialized text analysis programs designed for the educational needs of specific types of students. For example, Liou (1992) developed an English grammar text analysis program designed specifically for Chinese students in Taiwan who are learning to write in English. As part of the development process Liou analyzed hundreds of papers written by students, identified the most common types of errors, and developed software that identified those errors and made appropriate suggestions for revision. Liou's software, unlike many other text analysis programs, contains a special dictionary of problematic English words because the Taiwanese students needed that type of electronic support.

Text analysis programs do have a place in classrooms. They can be used in several ways. Individual students, and collaborative writing groups, can use them to analyze drafts of their papers. Teachers can use them in group editing sessions and in conferences with individual students. They are typically used to support teacher-supplied feedback. Could they replace teacher feedback? One study on this topic is somewhat negative. Dwyer and Sullivan (1993) studied the word processed compositions of high school students, some of which were evaluated by a teacher, some by a grammar checking program. Students preferred feedback from a teacher because it was more personalized. We tend to agree with the high school students. Text analysis software is probably best used as a support for, rather than a replacement of, teacher feedback.

INTEGRATED TEXT ANALYSIS FEATURES

Tools for Writers is a program designed specifically for just-in-time use, but many standard word processing programs include just-in-time features. Microsoft *Works for Windows*, a popular integrated program that includes a word processor, has three features in its Tools menu that can be used for just-in-time instruction: Spelling, Thesaurus, and Word Count (see Figure 5-4). Word Count, as you might expect, tallies up the number of words in the current document. Thesaurus provides alternatives for the word you have highlighted.

Figure 5-5 illustrates how *Works for Windows* handles a thesaurus request on the word *display*. The list of words on the left side of the dialog box are alternative meanings for the word *display*. As you can see this word has a number of different meanings. The list of words on the right are potential synonyms for the *exhibition* meaning of *display*. You can call up synonyms for other meanings by clicking a word in the word list on the left. Click the Suggest button on the right side of the dialog box and different meanings of the highlighted meaning are shown on the left with synonyms on the right (see Figure 5-6). At any point in the process, you can click on a word and then click the Change button to substitute it for the word highlighted in your document.

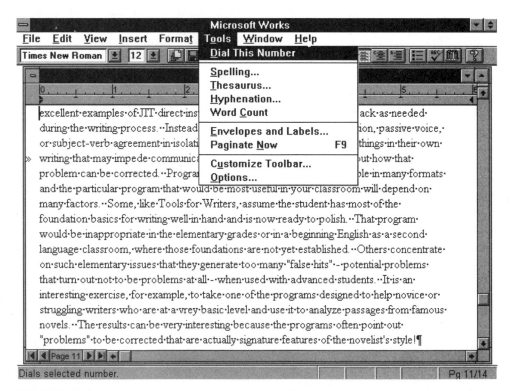

FIGURE 5-4 Microsoft *Works for Windows* provides several just-in-time features in the Tools menu.

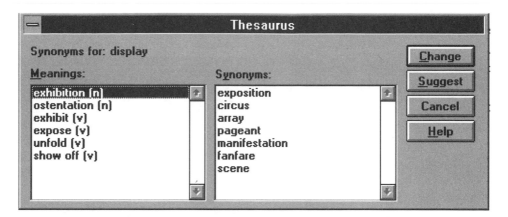

FIGURE 5-5   The Thesaurus command displays alternative meanings and synonyms of the highlighted word.

The Works spelling checker is typical of those found in word processing programs. It scans the document and highlights any word that seems incorrect. Sometimes the word is spelled correctly but Works does not have it in its dictionary. In that case you can click the Ignore button and the spelling check will continue. If you know the word is used several times in the document, you might want to click Ignore All instead. Then Works will ignore other occurrences of the word as it checks spelling. If it is a word you know you will be using frequently in other documents, you might want to click the Add button. Works will add it to its dictionary.

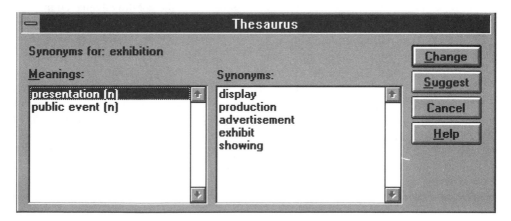

FIGURE 5-6   The Thesaurus command will suggest alternatives for the word you have highlighted.

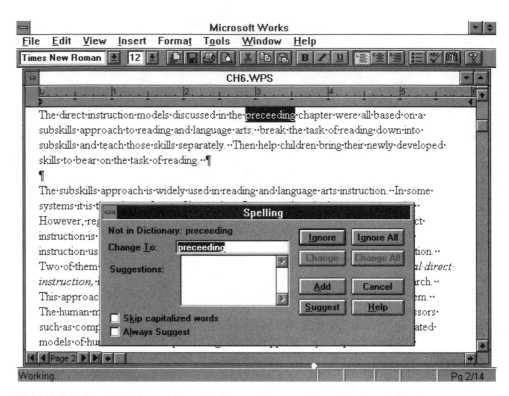

FIGURE 5-7   The Microsoft *Works for Windows* spelling checker dialog box.

Let's assume, however, that the word is not spelled correctly. When Works finds a word that may have been misspelled, it tries to guess which word you meant and displays it in the Change To text box. In our experience, the spelling displayed there is the one you want about 70 percent of the time. When Works guesses correctly, you can click the Change command and make the correction. However, in Figure 5-7 the word in question has simply been repeated in the Change To box. Works did not guess a correct spelling. If you click Suggest, the dialog box changes to the one shown in Figure 5-8. With prompting, Works guessed you meant *preceding*. Click Change and the change is made. The Works spell checker will occasionally have no guesses, even when prompted to make one. In that case you will have to type the correct spelling yourself and then click Change.

Some programs offer even more types of support than a spelling checker and thesaurus. Figure 5-9 illustrates the grammar checking facilities of the Word for Windows program, which in this case has identified a potential problem—the use of *there* when *their* is the correct word. Note, however, that the grammar program did not catch another problem in this sentence—*I thank we* instead of *I think we*. Grammar checkers find some, but not all, potential problems.

The Word for Windows grammar checker has other options. It can be customized for formal, business, or casual writing styles, and you can select the types of grammar prob-

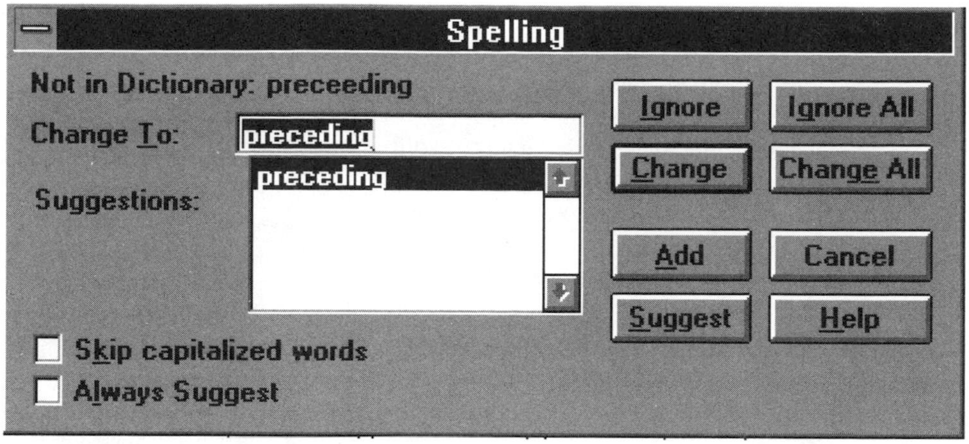

FIGURE 5-8   When prompted, the spelling checker will try to guess the correct spelling of the word.

lems it checks. This program also generates a readability report (see Figure 5-10). In addition to standard counts and averages, it computes several types of readability measures.

Most popular word processing programs include at least a spelling checker and a thesaurus. Others include full-fledged electronic dictionaries and grammar checkers. For classes in which students regularly write, the just-in-time tools of a good word processor can provide outstanding support to students as they write. Keep in mind, however, that the quality and fit of JIT features such as spelling checkers vary widely from program to program.

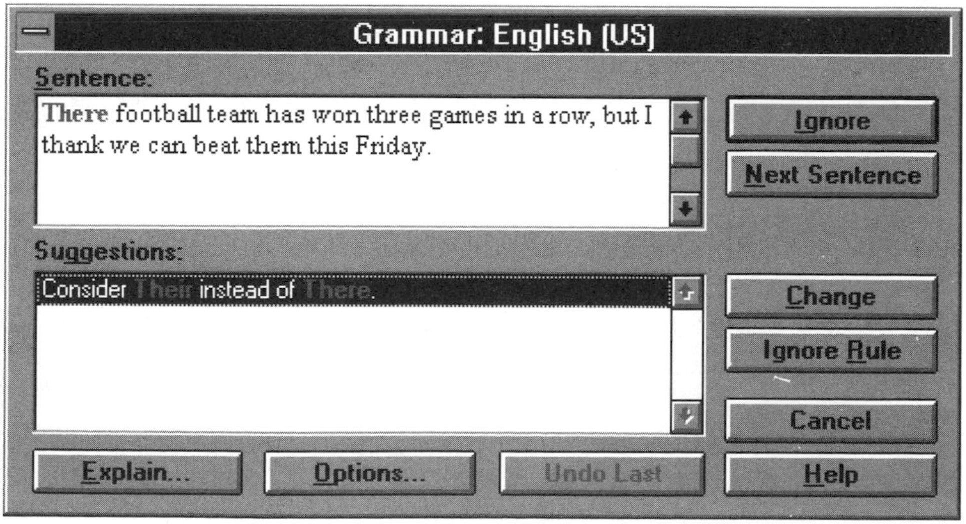

FIGURE 5-9   Word for Windows includes a grammar checking tool.

JIT features are built into many word processing programs. A number of stand-alone programs also support writing. Stand-alone grammar programs work independently of a particular word processor and generally will process files created by a range of word processors. *Grammatic* and *Correct Grammar* are two examples of stand-alone grammar checkers that are widely used in schools. These look for and make suggestions for correcting many different types of common grammar problems. For example, *Correct Grammar* checks:

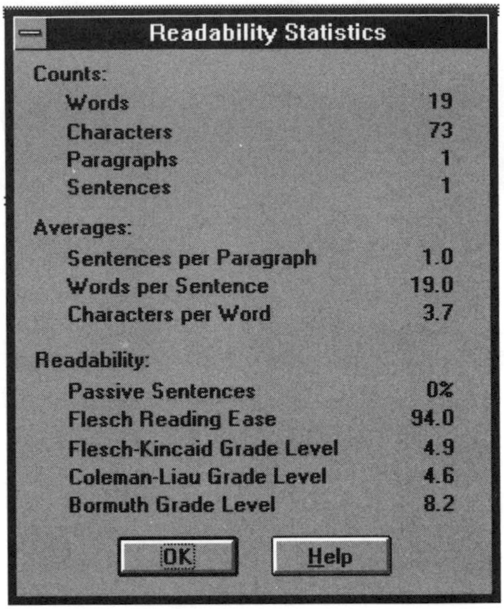

Spelling

Punctuation

Capitalization

Proper nouns

Spelling format (e.g., odd patterns such as *cApitals*)

Jargon

Inappropriate use of *-wise* and *-ize* endings and *well-*

Redundancies

Pretentious words

Colloquial usage

Informal usage in formal writing

Archaic language

Frequently misused or confused words

Wordy style

Inappropriate use of *which* and *that*

Inappropriate use of certain types of prepositional phrases

Split infinitives

Sentence fragments

Run-on sentences

Inappropriate use of *and*, *or*, and *but*

Inappropriate use of *instead of*

Passive main clauses

Passive subclauses

FIGURE 5-10   The Word grammar tool can generate a readability report for a document.

Another stand-alone program that has a place in the classroom is an electronic dictionary. Figure 5-11 shows the dialog box for the electronic version of *The American Heritage Dictionary* with the word *penultimate* entered. You can get several types of information on a word. The program will create a list of words that use the same letters (anagrams), and you can use a thesaurus feature. However, the most common use of the dictionary is for a definition. Figure 5-12 shows the definition for penultimate. This program also has a word hunter feature that might be useful in classrooms. You can use the Boolean search strategies AND, OR, and NOT to find words that are associated with two or more characteristics. In Figure 5-13 the search strategy tells the program to look for words that involve both *game* and *ball*. Figure 5-14 shows the result of that search through the dictionary. There were 14 hits—words whose definition involves both game and ball. The standard computer version of *The American Heritage Dictionary* comes on two diskettes. A new CD-ROM version, *The American Heritage Talking Dictionary*, includes spoken pronunciations of all the words in the dictionary—an excellent feature that would be impossible without the huge storage capacity of CD-ROMs. At $60 this program is more expensive than most printed dictionaries in classrooms, but it delivers additional resources to students, such as the ability to hear a word pronounced.

Tool software for writing that provides feedback to students on their compositions is one type of JIT software. Another type is "pop-up help" or TSR software that can be displayed on the screen by pressing a key or clicking a Help button. TSR, short for "terminate and stay ready," refers to programs that load into the memory of your computer and then stay behind the scenes until you ask for them to come forward and help.

A TSR program designed specifically for use in schools is *Windows Middle School Grammar*. When called up, the program presents a list of topics like the one in Figure 5-15. The submenu that appears when you select Punctuation is shown in Figure 5-16. Once you have selected a topic, *Middle School Grammar* displays problems (really a series of

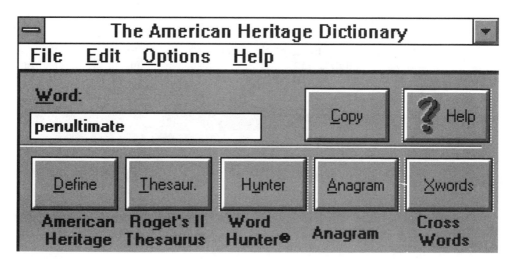

FIGURE 5-11   A startup screen from the *American Heritage Dictionary*.

test items) like the one in Figure 5-17. As students work through the problems presented, they have access to illustrative examples. The Example and Worked menus at the top of the screen take students to material that teaches important grammar concepts. Example items explain a point and then ask students to apply the point; Worked examples are explained and completed for the student. The Details menu contains just that— detailed information on different points of grammar (see Figure 5-18). One drawback to this program is the rather complex reading level of the detailed help. When the Word for Windows grammar checker scanned the material in Figure 5-18, it pegged the reading level at between the 10.6 and 12+ grade level and suggested some sentences were too complex. We

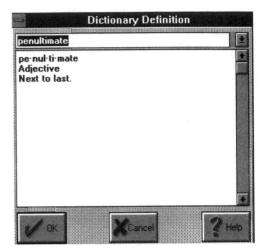

FIGURE 5-12   The dictionary program displays a definition when you click the Define button.

would agree. Software like *Middle School Grammar* has the potential to meet many of the instructional needs of students, but this particular program has several problems, including unnecessarily technical examples and illustrations. In addition, when students are in the middle of writing something that interests them, stopping to take a test and then read technical explanations of grammar points is not high on their priority list. A better format for a TSR program would be one that lets the student select the type of information needed, and then presents brief explanations with numerous examples that illustrate the point. Although not yet commonplace, this type of TSR is likely to be widely available in the near future.

The JIT software discussed thus far assists students with their own creations. JIT also is built into several forms of electronic books. While reading some electronic books, for example, a child can click a word and hear it pronounced. Some electronic books will

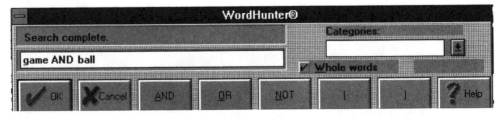

FIGURE 5-13   The word hunter feature lets you conduct Boolean searches for words that meet certain criteria.

define words, and some will translate the story into other languages.

Teachers are creating their own electronic books for classroom use. Several of the programs discussed in Chapter 7 (*HyperCard*, *SuperCard*, *Authorware Star*, *Action!*) can create electronic books. Intellimation distributes a program called *interText* that was designed specifically for the creation of electronic books. With *interText* and similar programs, teachers can create electronic documents that include text, graphics, photographs, audio, and digital video. With *interText* you can connect text and graphics on the computer screen to video clips on laserdisks or audio from CD-ROMs. The program's price, $39 for a single copy, or $169 for the right to give every teacher in a building a copy, is quite reasonable.

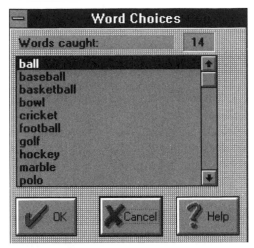

FIGURE 5-14   The results of a word hunter search.

Another way for JIT software to support students involves built-in help that is specific to the program. In addition to providing interesting reading material on the screen, the software provides built-in help and guidance that is available when the student asks for it. This type of software is not common, but the number of programs that use this model are increasing.

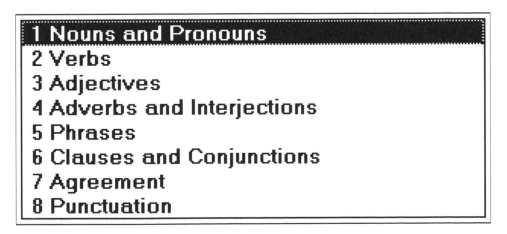

FIGURE 5-15   The initial menu from *Windows Middle School Grammar.*

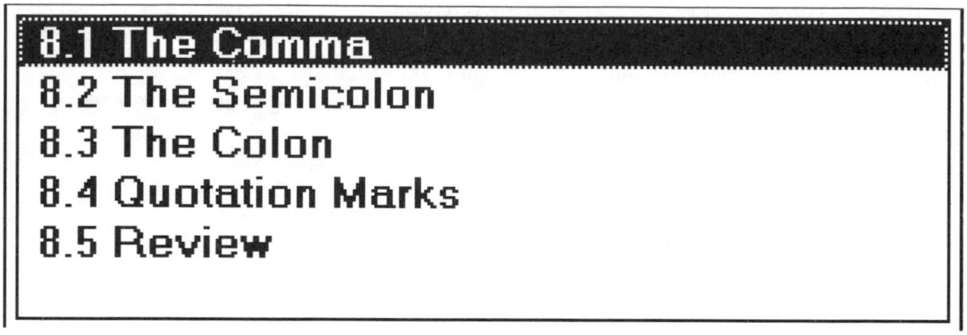

FIGURE 5-16   Select Punctuation and this menu appears.

AN ADULT LITERACY PROGRAM
WITH JIT DIRECT INSTRUCTION

A Day in the Life is an adult literacy program developed by the Institute for the Study of Adult Literacy at Pennsylvania State University. This program, which is based on the concept of authentic instruction, places students in contexts that have meaning to them. In authentic instruction environments, the reading tasks arise as a natural aspect of the context. In *A Day in the Life*, students take roles in simulations that adults with limited reading ability might actually face. The instructional package is designed specifically for adults who have at least a 4th-grade reading level but who do not have the literacy skills needed for many jobs. All the simulations involve jobs that require literacy skills such as:

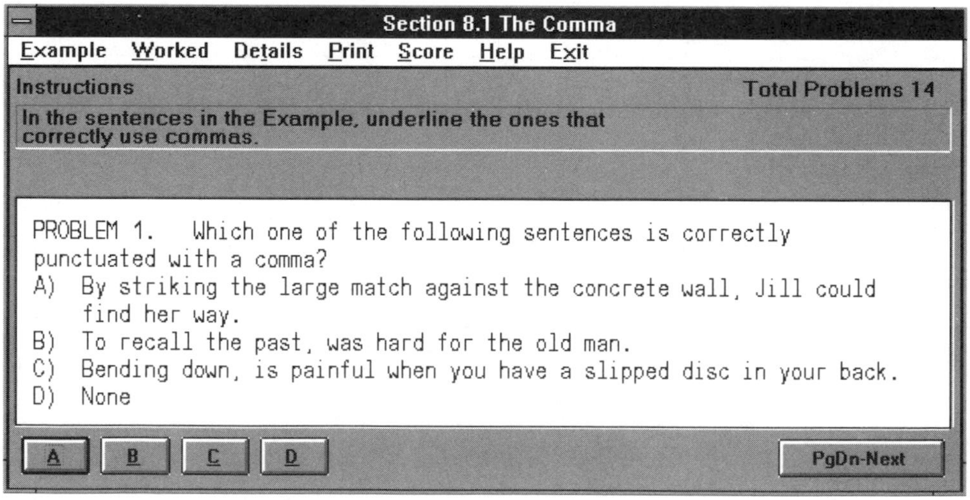

FIGURE 5-17   After you select a topic, the program displays a series of items that test your knowledge.

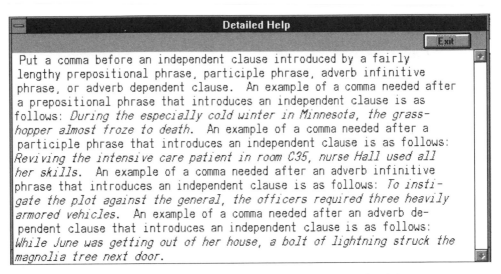

FIGURE 5-18   A Detailed Help screen from *Windows Middle School Grammar*.

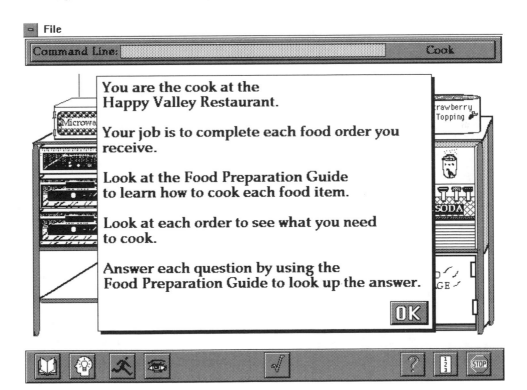

FIGURE 5-19   The beginning screen of a simulation in *A Day in the Life*.

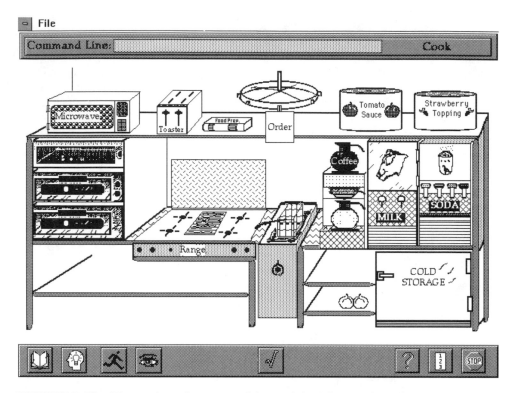

FIGURE 5-20   The work environment of the cook in *A Day in the Life*.

Reading: reading job-related notes, forms, or memos.

Writing: completing job-related forms, writing notes and memos.

Problem Solving: reading bids from vendors and selecting the most appropriate supplier.

Critical Thinking: thinking through options in multipath environments and making many decisions about how to proceed.

The program provides simulations for jobs in food service, health, maintenance, and clerical fields. Figure 5-19 illustrates a beginning screen from the simulation that puts the student in the role of a cook in a restaurant. The icons at the bottom of the screen are in the form of pictographs. The lightbulb icon, which is second from the left, is the Learn About button. Students can click on it when they need more information or help. Figure 5-20 illustrates the work environment for the simulated cook. Many of the objects on this screen are "hot," which means you can click them and something will happen. For example, to read the Order hanging on the spinner at the top of the screen, you would click the eye icon at the bottom of the screen and then click Order. Then the program would display a screen like the one in Figure 5-21, which shows that two entrees of spaghetti with meatballs have

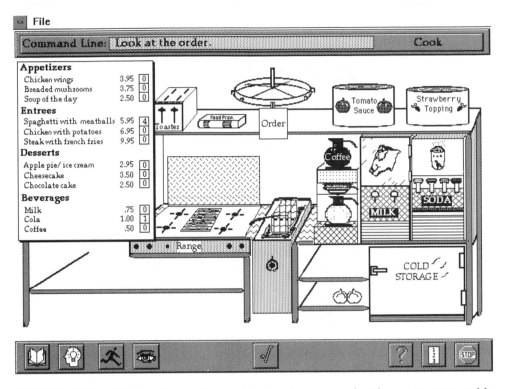

FIGURE 5-21   Clicking the eye icon and Order shows you what the guests at one table have ordered.

been ordered. To read the recipe for that dish, you would click the eye icon and then the book icon (see Figure 5-22). As the cook prepares the order, help is available by clicking the Learn About icon. After the order is prepared, clicking the checkmark at the bottom of the screen will display feedback as well as suggestions, if necessary, about what should have been done.

A Day in the Life provides students with reading instruction in an authentic context. The reading program has two unique aspects. First, it deals with routine tasks such as reading an order in a restaurant kitchen and preparing food according to directions in a book. This is just the sort of critical reading skill that can make the difference between holding a job that provides food, clothing, and shelter to a family and being homeless. If you are an unemployed or underemployed adult with limited literacy skills, the most important skills are not those that enable you to read the latest novel from Scribner's or understand the dual meanings of an Elizabethan poem. Instead, the most "authentic" skills are those that help you meet critical and immediate needs such as finding and holding a job, learning to get around using public transportation, or successfully traversing the dense jargon jungle in the "Please complete this form accurately and completely" requirements that litter the path to many public services available to the poor.

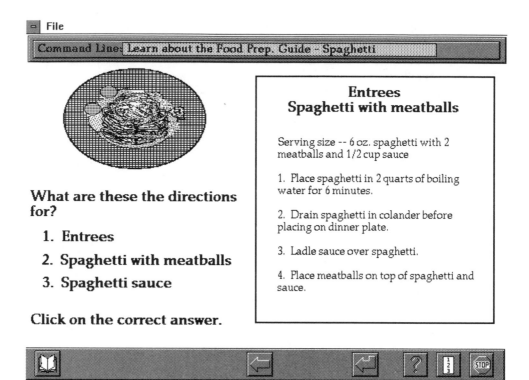

FIGURE 5-22   The program includes a detailed food preparation book that cooks must follow.

The second unique aspect of this program is the format of instruction. Students take a role and read what is required to be successful in that role. Help is provided as needed while the student completes real tasks in a simulated environment. Instructional time is often limited in literacy programs, and adults who use those services often have difficulty getting to a literacy center. This program can help provide the motivation to students who must overcome these barriers. Instead of teaching reading skills using general material that is not interesting or relevant to the student, it makes sense to concentrate on learning the precise literacy skills needed for survival.

Although *A Day in the Life* was designed for adults, it could be used profitably in many middle grades and high school programs. We expect many more reading simulations to become available over the next few years. Many will probably be designed for adults with limited literacy skills, but the approach also can be used with children.

SUMMARY

Just-in-time (JIT) direct instruction can be a supporting instructional strategy for a wide range of approaches to literacy instruction. Just-in-time direct instruction can take many forms, including mini-lessons, conferences, and group editing sessions. Several types of software, including spelling and grammar checkers, can be effective JIT instruction. In addition, a type of software based on authentic instruction models is beginning to appear that includes JIT instruction in simulation and problem solving software for literacy instruction. This relatively new type of software, and TSR programs designed to support literacy instruction, are likely to play much larger roles in the future.

MICROTEACHING ACTIVITIES

1. Use one of the grammar or writing style checkers to analyze passages from one of your favorite writers. Select an author who has a unique style that does not always fit standard usage conventions. Use an LCD panel (or make overheads of the printed feedback provided by the program) to lead the class in a discussion of the feedback provided by the program. Would the suggestions help a novice writer? A writer with experience? A writer with a unique but unconventional approach?

2. Select one of your own papers and run it through a grammar or style checker. Connect the computer to an LCD panel and lead the class in a group editing session. Have the class consider each recommendation the program makes and come to consensus on whether to accept the recommendation or not.

3. Assume you are the instructor for an adult literacy program and that you are using *A Day in the Life* as a primary instructional resource. Using the demonstration version of this program, deliver a microteaching lesson of 10 to 15 minutes to a group of 7 to 10 classmates who play the role of adult literacy students. After the microlesson, discuss the roles a teacher must play in a classroom using this software. What would the best physical organization be for the class? How would you deal with problems such as a student who cannot read the recipes and can't get enough help from the program?

REFERENCES

Atwell, N. (1987). *In the middle: Writing, reading, and learning with adolescents.* Portsmouth, NH: Heinemann–Boynton/Cook.

Balajthy, E. (1988). Can computers be used for whole language approaches to reading and language arts? Paper presented at the annual meeting of the Keystone State Reading Association, Hershey, Pa. (ERIC Document Reproduction Service No. ED300766)

Calkins, L. (1986). *The art of teaching writing.* Portsmouth, NH: Heinemann.

Dalton, B. (1990). "If you could just push a button": Two fourth grade boys with learning disabilities learn to use a computer spelling checker. *Journal of Special Education Technology, 10*(4), 177–191.

Dwyer, H., & Sullivan, H. (1993). Student preferences for teacher and computer composition marking. *Journal of Educational Research, 86*(3), 137–141.

Elkins, J. (1986). Self-help for older writers with spelling and composing difficulties: Using the word processor and spelling checker. *Exceptional Child, 33*(1), 73–76.

Fischer, R., & Grusin, E. (1993). Grammar checkers: programs that may not enhance learning. *Journalism Educator, 47*(4), 20–27.

Harley, S. (1994). Situated learning and classroom instruction. *Educational Technology, 33*(3), 46–51.

Hult, C. (1985). A study of the effects of word processing on the correctness of student writing. Paper presented at the annual meeting of the conference on College Composition and Communication, Minneapolis. (ERIC Document Reproduction Service No. ED260425)

Liou, H. (1992). An automatic text-analysis project for EFL writing revision. *System, 20*(4), 481–492.

Milone, M. (1990). Painless grammar: Revising with the help of a grammar checker. *Classroom Computer Learning, 10*(7), 18–20, 22–23.

Pennington, M. (1993). Computer-assisted writing on a principled basis: The case against computer-assisted text analysis for non-proficient writers. *Language and Education, 7*(1), 43–59.

Roberts, G., & Mutter, G. (1991). A celebration of literacy: Computer-assisted writing in the St. James–Assiniboia School Division No. 2. How it started and how it works. *Education Canada, 31*(2), 47–48.

SOFTWARE DISCUSSED IN THIS CHAPTER

A Day in the Life. Curriculum Associates, 5 Esquire Road, North Billerica, MA 01862-2589. Phone: 800-225-0248.

Correct Grammar. Writing Tools Group, WordStar International, One Harbor Drive, Suite 111, Sausalito, CA 94965.

Grammatic. Developed by Reference Software. Available from Computer Centerline (800-852-5802) and other software distributors.

interText. Developed at the University of Iowa. Available from Intellimation, 130 Cremona Drive, PO Box 1922, Santa Barbara, CA 93116-1922. Phone: 800-346-8355.

Microsoft Word for Windows. Developed by Microsoft. Available from most software distributors.

Microsoft Works for Windows. Developed by Microsoft. Available from most software distributors.

The American Heritage Dictionary. Writing Tools Group, WordStar International, One Harbor Drive, Suite 111, Sausalito, CA 94965.

The American Heritage Talking Dictionary. SoftKey International, 201 Broadway, Cambridge, MA 02139. Phone: 800-227-5609.

Tools for Writers. Intellimation, 130 Cremona Drive, PO Box 1922, Santa Barbara, CA 93116-1922.

Windows Middle School Grammar. Pro One Software, PO Box 828, East Lansing, MI 48826. Phone: 517-393-8100.

CHAPTER SIX

Cognitive Skills
Direct Instruction

Ms. Temple's Biology Class

"Did everyone get a copy of the advance organizer for 'The First Plants: The Thallo-phytes'?" Ms. Temple asks her biology class. Several heads bob up and down. "I'll flip on the LCD panel so that we can all see the organizer on the screen, and we can talk about this chapter before you begin reading. This advance organizer is to help you understand the structure of information in this chapter, and it should help you focus on the main ideas. Sam, what are the two main types of plants you will read about in this chapter?"

"Algae and Fungi," he answers.

"Janice, what are the subheadings under algae?"

"Chlorophyta and Other Algae Groups," she responds.

"Vicki, which one of those do you think you will learn the most about and why?" asks Ms. Temple.

"Chlorophyta," Vicki replies, "because of all the branches under the word."

"Do you recognize any of those words?" queries Ms. Temple.

"No, but I guess I will when I finish reading this chapter," Vicki responds.

"As you read, take notes on the points in this advance organizer. You'll find it a use-ful study guide," Ms. Temple assures them.

Ms. Temple's use of an advance organizer is one example of a teaching strategy that emerged from a type of learning theory discussed in this book. Throughout this century, but particularly in the past 30 years, two related families of learning theories, now known as *information processing* and *cognitive science*, have emphasized the need to study what goes on in students' minds while they are learning and to use the knowledge gained to improve instruction. We will call these two families *cognitive information processing theory*.

COGNITIVE INFORMATION PROCESSING THEORY

"Modern theoretical conceptions view learning as a set of processes having the function of information processing. Once the stimulation from external energy sources reaches the human receptors, it is transformed by them into patterns that can best be understood as conveying information" (Gagne & Glaser, 1987, p. 53). Much of the most influential work on information processing theory has involved computer modeling of decision making and learning with the assumption that what we learn from studying computers can be applied to humans. The researchers thus "conceive of the computer as a symbol-manipulating system, and draw the analogy with the operation of human cognition" (Gagne & Glaser, 1987, p. 53).

At the heart of learning in this theoretical tradition, which we will refer to as *cognitive information processing theory* (CIPT), is memory. Data received by our senses are processed and stored in memory. Most of the researchers in this tradition divide memory into two broad types: short term and long term. Short term memory (STM) has limited capacity and limited duration. For example, you might keep a phone number in short term memory for 20 seconds. You could keep it in short term memory longer by rehearsing it— saying the number over and over in your head—a process required by some types of memory chips in computers.

If everything we remembered for an extended period of time had to be rehearsed (for humans) or refreshed (for computer memory chips), our memories would be quite limited. We would quickly run out of space in STM even if we could rehearse many things at the same time. More information or longer durations of storage require that the information be organized and stored in long term memory (LTM).

In many ways short term memory is really a decision point along an information pathway. Some data in short term memory will be discarded and never heard from again. Some will be organized and forwarded to long term memory for extended storage and use. The data transferred to LTM usually will be compared with and matched to data already in LTM. Some of the new information from STM will be integrated or merged with material already in LTM. Some may actually replace material that has been disproved or outdated by new information. Still other data may cause a reorganization of existing data in LTM.

Regardless of whether the new information replaces (accommodates) or reorganizes or updates (assimilates) old information, it becomes part of an information web in LTM. The data are in the nodes of the web, and each node is connected to many other nodes. Thus, when you access one piece of information, many others also may be retrieved from LTM because they are connected to the data you pulled out. Just how easily the information in LTM can be retrieved depends in part on how it was stored.

Data are stored in long term memory in two different formats: *episodic* and *semantic* (Hamilton & Ghatala, 1994). Data in episodic memory are organized by place and time. For example, one of the authors of this textbook remembers listening to a books-on-tape version of *The Bridges of Madison County* while driving through the middle of a blinding snowstorm. Each time he has listened to that tape since the snowstorm, vivid memories of the snow blowing across the road, the jack-knifed truck on the shoulder, and the lonesome coldness of the rivers he crossed come to mind. Because passages from the book were stored in memory as part of an intense experience, coming in contact with any part of this memory, such as hearing portions of the book, brings back many other memories related to the same time and place. That is episodic memory.

Data stored in semantic memory are organized around meaning. Your knowledge of U.S. history is stored in semantic memory (except perhaps for the parts of that history you actually lived through yourself). For example, information about George Washington is probably closely connected with information about the American Revolution because these two types of information are meaningfully related. "How to" information is also semantic. For example, information about things to do when you are stuck on the side of the road with a car that won't run might be organized into several tightly related nodes even though the information was acquired over many years in different contexts.

The data in both types of LTM are organized into *nodes* and *networks*. However, the nodes of episodic LTM relate to times and places, whereas the nodes of semantic LTM involve cognitive or meaning relationships. Nodes in LTM are connected by *links*. The links of episodic memory connect nodes according to time and place. A memory of going to a football game may be linked to memories of sitting in the stands watching the game.

Links of semantic memory units connect meaningfully related material. For example, after you study this book, the information you have acquired about teaching reading with the support of technology might be organized into networks for strategies that grew out of cognitive constructivist, social constructivist, behavioral, and cognitive information processing theories. Each of the semantic networks might have several nodes for individual strategies. Moreover, because many strategies fit under several theories, there would be interconnections between these semantic networks.

Perhaps one reason for the frequently discussed theory/practice dichotomy in teacher education is that much of the professional practice knowledge a teacher acquires over the years is episodic—it is organized by time and place. Most of the theories about how to teach effectively, however, are organized semantically. Although LTM stores information in both formats, it is a little like Beta and VHS videotapes. They have many things in common, but they are different enough to be incompatible. Playing Beta video back on a VHS player takes some effort—you must first transfer video from one tape format to the other. Likewise, relating semantically organized information, such as the theories of classroom management you learned in your teacher education classes, to episodic information, such as student teaching experiences, is not easy.

Exactly what is in LTM is still subject to considerable debate. Researchers have used terms such as *propositions*, *mental models*, and *concepts*, but currently one of the most popular terms for the contents of human memory is *schemata*, which Gunning (1992, p. 188) describes this way:

> Our knowledge is packaged into units known as schemata. A schema is the organized knowledge that we have about people, places, things, and events. . . . A schema may be very broad and general—our schema for animals—or it may be fairly narrow—for Siamese cats.

Several theories use the term proposition for simpler relationships between items in memory and reserve the term schemata for more complex organizational mental structures.

Here we use the term schemata broadly to include what is termed propositions in other systems as well as more complex mental constructions that include several propositions.

The idea of schema helps us think about mental processes such as thinking and problem solving. A more detailed answer to the question of what is in the human mind might divide the schema into different types based on the type of knowledge they represent:

Declarative Knowledge. This is factual or verbal knowledge. Gagne and Glaser call it *knowing that* knowledge. This is the type of knowledge usually required to answer multiple choice tests. A kindergarten student who can say the names of the letters is demonstrating declarative knowledge. An 8th-grade student who summarizes the plot of a short story read in a literature class is demonstrating declarative knowledge.

Procedural Knowledge. This is *how to* knowledge, sometimes called *intellectual skill.* Students who can use context clues to puzzle out the meaning of an unfamiliar word are using procedural knowledge. Procedural knowledge generally involves applying a set of rules to a problem or process.

Conditional Knowledge. This is *when to* knowledge. For example, students may know several procedures for decoding unfamiliar words, such as determining if the word looks like a familiar word, using sound-letter relationships to sound out the word, and looking for root words. Depending on the reading context, they can select the more appropriate procedures to apply when puzzling over an unknown word. They are demonstrating conditional knowledge because they can select from among a number of alternative procedures and make appropriate selections. Problem solving could be described as a combination of procedural knowledge and conditional knowledge.

Metacognitive Knowledge. This is the ability to monitor your own thinking and make adjustments. It is sometimes called metacognitive awareness, self-awareness, or self-regulation. An example of this type of knowledge is found in the current emphasis in teacher education on reflective practice—thoughtful analysis of practice with an emphasis on what you want to keep and what you want to change the next time.

These four types of schema are not organized from simple to complex. Declarative knowledge, for example, can be very simple—such as being able to name the year the Battle of Hastings occurred—or quite complex—such as being able to name, classify, and describe the growth patterns of most of the plants in your neighborhood. It is important to note that the terms declarative, procedural, conditional, and metacognitive represent different types of knowledge, not different levels of complexity.

Recognizing that there are different types of knowledge is important because different types may call for different instructional strategies or learning environments. This has significant implications for teaching reading, language arts, and composition.

Another point to keep in mind is that approaches to literacy instruction based on cognitive information processing theory (CIPT) are still skills-based direct instruction. However, instead of breaking down the act of reading into component parts, CIPT direct instruction looks at the cognitive skills and knowledge that underlie reading. Those skills are the focus of instruction. Underwood and Underwood (1990) talk about using computers to "equip children with a toolkit of basic mental skills" (p. 29). They call those basic mental skills the "cognitive toolkit" students need to solve problems. For the Underwoods, problem solving can be almost any reasonably complex activity, such as solving a practical math problem. "In the case of reading, the problem is to understand what the writer has intended us to know" (p. 33). Basic cognitive skills are needed to read, and the Underwoods suggest that there are two critical factors about those skills. First, students must have them. Second, they must have become automatic so that "component sub-skills of problem-solving activities are performed effortlessly and without attention" (p. 33). "The value of the cognitive toolkit is that it releases the mind of the user for more general problem-solving activities" (p. 34). Underwood and Underwood believe that the development of a cognitive toolkit is one of the most critical responsibilities of education. The skills in the cognitive toolkit are, in the categorical scheme used in this chapter, primarily procedural, conditional, and metacognitive. Underwood and Underwood are critical of what they see as a continued emphasis on "facts" or declarative knowledge. "We are being tyrannised by curricula which fossilise information into facts to be known, rather than into material to be manipulated and thought about" (p. 61). In this chapter we will explore some computer-supported approaches to building the cognitive toolkit.

APPROACHES TO BUILDING THE COGNITIVE TOOLKIT

Although it may be necessary to learn some things by memorization or "rote," CIPT predicts that students will learn both more quickly and more information if they learn in meaningful contexts. CIPT and constructivist approaches hold this perspective, but for slightly different theoretical reasons. In CIPT, meaningful learning facilitates the creation of links between material already in LTM and new information. The more links to the new information stored in LTM, the easier and more likely it will be retrieved from memory when needed. One of the best examples of the problem with meaningless or rote learning is illustrated in a story told by William James (1912, p. 150), one of the pioneering American psychologists:

> A friend of mine, visiting a school, was asked to examine a young class in geography. Glancing at the book, she said: "Suppose you should dig a hole in the ground, hundreds of feet deep, how should you find it at the bottom—warmer or colder than on top?" None of the class replying, the teacher said: "I'm sure they know, but I think you don't ask the question quite rightly. Let me try." So, taking the book, she asked: "In what condition is the interior of the globe?" and received the immediate answer from half the class at once, "The interior of the globe is in a condition of igneous fusion."

Rote learning often leads to learning that merely associates questions with answers without any real understanding of what the answers really mean. This type of learning has been called by some "inert learning" (Risko, 1991) because it involves formalized learning that cannot be applied or used. Underwood and Underwood (1990, p. 34) suggest that out-of-context computer activities such as drill and practice exercises often concentrate on just the sort of "inert learning" we should avoid.

> Some of us still have memories of classes in which rooms of children could be heard to be reciting multiplication tables, or seen to be writing row after row of the same perfectly formed letter of the alphabet. These methods certainly present the child with a toolkit of sub-skills, but it is difficult to imagine a less motivating form of education. Of course, it is also questionable whether these are the sub-skills which should receive such emphasis. This educational philosophy has little to contribute to the development of flexible problem-solving.

Many of the teaching models and strategies presented in previous chapters—anchored instruction and reading/writing workshop to name just two—are also efforts to provide instruction in formats that fit our understanding of the cognitive structure of humans.

In this chapter we will explore approaches designed to develop, improve, and make automatic the cognitive skills needed for literacy. These approaches fall roughly into three different categories: (1) big-picture and structure strategies, (2) focus strategies, and (3) word- and sentence-level strategies. Consider the list of instructional approaches below, which were taken from Tierney, Readence, and Dishner's (1990) chapter on methods to enhance content area and text-based comprehension:

Graphic Organizers	Study Guides
Selective Reading Guide	Guided Reading Procedure
Idea Mapping	Text Structure Strategy
Story Grammar and Story Maps	Sentence Combining
Cloze Techniques	

Using only what you already know about these nine instructional approaches, place each of these into one of the three general categories below:

Big-Picture and Structure Strategies. These "wide-angle" or "macro" approaches help a student see the overall structure or context of the text.

Focus Strategies. These help students concentrate on learning the most important or relevant information for the task at hand.

Word-Level and Sentence-Level Strategies. These "close-up" or "microscope" strategies have as their goal increasing students' vocabulary and understanding of both sentence structure and meaning.

Our categorization of the nine methods listed above is included at the end of the chapter. Compare your categorization with ours and see if they agree. In the sections that follow, we explore some of the ways in which technology can support cognitive information processing theory approaches, and you will find that many of the strategies in the list above are discussed, as well as others that seem particularly suited to computer support. We have organized this material into three sections—Big-Picture and Structure, Focus, and Word-

Level and Sentence-Level Strategies—but this is a rather rough and fuzzy categorization. Many of these strategies cut across several categories.

BIG-PICTURE AND STRUCTURE STRATEGIES

At every level of literacy, students find it all too easy to get lost in the details of a text or composition. Fortunately, several effective strategies can help students rise above the details of a text and grasp the structure. The strategies covered here are advance and graphic organizers, semantic mapping or webbing, and story grammars.

Advance Organizers and Graphic Organizers

The advance organizer conceived by Ausubel (1968) was introductory text that would provide a cognitive scaffolding or framework within which students could organize the information they were to learn. Ausubel's advance organizer may be compared to framing for a house. The framing is put up first and determines the general shape and format of the house. Much work remains to be done after a house has been framed, but the general size, shape, and organization has been determined. The purpose of an advance organizer "is to prepare a student for a reading task. The student reads a short passage that precedes a selection or chapter of a text; the passage is written at a higher level of generality and abstractness than the text that follows" (Daines, 1982). The concept of an advance organizer has become a bit more general over the years, and the term has been applied to virtually any type of introductory information provided before students study a lesson. Moore (1989, p. 79) defines advance organizers as "generalizations, definitions, or analogies"; for example, "a second grade teacher might start a math lesson with definitions of the new vocabulary words." Simply defining new vocabulary words is not what Ausubel had in mind because that might get students deep into details before they had a good grasp of the general framework of a topic. That would be like trying to finish the living room of a new house, including painting walls and laying carpet, before the framework for the house was completed. Ausubel's idea is to create a scaffolding or mental structure for the information students will be learning. This should help students connect the new information to their existing knowledge and, where needed, help them develop new schemas. Research supports this assumption. In a study of 7th-grade students, Rinehart and Welker (1992) found that presenting an advance organizer, followed by teacher-led discussions, facilitated recall of reading assignments. Another typical application involves giving students written copies of the advance organizer without an introduction by the teacher or class discussions, but simply distributing copies of advance organizers may not be that helpful. Availability does not necessarily mean use. Snapp and Glover (1990) found that middle school students, as well as college students, profited from reading and then paraphrasing an advance organizer before studying a reading assignment.

Originally, advance organizers were text only, and they tended to be somewhat abstract. In their review of advance organizers, however, Hamilton and Ghatala (1994, p. 96) conclude that "recent research indicates that organizers containing concrete examples of things that students will encounter in the lesson are better than abstract organizers. In addition, the organizer should contain material familiar to students. . . . Aside from being concrete and familiar, advance organizers can take a variety of forms, including discussions, outlines, drawings, diagrams, and short passages from texts."

The terms *structured overview* and *graphic organizer* are often used when the organizer involves drawings, diagrams, or other visual representations of the information structure. A typical use of an advanced organizer or graphic organizer involves introducing the organizer to students in a teacher-led discussion that encourages students to think through the various components of the organizer and their relationship to each other. When students already understand aspects of the organizer, teachers sometimes have students create or fill in that part of the organizer during class discussion. The case study that began this chapter illustrates one use of a graphic organizer.

The graphic organizer in Figure 6-1 was created by a teacher with ordinary drawing software. Teachers use graphics and drawing software, as well as integrated programs such as *Microsoft Works*, to create many types of organizers. There are even specialized programs for visually representing concepts and relationships. Some of these use a traditional flowchart or organizational chart format, but several can be used for many types of organizers. For example, *Inspiration*, a Macintosh program, can be used to create anything from traditional flowcharts to what the manual calls "mindmaps." *Corel Flow*, a program for computers that run Windows, is a powerful and versatile program for making many types of charts and organizers. *Corel Flow* comes with 2,000 clip-art images and over a 1,000 photographs that can be incorporated into semantic maps and graphic as well as advance organizers. Another program students can use to create graphic organizers is the popular *Kid Pix* drawing program from Broderbund. Computer-generated organizers can be printed, duplicated, and distributed to all students or displayed on a screen via an LCD panel and overhead for class discussions.

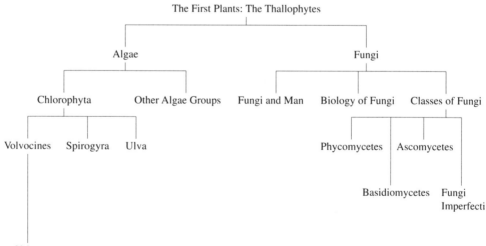

FIGURE 6-1   This graphic organizer was created using ordinary drawing software.

In Ms. Temple's biology class, students were instructed to use the teacher-produced graphic organizer as they studied. That is a common use of teacher-created organizers. A variation on this approach was described by Alverman and Boothby (1982). They illustrate how graphic organizers can be created by teachers with empty slots that students must fill in as they read. The graphic organizer helps students see the structure of the material they are reading, and it requires students to become actively engaged with the material in order to fill in the empty slots.

Although some research supports teacher-created organizers, the approach is somewhat anti-constructivist because a structure is imposed on the student. In their review of graphic organizers, Tierney, Readence, and Dishner (1990, p. 231) comment that "One wonders whether a strategy that imposes upon students a structure for thinking and reading would be as beneficial as a strategy that might activate students' own ideas. To this end, an organizer might be developed from a student's own ideas prior to, during, or after reading. In this way, the organizer may become more personalized and less abstract." Several studies have looked at student-created organizers. Hawk (1986), for example, reports significant improvements in the retention of information among 6th- and 7th-grade students when they created their own advance organizers. Another interesting study of graphic organizers created by students was reported by Weisberg and Balajthy (1987). Students with reading problems were given five hours of training in the use of graphic organizers with expository text. Students were taught the basics of creating graphic organizers, teachers modeled creating graphic organizers, and each student had an opportunity for guided practice. Students significantly improved their ability to identify and organize main ideas and to summarize the text they read.

Organizers can be created with outlining software, which often is used by writers to create and revise an outline before beginning to write. Outlining software generally has several views so that writers can display only the main headings, other levels, or the entire outline. In addition, outlining software generally has a way of easily rearranging whole sections of the outline. For example, when a main heading must be moved to another location, the writer usually has the option of automatically moving all the subheadings under that main head or leaving them at the original location. Organizers are sometimes called "thought organizers" because they help you move from confused and fuzzy ideas about a topic to a more organized and detailed understanding. Programs like IdeaFisher for the Macintosh are thought organizers. An "outline style" graphic organizer is more appropriate for text that involves the clear presentation of a main idea and supporting details. However, semantic mapping "may be more effective in illustrating relationships when the organization does not consist of main ideas and supporting details" (Askov, 1991, p. 97). Semantic maps are discussed in the next section.

Although there are many types of organizing software for writers, they are less popular today than they were a few years ago. That is because many of the more powerful word processing programs now have organizers built in. In classes where students have routine access to such programs, they could be used to create advance organizers. Computer-based creation of organizers may be particularly useful when, as Barron (1979) suggests, students create organizers in small groups *after* they have read an assignment.

Semantic Mapping or Webbing

Semantic mapping, or semantic webbing, is another way to help students assimilate information. A semantic map is a visual display of relationships among words or concepts in text. Semantic mapping is sometimes used as a substitute for vocabulary building activities that focus on the meaning of individual words out of context. Semantic mapping emphasizes meaning in context and helps students organize new learning and relate it to their prior knowledge. As Pittleman and Heimlich (1991) state, semantic mapping and similar procedures "influence students to become active readers by triggering the brain to retrieve what is known about a topic and use this information in reading. This activation of prior knowledge is critical to reading comprehension. When a specific concept is activated, the entire memory structure for that concept is reawakened and becomes available to facilitate the comprehension process" (p. 44). The case below illustrates how computers can support semantic mapping.

Ms. Morse's Class

The 3rd-grade students in Ms. Morse's room are seated on the floor, intently staring at the video monitor. Connected to that monitor is a computer with a CD-ROM player. Today, they're going to read the CD-ROM version of Arthur's Teacher Trouble. Before they begin reading, Ms. Morse is interested in finding out how much they already know about spellathons, a word in the story. She's creating a semantic web on the monitor using a drawing program. She draws an oval in the center of the screen, then clicks on the text tool and types spellathon.

"Does anyone know another word for spellathon?" she asks. Blank faces stare back at her. "Look for smaller words inside of spellathon," she encourages. "Zaheed, what word do you see?"

"I see spell," he replies.

"What do you know about spelling?" she inquires.

"You know, when you say the letters that make up words," offers Monique.

"Great! Now lets look at the rest of the word, 'athon.' Does that sound like any word you know?"

Undaunted by the 22 blank faces, she asks, "Does anyone know what the word marathon means?" She draws a second oval above the first, types in marathon, and draws a line to connect both words.

"Let's see if this helps," she says, creating another oval. In this one she types a "long race" and says the words out loud as she types. "A marathon is a long race with lots of people watching. Does that give you any ideas about what a spellathon is?" she asks.

"A long spell?" offers Gerald.

"You're on the right track. When might you spend a lot of time spelling with lots of people watching? What do we call that?" Several hands shoot up into the air. "Damone, what do you think a spellathon is?"

"Is it like a spelling bee?" he asks.

"That's exactly right! I'm going to type that under the word spellathon."

"Now, tell me all the words that come to mind when you think about a spelling bee."

"Spelling hard words," suggests Tina.

Ms. Morse creates another oval, types in Tina's phrase, and draws a line attaching it to the web. Then she asks, "What can happen when you spell hard words?"

"You make mistakes," says Brian.

"That's right. Let's connect those two groups of words," says Ms. Morse as she draws a line between the two ovals. The class continues filling in phrases to describe a spellathon before reading Arthur's Teacher Trouble.

Ms. Morse's use of semantic mapping is typical. The teacher selects a word or topic, presents it to the class, asks students to contribute information about the word or related words, and creates a visual map that is the focus of class discussion. There are, of course, variations. Instead of the whole class discussing the word or topic as the teacher creates the semantic map, much of the work can be done by students individually or in small groups. Or, once the basic semantic map has been created, students can explore a topic and add more details to the map. Another variation is the point of use. Originally semantic mapping was a prereading activity that helped activate a student's prior knowledge. Today it is often used as a post-reading activity that helps the student consolidate and organize what has been learned. Semantic maps or webs are often created with text and straight lines, as shown in Figure 6.2. Programs designed to create flowcharts and organizational charts can be adapted easily to create text-based semantic maps. However, with clip art, desktop publishing programs, and drawing software, it is much easier today to create more visually appealing semantic maps, like the one in Figure 6-3.

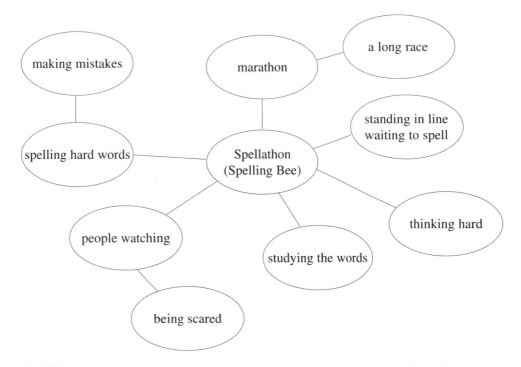

FIGURE 6-2   Semantic webs are one way of activating students' prior knowledge before reading.

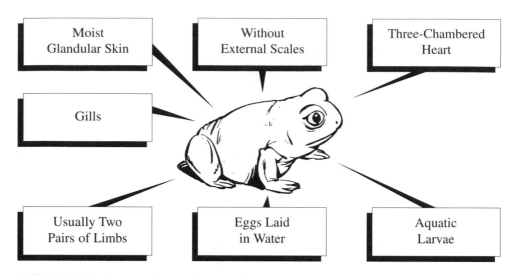

FIGURE 6-3   A semantic map for amphibians.

Source: E. Askov and K. Kamm, *Study Skills in the Content Areas.* Copyright 1982 by Allyn & Bacon. Reprinted with permission.

Story Grammars

Story grammars are another way of visually presenting a scaffolding for students. In the following case, a story grammar provides the scaffolding for looking at plots and other key elements of a story.

The War with Grandpa

Four 4th-grade students are clustered in front of a computer screen, examining the story map they created for the book The War with Grandpa. At the beginning of the year Ms. Foster used a draw program to create story maps for her students to complete when they finished reading books. However, it was not long before the students assured her they could make better ones themselves. Delighted to see them wanting to take control of their own learning, she let them.

"We've got the house drawn. Now let's go back and fill in the roof and windows with words," says Pete.

"You did most of the drawing, Pete. Let us do some of the typing," insists Fran. Peter reluctantly slides the keyboard over to Fran. Next to the heading for Characters, she types in Peter and Grandpa. Then, she types in Peter's House for the setting before moving aside so Megan can get to the keyboard.

"The problem was Grandpa moving in. How do I write that?" asks Megan.

"What about 'Grandpa comes to live with them, and Peter moves out'," offers Erin.

"But he didn't move out of the house," counters Fran. "Say that he had to give up his room."

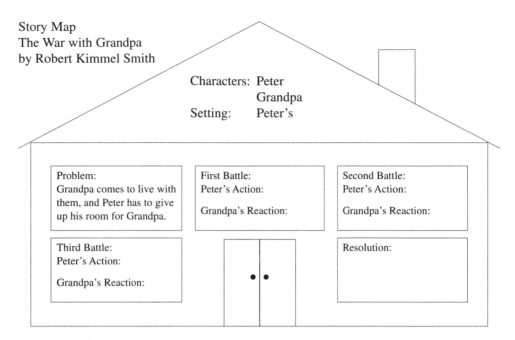

FIGURE 6-4   Students design story maps to help them remember key parts of the story.

Megan types Grandpa comes to live with them, and Peter has to give up his room for Grandpa. Then she slides the keyboard toward Erin.

"I don't remember the first battle," says Erin. "We'd better look in the book to be sure we get it right."

"He set Grandpa's alarm to ring at 3 a.m., and Grandpa just talked to him about why he was living in Peter's room," says Fran. Erin types that in under the heading First Battle. They continue flipping through their books and find that the next battle began with Peter stealing Grandpa's slippers.

"My turn to type," says Pete. Erin moves the keyboard toward him and he begins typing.

"I remember what Grandpa does. He takes his slippers out of Peter's closet and gives him a kiss," says Erin. Peter types this information onto the screen.

"We're not going to have enough room for all the battles," remarks Megan.

"Well, where do we have extra room?" asks Fran.

"On the roof. We'll put problems and resolutions up there," suggests Pete as he begins moving words around on the screen.

The story grammar in Figure 6-4 is one of many different types. A typical story grammar will break down a story into categories such as setting, plot, events, and themes. Each of these main divisions can be further subdivided. Events, for example, could be divided into episodes and episodes further divided into initiating event, reaction, and resolution (Tierney, Readence, & Dishner, 1990). The form and structure of story grammars vary with the age of the student, but the strategy can be used at virtually any level. As with semantic maps, there is considerable variation in the way story grammars are used. Teacher-developed story grammars can introduce students to a reading assignment. After an initial reading, student-developed story grammars can help consolidate a student's understanding and perspective. Questions arising from a story grammar can serve as guides for students as they read.

Traditional software such as drawing software and organizers are useful tools for creating story grammars. Another type of software, hypermedia, also has considerable potential. Hypermedia authoring programs like *HyperCard* and *SuperCard* can create nonlinear material that includes text, graphics, sound, and video. Nonlinear refers to the ability to move about in a hypermedia document and choose what to explore next. Nonlinear documents typically make extensive use of graphics, and they allow students to move about freely in a story or information database. Some teachers have taken advantage of the flexibility of hypermedia to support instruction with story grammars. For example, Heller and McLellan (1993) used a nonlinear computer document they wrote in *HyperCard* to help children understand the structure of multicultural children's literature. Their approach used three types of instruction: direct instruction on story structure, reader response to stories, and student exploration of *HyperCard* documents that helped them visually explore the story structure. *HyperCard*, which is available only on the Macintosh computer, is probably the best known of the hypermedia authoring programs. There are many others, however, including a Windows program named *Toolbook*. *HyperCard* is discussed in more detail in Chapter 7, along with several other programs for both Windows and Macintosh computers. Two programs we particularly like are *HyperStudio*, which runs on Macintosh, Apple IIGS, and Windows computers (it is discussed in more detail in Chapter 7) and *SuperCard*, a program for Macintosh and Windows computers. *SuperCard* is really an enhancement of *HyperCard* (better graphics and color features), and it can import files written in *HyperCard* for editing and revision.

The increasing popularity of hypermedia raises issues about the traditional structure of stories. Although traditional children's stories are linear, hypermedia is nonlinear. Traditional stories are generally static text supported by artwork; hypermedia stories can include text, artwork, animation, video, sound effects, music, and dialog. Traditional stories are not interactive; that is, they are the same story each time a child hears or reads them. Hypermedia stories can be interactive; many involve the child in the story and can be different from one reading to another. As hypermedia children's literature becomes more popular, will children learn traditional story grammars as well as hypermedia story grammars? Will they learn to write their own stories in traditional and hypermedia formats? McLellan (1992) addressed this question in an interesting study of 5th-grade students' responses to interactive, nonlinear *HyperCard* stories. Their language arts program included a wide range of traditional story books as well as hypermedia stories. The teacher read traditional stories to them, and the class discussed story structure. Then small groups of students read nonlinear stories written in *HyperCard* at the computer. These stories had graphics, animation, and sound effects. The children also explored the story grammar of the *HyperCard* stories. Finally, students wrote and illustrated their own stories, which were made into *HyperCard* stories with the teacher's help. McLellan concluded that hypermedia stories have a different story grammar than traditional stories and that children can use the new structure themselves if they have practice and support.

FOCUS STRATEGIES

The purpose of big-picture strategies is to help students situate concepts, ideas, or facts within a larger web of information and see the relationships between nodes of information in the web. Strategies that emphasize the structure of knowledge evolve naturally from the cognitive information processing theories, with their emphasis on the importance of viewing knowledge as an interconnected landscape.

Although they do the opposite, focus strategies are also an outgrowth of cognitive information processing theories. Focus strategies draw the students' attention to specific components or issues. They are often helpful when students are struggling with reading or writing tasks that are complex or relatively advanced in comparison to their skills. In many ways they help the student move from random, ineffectual efforts to derive meaning from text to organized, almost automatic meaning making. Focus strategies provide structure and guidance as the student is mastering difficult or new types of material. There are many ways of helping children focus, and in this section we will explore three: study strategies, prewriting activities, and process writing activities.

Study Strategies

The literature is filled with strategies for studying—from the classic SQ3R—Study, Question, Read, Recite, and Review—of Robinson (1946) and its many variations to computer-supported study systems. Two study strategies, the herringbone and specialized uses of computers, will be discussed here.

Something Fishy in Mr. Dupre's Class

Mr. Dupre's class has just finished reading an autobiography of Ben Franklin. To help students organize their thoughts before writing about their favorite incident in his life, he has created herringbone charts (Tierney, Readence, & Dishner, 1990) for them. Now he projects one onto the computer screen from the LCD panel. As his students check out the herringbone, Mr. Dupre tells them how to create and complete one of their own.

"Obviously, we're putting Ben Franklin down for the Who category," he says as he types in Ben Franklin.

"Would someone else like to create the text fields and type the information into the computer?" asks Mr. Dupre. "Okay, Todd, come up and take a seat at the computer."

"Any volunteers to tell me one thing Ben Franklin did?" asks Mr. Dupre.

"Created public libraries," offers Kara, and Todd types in that phrase under the What heading.

"When did he do that? What year?" queries Mr. Dupre.

"1731," responds James.

Herringbone

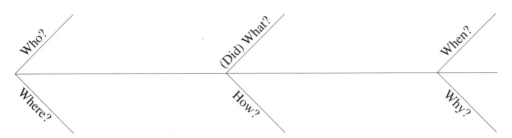

FIGURE 6-5   Herringbone charts are one way to organize information.

"Nice job of keeping up with typing all this in, Todd. Don't worry about spelling. We'll check that when we finish. Where did Franklin open the first library?"

"Philadelphia," replies Melanie.

"How did he start a library?" asks Mr. Dupre.

"He got his friends to bring books to put on shelves in a room they rented," says Carol.

"You are doing great with this. Now, why did he start libraries?"

"I know," Butch says. "Because books were scarce. Most of them were printed in England, and most people didn't have very many books. Ben Franklin and his friends decided to put all their books together to share them. Then they set up libraries for others in the city to use."

"Great answer, but a little long to go here. Let's shorten it to 'share books because they were scarce'," suggests Mr. Dupre. "Thank you, Todd, for your typing. Now, are there any questions before you complete your own herringbones on the next reading assignment? Remember, when you finish, share yours with a friend, then use the information to write one or two paragraphs about the topic. If you don't finish before the bell, consider it homework."

Mr. Dupre's use of the herringbone strategy is typical. Questions such as who, where, and how are on the ribs. Sometimes the main idea or purpose is on the backbone. The primary purpose of study strategies like the herringbone is to help students as they read to focus their attention on critical information. The herringbone is really a graphical outline. Since most classrooms do not have enough computers for every child, students usually draw their own by hand or write their information about who, what, and so forth on copies of a blank herringbone form created by the teacher.

Other study strategies are available through specialized uses of computers for study and study skills training. In his review of the personal computer in reading instruction, O'Byrne (1989, p. 16) expresses his disappointment with the tendency to use computers as tutors rather than as tools:

The ability of the personal computer or PC to handle information is denigrated by the very name "computer." How much better the French word, *ordinateur*, for it is the ability of the machine to move information that makes it the indispensable tool for the modern information worker.

Teachers like O'Byrne have made the point that many types of readily available programs can be used to support studying. Traditional commercial software such as word processing programs as well as thought organizer programs can be used to take notes and write summaries of reading assignments (Anderson-Inman, 1992). They have advantages over handwritten notes and summaries, including the ease with which material can be reorganized, moved, and edited. Tenny (1992) described how the program *Inspiration*, which was mentioned earlier, can be used by learning disabled students to improve their study strategies.

Hypermedia software has also been promoted as a powerful tool for studying. Horney (1991), for example, describes how hypermedia programs like *HyperCard* can be used to create linked note cards. Linking allows a student to create connections between study notes on an electronic card and any number of other cards. Any particular card, therefore, might contain information relevant to several topics, and that card would be linked to all the other cards on those topics.

The flexible nature of hypermedia appeals to teachers who are creating study guides for their students. For example, Higgins and Boone (1990) created a hypermedia study guide for their 9th-grade students. For suggestions on how to create hypermedia study guides, see Anderson-Inman (1989).

Prewriting Activities

Another focusing strategy is prewriting, the activities that come before the actual writing of a composition. One computer program that assists prewriting is described in the case that follows.

Writer's Helper

Ms. Barton's 8th-grade class has come to the computer lab to try out Writer's Helper. She demonstrated the program to her students on the computer in the classroom, and now they are going to get some hands-on experience. "Remember, today we are working on prewriting activities. Take about ten minutes to explore the activities that are available. Then, I need to see you choose one and get started," she instructs.

"I already know the one I want to use," states Connie. "Idea Wheel." On her computer screen, words spin around and around. When they stop, three words are highlighted: Love enjoys success. Connie types them onto the screen, then stops and ponders them. "I'm not sure what that means, or what to write," she mutters. She begins typing phrases and sentences that come into her head when she reads the words. She's not sure where this is going to take her. Once she has the screen filled, she'll stop and find a train of thought she wants to follow.

Next to her sits Matt, who has settled on the option called Starters. The minute he reads the phrase Without a moment's hesitation, we . . . he knows what he has to write

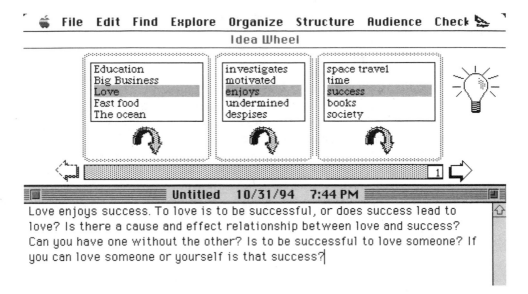

FIGURE 6-6   Idea Wheel generates some interesting phrases that can spark interesting ideas.

about. He had pushed that wreck out of his mind, but now it is back and he has to write about what he saw. The words come quickly and easily. For now, he will just write. Later he will go back and revise.

Programs like *Writer's Helper* help children select topics, organize what they want to write about, brainstorm, and begin setting down their ideas. A growing number of word processing programs for students include features such as story starters. *Creative Writer*, a colorful Microsoft program designed specifically for elementary and middle grades students, is a combination word processing and desktop publishing program that includes a large set of story starters as well as clip art and predesigned formats for creating everything from a traditional report to a comic strip or a multimedia presentation. Programs like *Discovery Toolkit* and *Storybook Theatre* actually go beyond the story starter concept. *Discovery Toolkit* includes ideas for projects in several categories, including ecology and seasons as well as a collection of photographs, sounds, animation, text, and movies organized according to topic. *Storybook Theatre* can be used to create multimedia stories from scratch, but it also uses existing storybooks such as *Mr. Murphy's Chowder*, a multimedia story about an unusual soup. Students tell this story, with the help of animation and sound from the computer, and can then create their own version of the story with new characters and settings.

Story starters are part of the resources in several programs designed to help young children create and illustrate their own storybooks. Most of these programs include collections of artwork as well as storybook formats and the ability to print to color printers, if

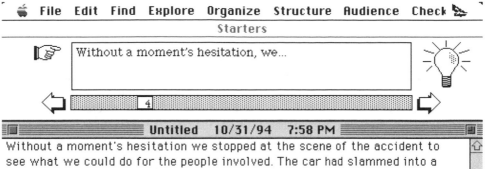

FIGURE 6-7   Starters provide intriguing sentences and phrases to get students started.

available. Some of the better-known storybook programs are *Story Book Weaver* and *Storybook Maker CD*. A few specialized programs support a particular type of writing, such as poetry (*Poetry Palette* and *Poetry Express*) and plays (*Author! Author!*).

Process Writing Activities

Process writing is "an instructional methodology that reflects the stages through which successful writers produce pieces that communicate clearly and effectively" (Barr & Johnson, 1991, p. 194). This approach is constructivist in that children select their own topics. However, the teacher plays many roles during the process:

> Helping students select topics and approaches that fit their abilities and interests.
>
> Encouraging students as they write.
>
> Offering suggestions for revision during conferences.
>
> Teaching mini-lessons as needed to individuals, small groups, and the whole class on aspects of writing, such as punctuation and grammar.
>
> Modeling effective approaches to editing and revision.
>
> Securing and arranging the resources needed to publish student work.

We have classified process writing as a focus strategy because it helps students concentrate on different tasks at different points in the writing process. Several versions of the process writing stages have been proposed. Barr and Johnson (1991), for example, divide the process into six stages: developing a topic, writing a draft, conferencing, revising, editing, and publishing. Pon (1993), an elementary teacher, combines conferencing, revising, and editing into one step that she calls editing. Her phases, which are summarized below, include some of the ways in which she and other teachers at her school use a computer during each stage of the writing process.

Prewriting.   Use brainstorming and clustering to select a topic and plan for researching. Brainstorming can be done with the whole class or in small groups with a student or teacher using a word processor to enter ideas. "Then the teacher need only print the list of ideas, make copies, and distribute it to the class" (p. 131). Individual brainstorming activities can also be done with a word processor with each student's brainstorming ideas stored in a separate file.

Clustering, which is brainstorming with some organization and categorization of ideas, also can be done with a word processor. A word processor's ability to insert new material at any point in a document can be invaluable as students brainstorm new ideas in no particular order. Clustering, as Pons notes, "is good cognitive skill practice for all students. It can be used in a more advanced way for older students by letting them move text around as their lists grow, putting terms that belong together in groups and then naming the groups. I like to tie this activity in with grammar. Having students cluster terms by nouns, verbs, and adjectives is one way to do this" (p. 132).

As noted earlier, another way the computer can be used in prewriting is to create files of story starter questions. Students can load the file created by the teacher, answer the questions, and then save the file under their own name. Figure 6-8 shows one of Pon's story starter files.

More Ideas for Writing at the Computer

A Science Fiction Story Starter

Directions: Make sure your cursor is in the insert mode. Then, put your cursor on the first arrow after each question and answer it. When you are finished, move your arrow key to get to the next question. Save your work under your name + SCI (Kathy.SCI).

1. Where on earth or in the universe is the setting of the story?
→

2. Who is the main character of the story? Describe him or her or it.
→

3. What happens to the character?
→

4. Who or what stands in the way of the character?
→

5. How does he or she or it solve the problem?
→

6. How does the story end?
→

FIGURE 6-8.   A story starter for a standard word processor.

Writing.   Several word processing programs for students are now available for classroom use. For example, *Student Essentials*, a program created by WordPerfect, includes 50 pre-formatted templates for many types of writing, including term papers that follow the MLA, APA, or Turabian formats. *Student Essentials* also has grammar, spelling, and style checkers as well as a large electronic dictionary.

If all of your students had sufficient access to computers, they could word process their writing. Access, however, may be limited. In a one-computer classroom, students would do most of their in-class writing with paper and pencil, but Pon suggests that they get some experience with a word processor and that some activities during the year include short writing activities on the computer.

Editing.   In a computer-rich classroom some of the editing work can be done by students on the computer using grammar and spelling checker software. Pon, who works with young children, finds that students sometimes feel overwhelmed when they are asked to edit a full screen of text, so for practice she has them edit sentences and paragraphs before they tackle longer text. When her students edit their own material (or that of another student), she encourages them to work on one or two elements at a time, such as punctuation.

Publishing.   "It often seems that, by the time students get to the publishing stage of the writing process, it's time to move on to a new assignment. However, this is the most fun part of the experience for most students and it should never be left out. The published paper may be hung somewhere for others to see. Perhaps it is read to a PTA or senior citizens group, or just to classmates. Or it may be incorporated into an art project which is set out for Parent Night, displayed in a local bank for the community to see, or placed in the school library for others to enjoy. . . . One popular option is for students to publish a book" (Pon, 1993, p. 137). Many programs, including the *Children's Writing and Publishing Center*, support this aspect of the writing process.

WORD-LEVEL AND SENTENCE-LEVEL STRATEGIES

Several methods of teaching vocabulary development and understanding sentences have already been discussed. Two additional approaches, which are based on cognitive information processing theories, are covered in this section: cloze techniques and hypermedia reading support.

Cloze Techniques

The basic idea of cloze techniques is quite simple. Take text students are to read, leave out some of the words, and then ask students to read the passage and guess what the omitted words are. Cloze techniques often are used to assess whether material can be read by a student or is too difficult. Clariana (1991), for example, in a comparison with standardized reading tests, found that a computer-administered cloze placement test was an appropriate way to assess student reading ability. The techniques also are used as instructional strategies. Cloze activities may improve students' comprehension skills because they require them to use the structure of the sentence and the context to make predictions about the meaning of omitted words.

Although books of cloze exercises are available, teachers can easily create their own with a word processor. Procedures for creating cloze techniques on the computer have been published by Butler (1990) and Montgomery (1984).

Cloze techniques are used for students at all levels, including adults. Eichel (1989) used computer-assisted cloze exercises in English-as-a-Second-Language classes for adults. Students who completed cloze exercises on the computer scored significantly higher on comprehension tests compared to a control group that studied the same material using traditional methods. In a second study, some ESL students completed standard cloze exercises on the computer while others completed exercises that were culture-specific. The students who used the culture-specific exercises read material more quickly and had higher comprehension.

Hypermedia Reading Support

Electronic books have been available for several years. They come in many forms, including simple copies of traditional books that put each page on a computer screen. Simple copies take away all the advantages of traditional printed books, such as portability, and add no advantages. More sophisticated electronic books, however, add many advantages. For example, the computer can read the story aloud in a variety of voices, change the appearance of text, or use background music and sound effects. Some electronic books let students identify problem words, hear them pronounced, and have the meaning explained. Others allow students to see and hear the text in more than one language. Martin (1992) describes primary-grade reading and language arts activities that take advantage of electronic book features, and Standish (1992) explains how they can be used as supplements to a basal reading program.

Many books take full advantage of the multimedia and hypermedia capabilities of computers. They are nonlinear; they use graphics, animation and video; and they support many types of interaction. Electronic children's books are one of the most popular types of software today. The best-known of this genre is the *Living Books* series from Broderbund. Many are based on the print books of well-known children's book authors, but quite a few are original creations by established authors. Perhaps the best-known thus far in this genre is Mercer Mayer's *Grandma and Me*, a CD-ROM storybook about a child's trip to the beach with his grandmother. Children can read the electronic book in much the same way that they would read a print version. Each page contains detailed illustrations and some text at the bottom. But electronic books like *Grandma and Me* can be used in interactive ways. For example, the child can select to have the story read in English, Spanish, or Japanese, and the rich drawings on each screen contain many "hot spots," objects that react when they are clicked with the mouse cursor. If you click on the knothole in a tree, a squirrel peeks out and then runs around the tree trunk. Click the mailbox and it pops open. None of these objects is marked as "active" or "clickable." Part of the appeal is finding the "live" objects.

Some objects add additional material to the story. Click on a balloon at the beach and Grandma buys one. When she hands it to the child, it flies into the air taking the child with it, complete with appropriate sound effects and comments. The rich, creative interactivity of the *Living Books* makes them popular. On any page, 10 or 20 objects may react when clicked. Electronic books like *Grandma and Me* offer some of the action and color of television, with the added benefit that they are interactive. Because books frequently compete with television for a child's attention, electronic books may push reading a few rungs higher on the priority list of many children. The genre is too new for us to predict all the ways in which these books will be used in education, but interactive books like *Grandma and Me* seem to have a bright future. The cases below illustrate how electronic books might be used in schools to improve reading and vocabulary skills.

CD-ROM Books and Reading

The library at Ames Elementary School has several computer stations where children can sit and read CD-ROM books. These are popular with all the students, who enjoy listening to the books and then interacting with them. The librarian encourages the children to read the books by themselves, once they have listened to the computer read the book to them.

Thuy and Linh, who are reading Jack Prelutsky's New Kid on the Block, are fascinated by the animated line drawings that act out the poem as it is read. The computer has just read a poem from the book, When Tillie Ate the Chilli, and now they are reading it softly to themselves.

FIGURE 6-9   Discis Books such as *Mud Puddle* can be customized to include words in Spanish.

"Click on coughs, wheezes, and sputters," urges Thuy.

Linh clicks and the words are highlighted, then pronounced as Tillie comes to life coughing, wheezing, and sputtering.

"I like the way the words are acted out," says Thuy, *"It helps you know what they mean."*

At another computer Diego and Brad are reading Mud Puddle by Robert Munsch. Softly they read, "She scrubbed Jule Ann till she was red all over."

"What does scrubbed mean?" asks Diego.

"Press and hold the mouse button," replies Brad.

Diego complies and hears scrubbed pronounced in English. Then the word is translated into Spanish. Next he hears the sound of a scrub brush at work, and finally the definition in English.

"Oh, now I know," he says. *"When you take a bath and rub all over with soap to get clean."* His words are accompanied by hand motions as he pretends to scrub himself.

Tucked away in a cozy corner of the library, Selenne and Ramon are seated in front of a computer listening to The Tortoise and the Hare in Spanish. After they have listened to the book in Spanish a few times, they will listen to the book in English. These books help the children make the transition from reading in their native language to reading in English.

FIGURE 6-10   With the click of a mouse, *Living Books* can be read in either English or Spanish.

FIGURE 6-11   CD-ROM storybooks can help children develop automatic word recognition skills.

Mr. Sanderson and Practice

Allen and Gene are making progress in their reading, but they read slowly and laboriously. They're embarrassed by the fact that others in the room read better than they do. Mr. Sanderson, their teacher, wants them to practice their reading on easier books to develop their automatic word recognition skills. They want no part of baby books, as they call the easier books he has gathered for them to read. Yesterday, in the library, he discovered a Discis CD-ROM book of poetry by David Harrison. He knows they will enjoy the poems, and the short verses will be easy for them to read. He knows that reading along as the computer reads the poems will help them improve their word recognition skills.

Allen and Gene's eyes focus on the lines of the poem as they are highlighted on the computer screen. They're reading the poems softly with the computer. "Last night I was a genius. So where were you last night!"

"I like that one," says Allen. "Let's read it again." He clicks on the speaker icon at the beginning of the poem, and the boys again recite the poem with the computer.

"Hey, the next one is about a test," says Gene.

"This one will be good," says Allen as he clicks to start the poem. The boys are oblivious to the other students in the classroom. They're happily reading and reciting the clever, funny poems on their computer screen.

SUMMARY

Cognitive information processing theories of learning emphasize the "connectedness" and "relatedness" of knowledge. Many types of instructional strategies emerge from this family of theories—from advance and graphic organizers to semantic webs, story grammars, study strategies, process writing, and many more. These strategies fall roughly into three different categories: big-picture and structure strategies, focus strategies, and word- and sentence-level strategies. Technology, from standard word processing software to specialized drawing and organizing programs, can support the instructional strategies based on cognitive information processing theories.

MICROTEACHING ACTIVITIES

1. Select a topic from your subject area, or from one of your teacher education courses, that has a main topic and subtopics related to it. It should be a topic unfamiliar to many students in the class. Microteach a prereading activity that involves creating an organizer (advance or graphic). Decide whether the organizer will be complete prior to the microteaching and discussed by students or developed with open slots that students will fill in during class discussion or small-group activities. Use a word processing organizer, draw, or paint program to create the organizer, and use an LCD panel to display it to students in the class.

2. Select a relatively complex topic from your subject area, or from one of your teacher education courses, that is not organized in the "main idea–supporting material" format. Microteach a prereading activity that involves creating a semantic map. Decide whether this should be a teacher-led, whole-group activity, a small-group activity that concludes with summaries from the small groups, or an independent student activity.

3. Use a program like *Grandma and Me* as the focus of a microteaching activity for teaching students a second language. Divide the students in your course into small groups of 3 to 5 and ask them to take the role of English-speaking students in a Spanish country. Organize a lesson around *Grandma and Me* that lets students work with the electronic book in their native language first and then switch them to Spanish.

REFERENCES

Anderson-Inman, L. (1989). Electronic studying: Information organizers to help students to study "better" not "harder"—Part 2. *The Computing Teacher, 16*(9), 21–23, 25–29, 53.

Anderson-Inman, L. (1992). Electronic studying: Using computer-based outlining programs as study tools. *Reading and Writing Quarterly: Overcoming Learning Difficulties, 8*(4), 337–358.

Alverman, D., & Boothby, P. (1982). Text differences: Children's perception at the transition stage in reading. *Reading Teacher, 36*(3), 298–302.

Askov, E. (1991). Teaching study skills. In B. Hayes (Ed.), *Effective strategies for teaching reading* (pp. 84–102). Boston: Allyn & Bacon.

Ausubel, D. (1968). *Educational Psychology: A cognitive view.* New York: Holt, Rinehart and Winston.

Barr, R., & Johnson, B. *Teaching reading in elementary classrooms.* New York: Longman.

Barron, R. (1979). Research for classroom teachers: Recent developments on the use of the structured overview as an advance organizer. In H. Herber & J. Riley (Eds.), *Research in reading in the content areas: Fourth Report* (pp. 171–176). Syracuse, NY: Syracuse University Reading and Language Arts Center.

Butler, G. (1990). FrEdWriting with Bruce Fleury: Using FrEdWriter to create "cloze" reading lessons. *Writing Notebook: Creative Word Processing in the Classroom, 7*(4), 39.

Clariana, R. (1991). A computer administered CLOZE placement test and a standardized reading test. *Journal of Computers in Mathematics and Science Teaching, 10*(3), 107–113.

Daines, D. (1982). *Reading in the content areas: Strategies for teachers.* Glenview, IL: Scott, Foresman.

Eichel, B. (1989). Computer-assisted cloze techniques in the adult ESL classroom: Enhancing retention. *Texas Papers in Foreign-Language Education, 1*(3), 168–181. (ERIC Document Reproduction Service No. ED345493)

Gagne, R., & Glaser, R. (1987). Foundations in learning research. In R. Gagne (Ed.), *Instructional technology: Foundations* (pp. 49–83). Hillsdale, NJ: Erlbaum.

Gunning, T. (1992). *Creating reading instruction for all children.* Boston: Allyn & Bacon.

Hamilton, R., & Ghatala, E. (1994). Learning and Instruction. New York: McGraw-Hill.

Hawk, P. (1986). Using graphic organizers to increase achievement in middle school life science. *Science Education, 70*(1), 81–87.

Heller, M., & McLellan, H. (1993). Dancing with the wind: Understanding narrative text structure through response to multicultural children's literature (with an assist from HyperCard). *Reading Psychology, 14*(4), 285–310.

Higgins, K., & Boone, R. (1990). Hypertext computer study guides and the social studies achievement of students with learning disabilities, remedial students, and regular education students. *Journal of Learning Disabilities, 23*(9), 529–540.

Horney, M. (1991). Uses of Hypertext. *Journal of Computing in Higher Education, 2*(2), 44–65.

James, W. (1912). Talks to teachers on psychology: And to students on some of life's ideals. New York: Holt.

Martin, R. (1992). Discis Books: Adventures in learning. *School Library Media Activities Monthly, 8*(10), 42–43.

McLellan, H. (1992). Narrative and episodic story structure in interactive stories. *Proceedings of Selected Research and Development Presentations at the Convention of the Association for Educational Communications and Technology.* (ERIC Document Reproduction Service No. ED348012)

Montgomery, J. (1984). Cloze procedure: A computer application. *The Computing Teacher, 11*(9), 16–17.

Moore, K. (1989). *Classroom teaching skills: A primer.* New York: Random House.

O'Byrne, J. (1989). The personal computer: An information based study strategy. *Journal of Reading, 33*(1), 16–21.

Pittleman, S., & Heimlich, J. (1991). Teaching vocabulary. In B. Hayes (Ed.), *Effective Strategies for Teaching Reading* (pp. 35–60). Boston: Allyn & Bacon.

Pon, K. (1993). Process writing in the one-computer classroom. In T. Cannings & L. Finkel (Eds.), *The technology age classroom* (pp. 131–139). Wilsonville, OR: Franklin, Beedle & Associates.

Rinehart, S., & Welker, W. (1992). Effects of advance organizers on level and time of text recall. *Reading Research and Instruction, 32*(1), 77–86.

Risko, V. (1991). Videodisc-based case methodology. A design for enhancing preservice teachers' problem-solving abilities. *American Reading Forum, 11*, 121–137. (ERIC Document Reproduction Service No. ED340002)

Robinson, F. (1946). *Effective study.* New York: Harper and Brothers.

Snapp, J., & Glover, J. (1990). Advance organizers and study questions. *Journal of Educational Research, 83*(5), 266–271.

Standish, D. (1992). The use of CD ROM based books to improve reading comprehension in second grade students. (ERIC Document Reproduction Service No. ED352605)

Tenny, J. (1992). Computer-supported study strategies for purple people. *Reading and Writing Quarterly: Overcoming Learning Difficulties, 8*(4), 359–377.

Tierney, R. J., Readence, J. E., Dishner, E. K. (1990). *Reading strategies and practices* (3rd ed.). Boston: Allyn & Bacon.

Underwood, J., & Underwood, G. (1990). *Computers and learning.* Cambridge, MA: Basil Blackwell.

Weisberg, R., & Balajthy, E. (1987). *Effects of training in constructing graphic organizers on disabled readers' summarization and recognition of expository text structure.* Paper presented at the 37th Annual Meeting of the National Reading Conference. (ERIC Document Reproduction Service No. ED309386)

SOFTWARE DISCUSSED IN THIS CHAPTER

Author! Author! Available from MindPlay, PO Box 36491, Tucson, AZ 85740.

Corel Flow. Available in most computer software stores that carry Windows software and from most mail order software companies that advertise in magazines such as *PC Magazine* and Windows World.

Discis Books. Discis Knowledge Research Inc., PO Box 66, Buffalo, NY 14223-0066. Phone: 800-567-4321.

IdeaFisher. Available from MacConnection (Phone: 800-800-2222) and other Macintosh software suppliers.

Inspiration. Available from MacConnection (Phone: 800-800-2222) and other Macintosh software suppliers.

Kid Pix. Available at most software and computer stores in versions for Macintosh and Windows computers.

Living Books. PO Box 6144, Novato, CA 94948-6144. Phone 800-776-4724.

Mr. Murphy's Chowder. Available from Sunburst, 101 Castleton Street, Pleasantville, NY 10570-0100. Phone: 800-321-7511.

Poetry Express. Developed by Mindscape and available from many educational software suppliers, including Educational Resources. Phone: 800-624-2926.

Poetry Palette. Available from MindPlay, PO Box 36491, Tucson, AZ 85740.

Storybook Maker. Created by Jostens Learning and available from many educational software suppliers, including Educational Resources. Phone: 800-624-2926.

Story Book Weaver. Created by MECC and available from many educational software suppliers, including Educational Resources. Phone: 800-624-2926.

StoryBook Theatre. Available from Sunburst, 101 Castleton Street, Pleasantville, NY 10570-0100. Phone: 800-321-7511.

Student Essentials. Created by WordPerfect and available from most Macintosh software suppliers.

SuperCard. Available from Allegiant Technologies, 6496 Weathers Place, Suite 100, San Diego, CA 92121. Phone: 619-587-0500, Fax: 619-587-1314.

Our Categorization of the Strategies listed in "Approaches to Building the Cognitive Toolkit," in Chapter 6:

Big-Picture and Structure Strategies

Graphic Organizers

Text Structure Strategy

Idea Mapping

Story Grammars and Story Maps

Focus Strategies

Study Guides

Selective Reading Guide

Guided Reading Procedure

Word-Level and Sentence-Level Strategies

Cloze Techniques

Sentence Combining

CHAPTER SEVEN

Tools for Teachers

It's Wednesday morning at Samson Intermediate School. Ms. Lambert's 6th-grade students slowly file into the class after making stops in the hall to visit their lockers and friends. A math problem is on the board to give them a morning focus and start them thinking while Ms. Lambert gets ready for another busy day. "Please sign the attendance roll and sign up for a lunch option," she reminds the students.

The bell rings loudly to start the day. "Good morning students. Stand for the pledge," intones a disembodied voice over the PA system. When the pledge is finished, the voice has instructions for the teachers. "Teachers, by ten o'clock we need to have a copy of your homeroom class roster, and remember that progress reports are due in the office before you leave school today. Have a nice day!"

As Ms. Lambert heads for her computer, she reminds the students, "Please finish your math problem. If you need help, quietly ask a neighbor who has finished." After launching ClassMaster, Ms. Lambert enters her password at the prompt. Soon her homeroom class roster is printing out.

"Sandra, take this to the office," she requests as she tears the roster from the printer. She quits ClassMaster, knowing that during her off period she'll be back to enter the grades on the papers she checked last night and to print out student progress reports.

Morning announcements often consist of reminders to teachers about paperwork due. Their mailboxes inevitably contain another form to complete or a reminder of one that is late. Teachers are responsible for an overwhelming amount of paperwork, much of which must be done on short notice. Beyond keeping track of students' attendance and lunch requests, teachers create lessons and tests, record grades, track student progress, and send reports to the office, the counselor, the nurse, the diagnostician, and parents. On some days, paperwork seems to overshadow the real reason they are in schools: to teach.

Paperwork is an inevitable part of the teaching profession. Although it will never disappear, it can be managed and simplified by the effective use of information technology. This chapter presents several ways in which technology can assist teachers with templates for reports, electronic gradebooks and portfolios, and customized lessons. Word processing programs quickly and easily create forms. Electronic gradebooks automatically average grades, print progress reports and seating charts, and track attendance. Electronic portfolios store and organize authentic assessments of student progress. Tests, presentations, lesson plans, student handouts, and games can all be created with the assortment of programs available for teachers.

ELECTRONIC GRADEBOOKS

Gradebook programs offer a wide variety of options. Many offer more options than teachers have time to use. When faced with an array of options, teachers use the ones that benefit them the most. However, it's important to take time to explore all the options that come with the program and then decide on the ones that are useful. They're all designed to save time and effort.

It's Cheryl Ransom's first year of teaching. She has a self-contained 4th-grade class and is responsible for giving her students grades in language arts, math, social studies, and science. Her gradebook is divided into four sections, one for each subject. In each subject she must give grades for participation (10 percent), homework (15 percent), daily work (50 percent), and tests (25 percent). For the first three weeks of school she has been dutifully recording grades in her gradebook and now progress reports are due. Suddenly, she realizes that she must average grades for 26 students in five subjects and cope with figuring out those percentages.

"So this is why Karen Sherwood has been telling me to get on the school computer network and use ClassMaster to keep track of my grades," Cheryl mutters. "I remember her saying it does all of this for you." She sets off in search of Karen and soon is getting an after-school lesson on how to set up an electronic gradebook.

Opening up a new document, Cheryl clicks in the column on the left of the screen and a Student Information box appears. She will complete a box for each student. Each box contains cells in which she could enter quite a bit of useful information, but because she is in a hurry, she simply types in the student's name.

After Cheryl enters the names, Karen suggests she save the file as Social Studies Grades. A dialog box appears on the screen, recommending that she choose a password to prevent anyone else from having access to the students' grades. "Choose a password your students won't be able to guess," Karen advises. Cheryl chooses her grandmother's maiden name.

Cheryl is now ready to set up the categories for grades. Karen directs her to Setup on the menu bar. Cheryl chooses to record her grades as percentages and notes that the grading scale is correct. Then she chooses "Define final grade/activities categories" and sees that homework is set at 15 percent. She edits tests to reflect 25 percent and deletes the other two categories. Now she adds participation 10 percent and daily work 50 percent.

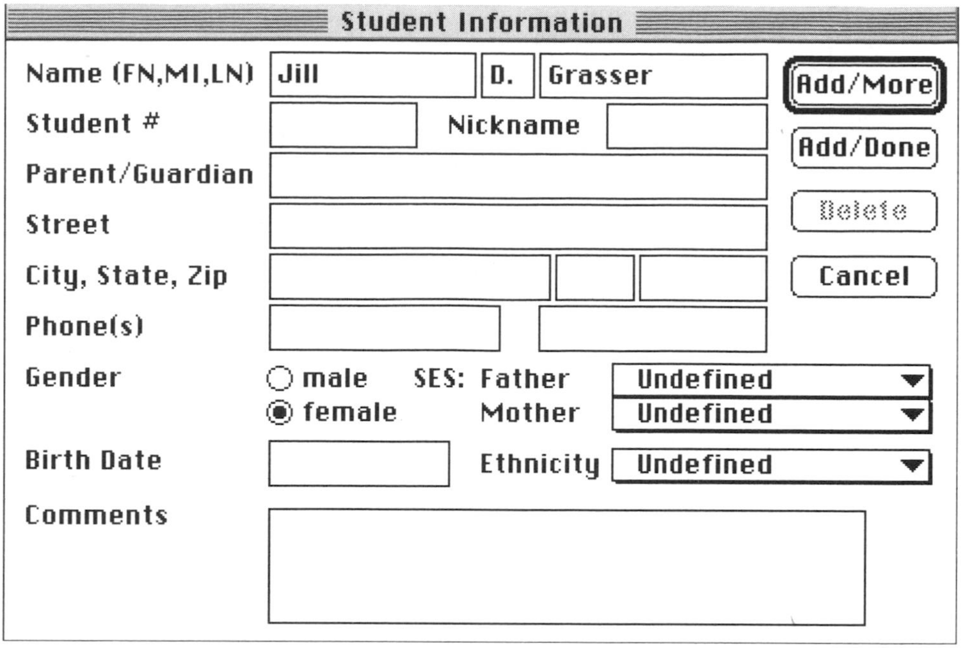

FIGURE 7-1 *ClassMaster* has spaces for a great deal of Student Information.

"Okay, let's enter all their assignments across the top of the page," says Karen. Cheryl clicks in the first space at the top of the screen. A dialog box appears, and she enters only the essential information on each assignment. She will enter additional information later.

As Cheryl types in the last activity, Karen says, "I think we are ready to enter grades. I'll call them out while you type." While she enters the grades, Cheryl remembers to save the file periodically.

"Did you notice how the program averages the grades automatically as you enter them?" asks Karen when they are done. "It takes care of figuring the percentages for you. Let's print out progress reports for social studies."

"How?" asks Cheryl.

"Click on Salma's total in the far right column."

Cheryl clicks and Salma Ali's progress report appears.

"Let's get these printed out and move on to science," says Cheryl.

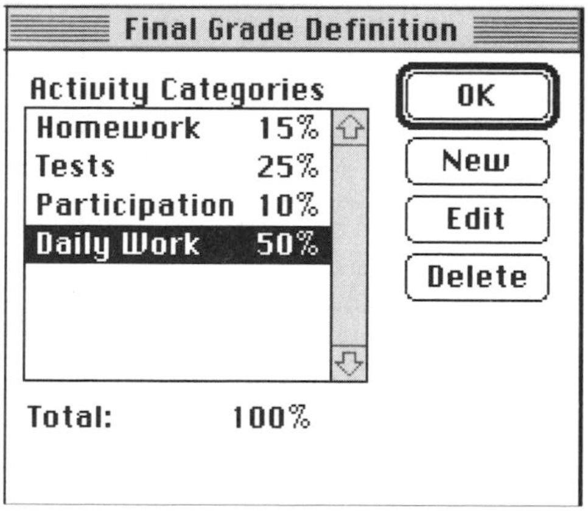

FIGURE 7-2 Final Grade Definition allows teachers to customize the program to suit their needs.

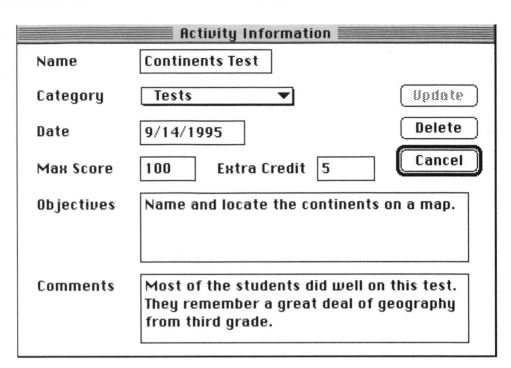

FIGURE 7-3   Activity Information gives teachers options for saving a great deal of information.

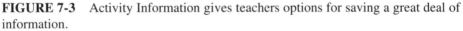

	Attendance	US Map	Continents	Oceans	Islands	Class Di...	Class Di...	Group W...	Oceans T...	Continen...		Totals
Ali, Salma		85	85	86	98	95	90	95	85	90		88.97
Anderson, Samuel		86	78	77	87	95	95	95	78	80		83.10
Dean, Harriet		97	93	90	95	100	100	90	95	85		92.46
Dickerson, Janice		88	90	85	87	95	95	95	95	85		90.25
Englund, Jason		78	83	87	90	85	95	90	93	88		88.60
Frillot, Jerome		93	90	95	86	90	95	95	94	86		90.97
Garcia, Maria		94	97	100	89	95	90	90	94	94		93.83
Grasser, Jill		96	91	94	97	100	95	95	96	94		95.18
Hymel, Joshua		94	87	80	94	100	95	90	90	80		88.12
Ingraham, Benjamin		86	94	75	100	100	95	95	90	85		89.71
Averages		89.7	88.8	86.9	92.3	95.5	94.5	93.0	91.0	86.7		90.12

ClassMaster 1.5a
Windom Ele. School

FIGURE 7-4   The social studies grades have been entered and saved.

Total for Ali			

Grades for Salma R. Ali (1/3/95)

Homework		Tests		Participation	
US Map	85.0 / 100.0	Oceans T.	85.0 / 100.0	Class Dis.	95.0 / 100.0
Continents	85.0 / 100.0	Continent.	90.0 / 100.0	Class Dis.	90.0 / 100.0
Oceans	86.0 / 100.0			Group Wo.	95.0 / 100.0
Islands	98.0 / 100.0				

Student Total

Weight	354.0 / 400.0	Weight	175.0 / 200.0	Weight	280.0 / 300.0	44.5 / 50.0
15%	x 88.5%	25%	x 87.5%	10%	x 93.3%	88.97%

FIGURE 7-5 *ClassMaster* creates and prints individual progress reports.

As the last of the progress reports are printing, Karen says, "Let me show you another useful feature. Click on the class average for Oceans Test at the bottom of the page." Cheryl clicks and a graph appears showing the distribution of the grades. "This gives you a picture of how the class did as a whole, and you can compare individual scores to the class average," says Karen.

"Now, we'll set up your science grades file. You can save the social studies file as a template and you won't have to retype all of the names."

Cheryl does this and a new file appears with the children's names. "I can work from here on my own. I know you have other things to do. Before you go, though, tell me some of the other things this program will let me do."

"By clicking in the box to the right of the students' names, you can mark attendance and print out daily attendance records to send to the office," Karen states. "You can also print out individual attendance records."

"Is there a way to make notes about individual student grades?" asks Cheryl.

"Sure," replies Karen. "Click in the top right corner of the grade cell and a box will appear for you to type in notes. I always type in notes about concepts students need to work on a bit more, or if they didn't do well because they had a headache. That sort of information. We'll sit down together another day, and I'll show you how to track attendance, put in notes about grades, and figure out what grades students need to bring up their averages."

"Thanks for your help. This is going to make keeping track of grades a whole lot easier."

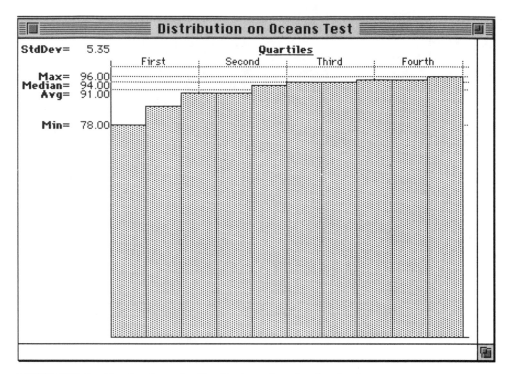

FIGURE 7-6 Graphs show the distribution of grades for the class.

A wide variety of gradebook programs are available, including some freeware and shareware programs. Freeware costs nothing; shareware requires a small fee if you continue using the program after an evaluation period. Many school districts purchase site licenses or network versions of gradebook programs, which makes copies available for all the teachers in the district. Some of the programs function on both Macintosh and MS-DOS Windows machines; however, not all can trade information between platforms.

Some gradebook programs have parent and student access options. Dialing up the school computer through a modem and typing in a personal identification number provides parents and students access to grades and teacher comments. The personal identification number is unique to each student and prevents anyone else from viewing that student's grades. Teachers have the option of deciding which information in the students' records can be viewed via the modem connection. The displayed information is "read-only" information; it can only be read, not changed. One program that has this option is Excelsior grade2.

ELECTRONIC PORTFOLIOS

Collecting and averaging students' grades is just one method of assessment. Grades are product-based assessments, which many teachers as well as school districts rely on for part of instructional measurement. Teachers, parents, and students realize that grades give a snapshot picture of one point in time. Learning is an ongoing process, however, and should be assessed in a manner that reflects the students' growth. Portfolio assessment provides a wide view of students' growth and progress in school. But storing materials in a portfolio means that students don't get to take home their prize work to post on the refrigerator, unless the teacher makes photocopies or prints another copy. Additionally, storing portfolios and organizing them often creates problems for teachers. For example, collecting student presentations may mean keeping cassettes or videotapes of their performances. Teachers then are faced with how and where to store these often bulky, cumbersome collections. Fortunately, many of these problems have been solved by electronic portfolios, which can save students' work in a variety of formats, such as text, graphics, audio, and video. They also provide a framework for organizing these collections. With district site licenses for electronic portfolio programs, children's work can follow them throughout their school careers.

The *Grady Profile* is one example of an electronic portfolio for the Macintosh computer. This program, which is a HyperCard stack, (a stack is a file created by HyperCard, a popular authoring program) works like a large database. Password protection allows teachers to decide which portions of the program parents and children can access. The profile can store a great deal of information about students, such as family facts, medical history, student services, student behavior, and standardized test scores. Assorted cards in this stack provide a framework for organizing students' work. The *Grady Profile* can store students' work as text, sounds, graphics, and video.

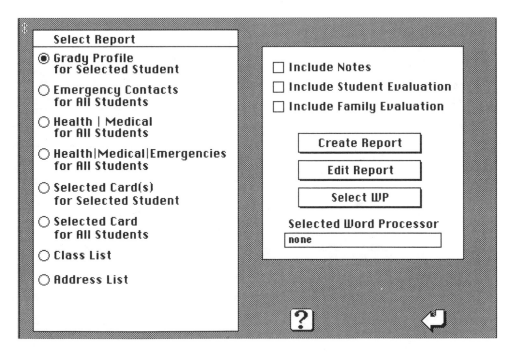

FIGURE 7-7   Computers can create a variety of reports.

Using a scanner attached to a classroom computer, students can create electronic copies of their drawings, stories, and photographs to store in their portfolios. By attaching a microphone to the computer, students can record samples of their reading or oral presentations.

Rubrics are a useful way to track students' growth and progress in school. They are a means of recording teachers' observations of students during the school day. The rubrics in *Grady Profile* can be customized by the teachers to reflect their curriculum and individual students' progress.

Learner Profile is another electronic portfolio for recording performance-based student assessments in a database. Anecdotal observations are immediately recorded using either a portable bar code reader (about the size of a credit card) or a Newton MessagePad. For the bar code process, teachers generate bar codes for each student and for each behavior they expect to observe. To record a behavior, the teacher swipes the bar code reader over the student's name and then over the bar code for the observed behavior (Barrett, 1994). For the Newton, the teacher simply taps the screen to bring up the student's file and then taps the observed behavior. The Newton's handwriting recognition feature enables the teacher to record unprogrammed responses and behaviors by writing notes on the Newton's pad. At the end of the day, information from the bar code reader or from the Newton can be downloaded to a Macintosh computer to be edited, summarized, and stored.

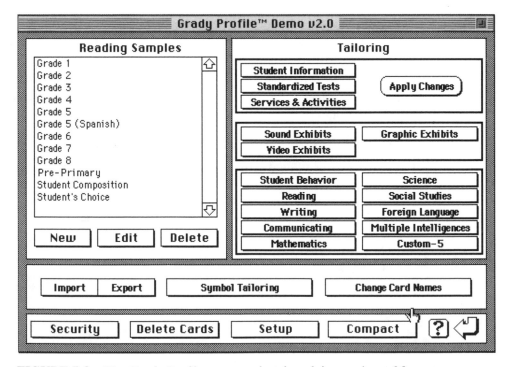

FIGURE 7-8   The *Grady Profile* stores students' work in a variety of formats.

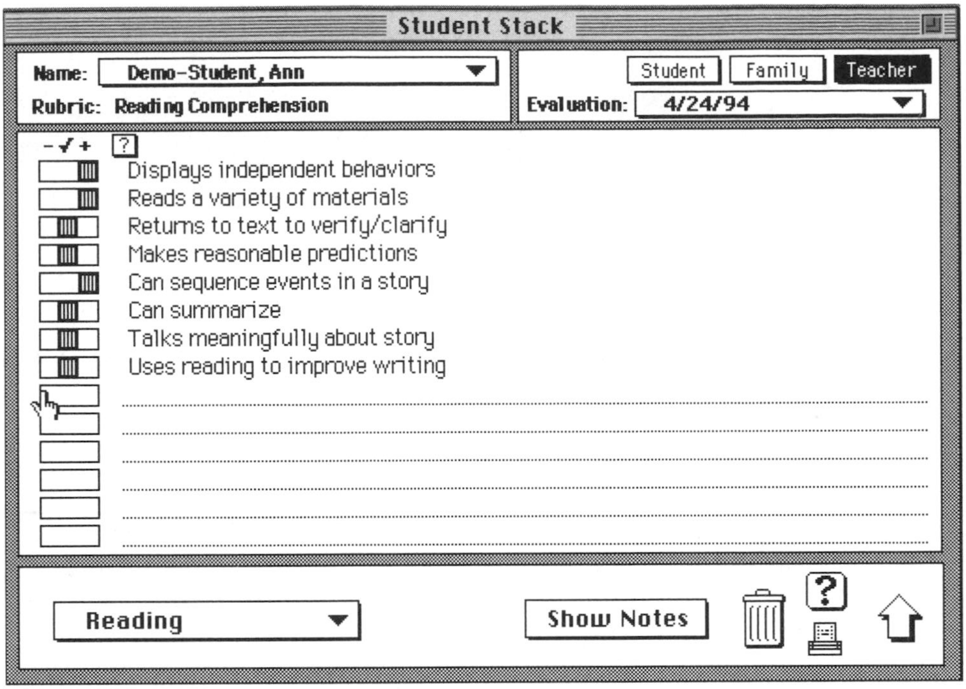

FIGURE 7-9 Rubrics are another way to note student progress.

AUTOMATING ROUTINE TASKS
USING INTEGRATED PROGRAMS

Fall parent conferences start next week at Adams High School. Teachers' off periods and after-school hours are booked, as well as Thursday from 1:00 p.m. to 7:00 p.m. Before the conferences begin, teachers must complete a parent conference form for each student's cumulative folder.

"There has got to be a way to complete these conference forms on the computer. There's just too many of them to write out by hand, and my handwriting is not the best. In addition, for many students it's a matter of turning in homework and lab reports. I have to write the same thing over and over," complains Mr. Sherwood.

"Let me look at that form again," Ms. Hernandez says.

Mr. Sherwood hands her a parent conference form and together they stare at all the blank lines that have to be completed.

"I know, we'll type this form into ClarisWorks and save it as a stationery template. Then, each time we open the file, we'll get a blank form to fill out. We'll type in the information about each student that we want to discuss in the conference and print out two copies, one for the parent and one for the student's cumulative folder," suggests Ms. Hernandez.

"That sounds like a winner to me. They'll be a lot neater and easier to read than if I write them out. Let's get started."

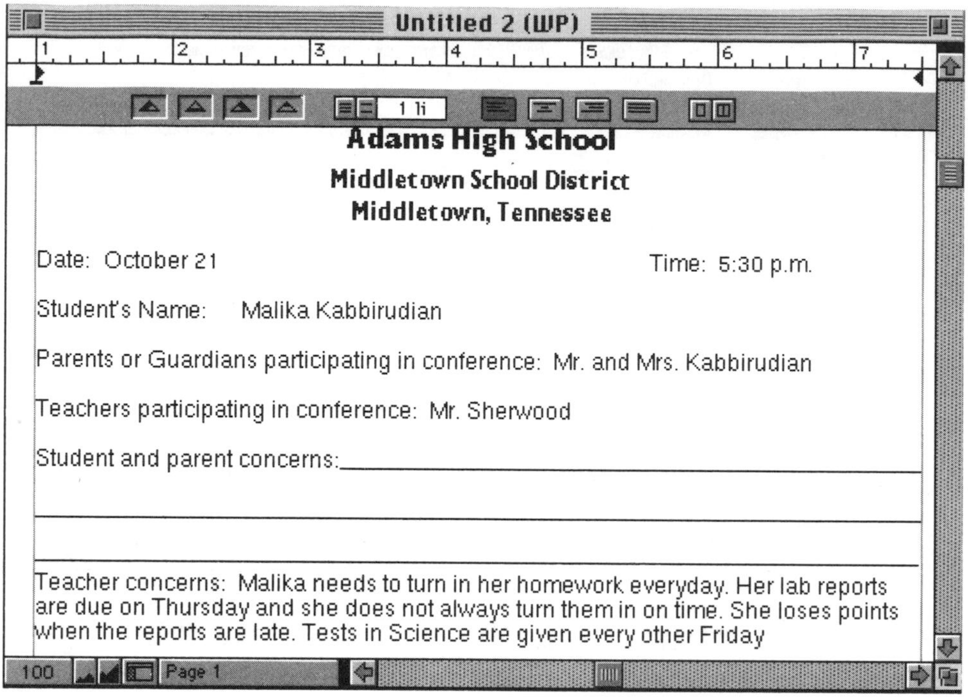

FIGURE 7-10   Parent conference forms can be created and saved as templates to be used again and again.

Integrated programs such as *ClarisWorks* and *Microsoft Works* offer an array of features that can simplify a teacher's paperwork at a reasonable cost. These integrated programs have word processing, database, spreadsheet, draw, paint, and communications modules. The word processing module can be used to create stationery templates for forms and letters. The database can be used to store, sort, and organize class rosters and other student information. The spreadsheet module can be used as a gradebook or to keep track of school picture money. The draw and paint modules can be used to create signs, posters, and cards. With the addition of a modem and a phone line, the communications module can connect one classroom to many classrooms around the world. Additionally, materials created in one module can easily be imported and exported to the other modules. For example, graphics created in the draw or paint module can be used to decorate nametags created with the database or letters written in the word processing module.

"Jury duty. Why is it that teachers always get jury duty?" asks Mr. Jacob, who teaches 2nd grade. "My students were awful the last time I had a substitute teacher."

"You know what helped the last time I was out? Nametags," offers his teaching partner, Ms. Garcia. "The substitute was able to call everyone by name, and she said that helped her get to know the students."

"Great idea. I'll write all their names on a piece of paper and put them on yarn necklaces," says Mr. Jacob.

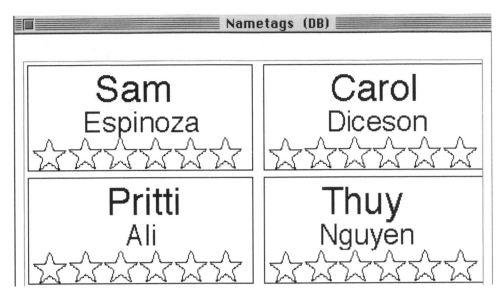

FIGURE 7-11   Nametags are easily created from a database.

"I have a better idea. Turn on your computer and open that database you have of your students, their parents' names, and phone numbers. We can use that to make name tags."

"But we don't need the parents names and phone numbers on the nametags," states Mr. Jacob.

"The database will let us select only the field we want, the student names," replies Ms. Garcia. *"We can add a graphic to dress them up and print them out on some gummed labels I have."*

LESSON PLANNERS

Teachers everywhere write lesson plans ranging from very brief statements to detailed multipage plans. Preservice teachers write them in methods classes as assignments. Student teachers write them in the evenings before they collapse exhausted into bed. Technology has made this teaching chore easier. Teacher-tested lesson plans can be downloaded from the Internet (see Chapter 8), and software programs help with creating, analyzing, and storing lesson plans. Lesson planners and lesson databases are a great way to organize and store lessons that teachers create and swap. *Lesson Planner for Windows* can be used to develop lesson plans and to key them to a master calendar. *Planalyst: The Lesson Plan Generator* for the Macintosh helps create, write, edit, and analyze lesson plans.

Educator's HomeCard for the Macintosh contains a lesson planner, a lesson database, and other teacher utilities. The program is a collection of *HyperCard* stacks that were created to help classroom teachers. *HomeCard* has three types of stacks: student management, lesson management, and ideas. *HomeCard* helps keep track of student information with a database. It also includes a gradebook and a seating chart. Seating charts are a great way

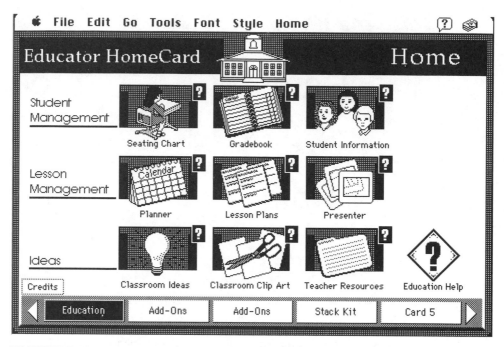

FIGURE 7-12   *Educator's HomeCard* has three types of HyperCard stacks.

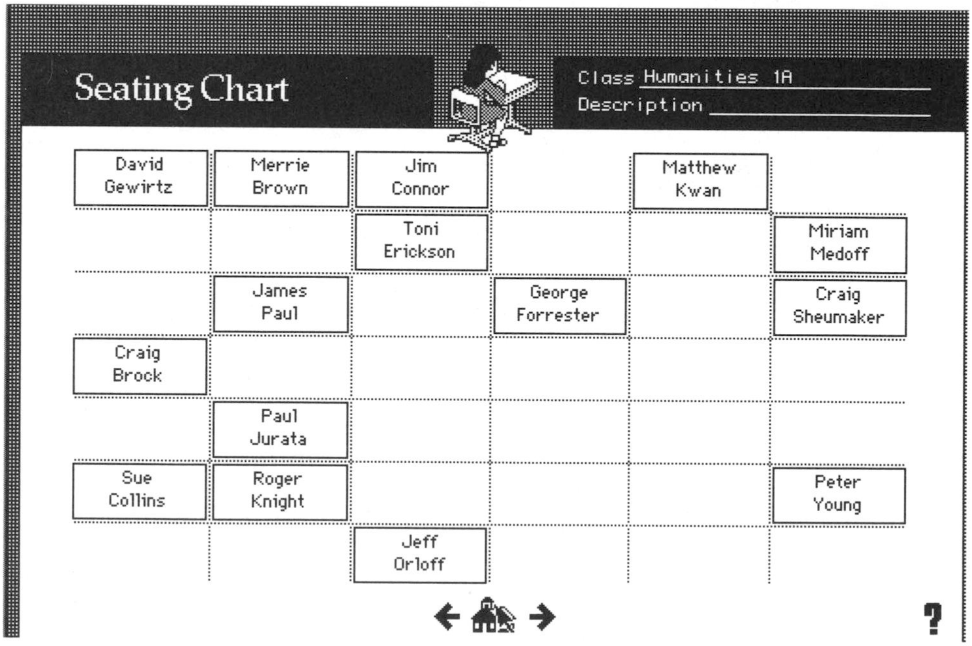

FIGURE 7-13   *Educator's HomeCard* also creates seating charts.

to help learn students' names in those first frantic weeks of school. They are also invaluable aids for substitutes.

A customizable planner is provided in the lesson management stack to help create lesson plans, and the presentation support program helps create overheads to print out or to display on screen via an LCD (liquid crystal display) panel. Each day is organized into periods, and there is space for brief descriptions of the plans for each period as well as after school.

The lesson management stack contains a stack for lesson plans that puts them into a hypermedia environment. This enables the lesson plans to be connected to other lesson plans and sources of information. Additionally, the lesson plans can be searched by title or keywords. Lessons can be organized by objectives, resources, preparation, activities, and evaluation.

PRESENTATION PROGRAMS

Madelyn Hanson and Julie Mendoza, two 6th-grade reading teachers at Darlington Intermediate School, have just emptied their mailboxes before leaving for the day.

"The note on pink paper is about Open House in two weeks," Madelyn announces. "It suggests we showcase the Macintosh computers the PTO purchased with money from the last fund raiser."

"Well, we can turn them on, but then what?" asks Julie. "What else does the note say?"

"Something about letting the parents know what we'll be doing in our classes this year," replies Madelyn.

"Does it say how? Parents just wander in, and it's hard to speak to all of them."

"Think about that ClarisWorks inservice we attended this summer. Remember

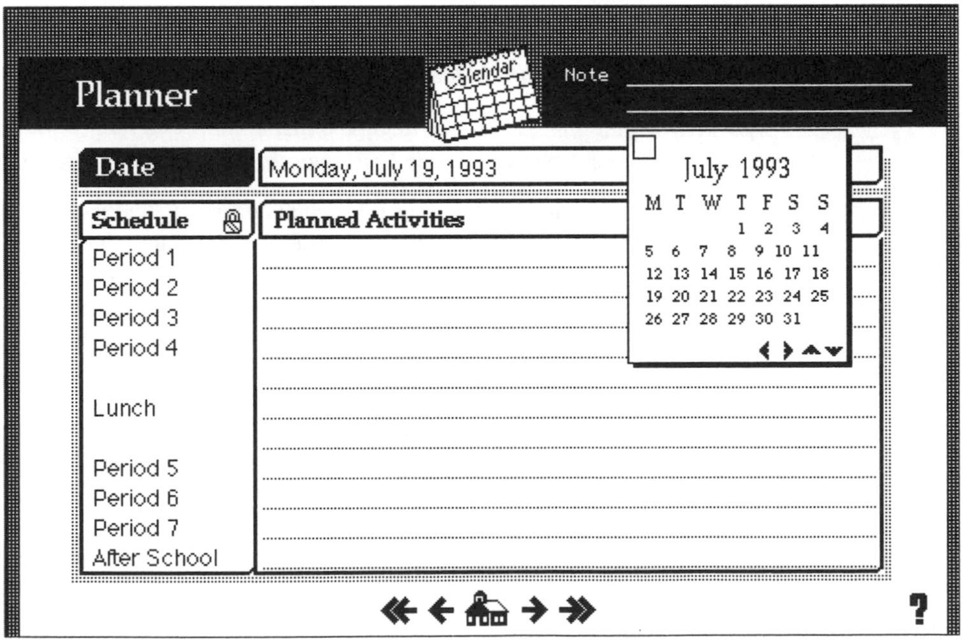

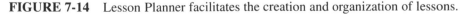

FIGURE 7-14   Lesson Planner facilitates the creation and organization of lessons.

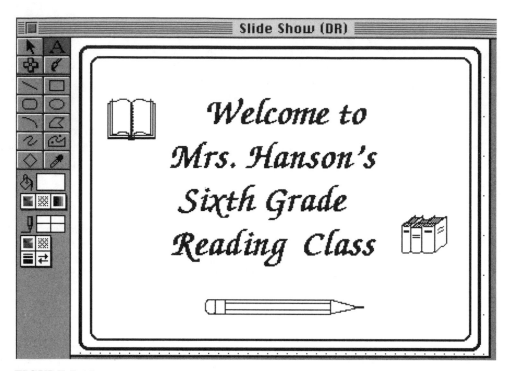

FIGURE 7-15   *ClarisWorks* slide show is a fast and easy way to create presentations.

how we made slideshows. We could make a slide show telling the parents what we will be doing this year and set it to run continuously throughout open house," suggests Madelyn.

"We'll be showcasing the Macs and telling parents what we'll be doing this year," says Julie.

"The instructions for creating slide shows are in that blue binder in my room. Let's get them out and see what we can do before we go home," suggests Madelyn.

Teachers periodically create presentations for special occasions, for example, an open house for parents. For their students, however, teachers create presentations almost daily to support lectures and discussions. Presentation software has emerged over the past few years as an alternative to the most common visual aids: overhead projectors and transparencies. Presentation packages produce electronic presentations that contain color graphics, text in many sizes and shapes, sound, video, and animation. *ClarisWorks* slide shows are quick and easy to create, and the software is readily available in many schools. However, there are many other more powerful presentation programs that create more sophisticated, eye-catching presentations. One of these programs is Microsoft's *PowerPoint*. Figure 7-16 shows a slide from a *PowerPoint* presentation for the book *Slave Dancer*.

PowerPoint is widely used in business as well as in education, and its strengths are as a sophisticated electronic replacement for traditional overheads. It is, unfortunately, designed for linear presentations. Slide 1 comes first, then Slide 2, then Slide 3. The sequence of the slides can be changed, but it was not designed to support nonlinear presentations. Because most classroom discussions are nonlinear, finding the slide that may help explain a student's question may require flipping through the slides until the appropriate one turns up.

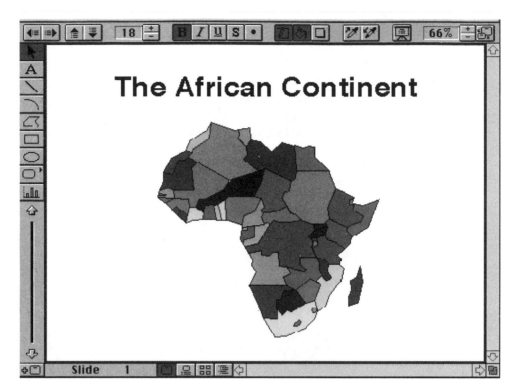

FIGURE 7-16   A slide from a *PowerPoint* presentation.

Some presentation programs support nonlinear presentations and also control laserdisk and CD-ROM players. These programs are available for both Macintosh and IBM-compatible computers. One such program is *PODIUM*, which was designed by Hofstetter (1989, 1994), a music professor at the University of Delaware. *PODIUM* was created specifically for teachers who want to support their lectures and demonstrations with multimedia. You can produce overheads that allow you to click on a topic and view a segment of video from a laserdisk. For example, one *PODIUM* program is a presentation on the Tacoma Narrows bridge collapse. Each line of text on one screen is linked to a portion of the video on a laserdisk about the bridge. When the text is clicked, the associated video clip is projected on a monitor connected to the laserdisk player (or, if you have special circuit cards in your computer, the video will be displayed on the computer screen). *PODIUM* also controls CD-ROM drives, plays several types of electronic music, and offers many of the features of *PowerPoint*. Additionally, it has extra features of special interest to teachers. For example, an *Electronic Chalk* option allows you to write with the mouse on the projected image as if it were drawn on a chalkboard. A demonstration version of *PODIUM* on CD is provided with Hofstetter's (1994) book on creating multimedia presentations.

Other programs for creating multimedia presentations include *Action!* and *LTC ClassMate*. *Action!* is less powerful than *PODIUM*, except in the area of animation, but is easier to use. It supports many types of animation as well as CD audio and digital video (e.g., video stored on a CD or the hard drive of the computer) but not laserdisks. *LTC ClassMate*

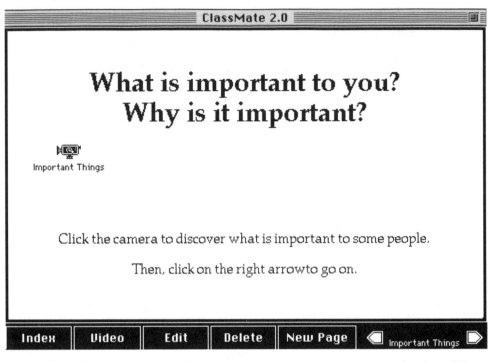

FIGURE 7-17 *LTC ClassMate* is an easy-to-use program for incorporating laserdisks into presentations.

is a very affordable shareware presentation program for creating presentations that incorporate laserdisks. Figure 7-17 shows a screen from a presentation that integrates laserdisk video clips with a story the students read.

AUTHORING SYSTEMS FOR TEACHERS

Until recently, authoring programs that let you combine video, animation, sound effects, high resolution graphics, and audio in one instructional program were expensive and difficult to use. Advances in both hardware and software, however, have led to the design of powerful and easy-to-use software for creating sophisticated instructional materials at affordable prices. Some of the authoring tools cost under $100. A few of the many authoring programs currently on the market will be discussed in this section and the next. Keep in mind, however, that new programs appear regularly that offer even more powerful features.

Authorware Star is a limited and much less expensive version of *Authorware Professional*, a powerful multimedia development program that is very popular with professional multimedia developers. Both programs are available for Macintosh and IBM-compatible systems, and both support a wide range of video and sound options. Several types of digital video, many models of laserdisk players, and CD audio can all be used in presentations created with *Authorware Star* and *Authorware Professional*.

Authorware has a graphical user interface, which means many options are selected by dragging icons. To create a screen containing text and graphics, an icon is dragged from the menu on the left side of the screen (see Figure 7-18). The icons represent the different types of material that can be added to the instructional program. For example, the three icons at the bottom are for linking computer video, music and sound, and video from a laserdisk player to the program. If the video icon is dragged to the courseline, the specified frames of the video will be played when the program reaches that point. Other icons represent text, graphics, animation, interactions, and decision points.

Authorware Star can create a variety of linear, nonlinear and multimedia presentations. *Authorware* is most suited to creating interactive materials such as tutorials, simulations, and databases that require responses from students. The program is a versatile development environment. Figure 7-19 shows a screen from an interactive resume created with *Authorware Star*. Click on one of the boxes on the left, such as Education, and that information is displayed. Click on the picture of one of the references on the left and you hear a quote from that person about the applicant.

Other authoring systems that are available include *HyperCard* for the Macintosh, *SuperCard* for the Macintosh and Windows systems, and *Toolbook* for computers running the Windows operating system. Teachers use authoring systems to create everything from presentations and tutorials for their students to interactive stories and electronic books.

STUDENT AUTHORING SYSTEMS

Distinguishing between authoring systems for students and teachers is somewhat artificial because they often use the same programs. Many student-centered classrooms using a

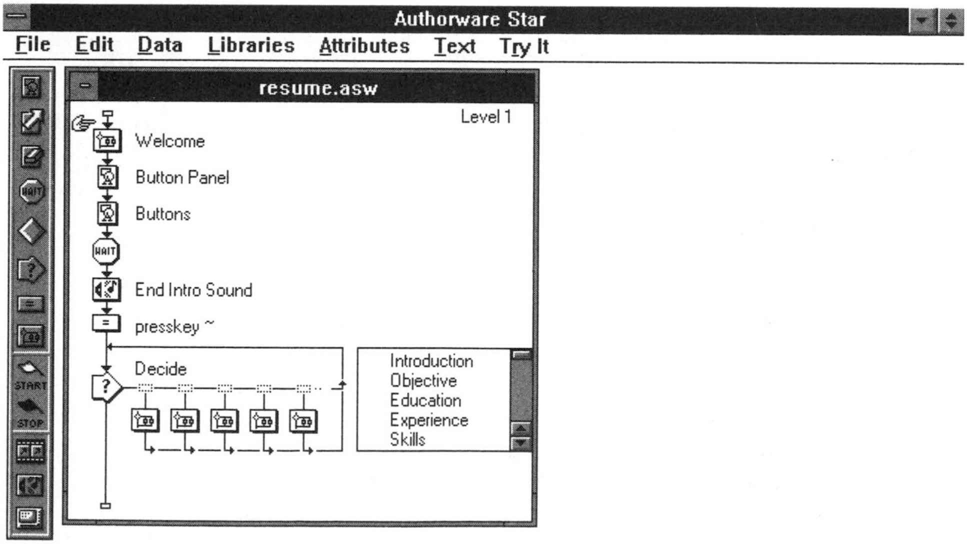

FIGURE 7-18   Programs are developed in *Authorware Star* by dragging icons to the courseline.

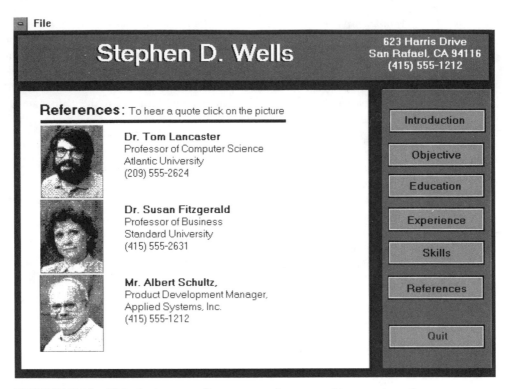

FIGURE 7-19   This *Authorware Star* program has several hot spots on the screen. Click one of them and something happens.

hands-on approach to learning find authoring programs essential. Authoring software enables students to create innovative presentations and reports that incorporate graphics, video, sounds, and photographs. *Authorware*, *HyperCard*, *SuperCard*, and *Toolbook* are all used by students, but easier to use programs have been created specifically for classroom use. Two such programs are *HyperStudio* and *The Multimedia Workshop*. *HyperStudio* is available for the Apple IIGS, Macintosh, and IBM PC-compatible systems.

TEACHER-CREATED MATERIALS

Teachers create many of their own materials to supplement and enrich their curriculum. Crossword puzzles, word searches, flashcards, and bingo cards can be created on the computer. Draw and paint programs can be used to create these customized activities. However, specific programs can be purchased to create student activity sheets quickly and easily. Programs like Crossword Wizard turn a list of vocabulary words and their definitions into a fun-to-do study guide in the form of a crossword puzzle.

Friday Afternoon is a teacher utility that creates customized word searches, bingo cards, crossword puzzles, flashcards, and worksheets. Students enjoy working together to solve word searches, crossword puzzles, and worksheets. They become very creative at

FIGURE 7-20 *HyperStudio* can be used to create many types of presentations and programs.

making up their own games to play with flashcards. Customized bingo games are perfect for a rainy-day recess or those long Friday afternoons that do not seem to end. (Dried lima beans are inexpensive bingo card markers.)

Calendar programs organize teachers' and students' lives. Paint programs such as *SuperPrint* and *Print Shop Deluxe* have a calendar that students enjoy customizing with their assignments and clip art. Teachers create calendars for students to let them know what material will be covered during the month and when assignments are due. Some programs, such as *Calendar Maker*, are strictly for creating calendars. These programs come with a wide variety of options for creating customized calendars in a wide array of styles.

TEST GENERATORS

Jennie teaches three different sections of 10th-grade English. Now that her students have gone for the day, she is working at the computer. Her students will finish reading Amy Tan's Joy Luck Club this week, and she wants to create three different versions of the test, one for each section.

Marty, another 10th-grade English teacher, sticks her head into Jennie's classroom and asks, "What are you up to?"

"Making tests," she replies.

Curious, Marty comes in for a closer look. "Are you using MakeTest?"

"Yes," replies Jennie. "I want to create three different versions of the test using the bank of questions I have in the computer."

"What do you mean by a bank of questions?"

"As we read the book and questions come to me, I type them into the computer. See, like this one," Jennie explains as she points to the screen. "By the time we finish the book, I have a bank of questions to choose from."

"I open up test editor and from the bank of questions I select some for each test. Some of the questions are the same for all three sections, but most are different. Then I scramble the order of the questions. I can easily create three different tests, one for each section," explains Jennie.

"That makes it difficult for your first section to tell the other two sections what is on the test," Marty observes.

"That's right," replies Jennie as she sends a test to the printer.

"Can you include graphics?"

"Sure. Also, you can create four different types of questions: multiple choice, true/false, fill-in the blank, and free response. I also put in a difficulty level for each question. Since my afternoon section tends to find the class somewhat harder, I choose easier questions for them."

"Does it create an answer key for you?" asks Marty.

"When I get ready to print, I specify that I want an answer key and it prints out a test with the correct answers marked," replies Jennie.

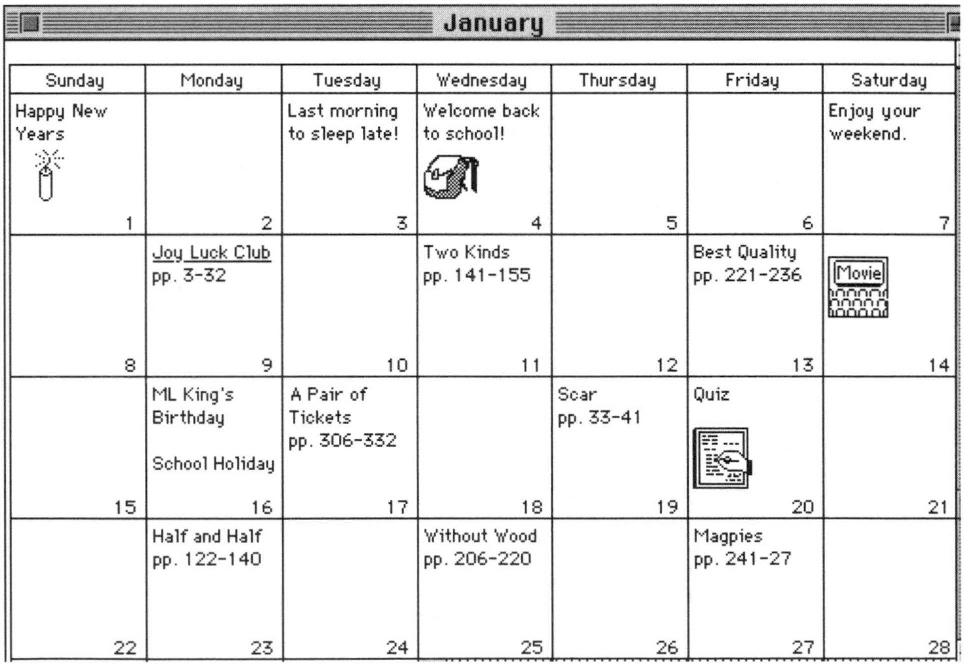

FIGURE 7-21 This customized calendar, created with *Calendar Maker*, helps 10th-grade students keep up with their reading assignments.

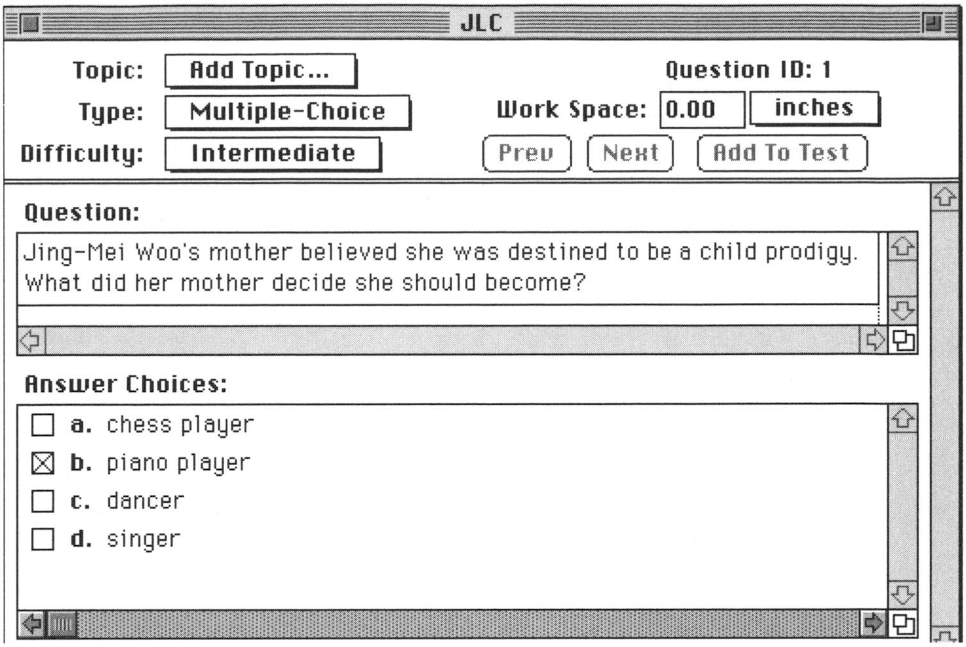

FIGURE 7-22   *MakeTest* enables teachers to create different tests for each section of students they teach.

The format and features of test programs vary considerably, from simple systems that do little more than organize a database of test items to sophisticated packages that can match test items to different sets of objectives and keep track of individual item statistics. *MakeTest* is a simple system. More complex is *Educatabase*, which was developed by a teacher who wanted a way of managing collections of ordinary test items and a system for administering tests on the computer. *Educatabase* has two components, one for creating tests and one for administering the tests.

To create a test in *Educatabase*, you begin with a simple screen with space for question stems and answers. The question stem is entered at the top of the screen and the possible answers in the spaces below. The item number is indicated at the top of the screen. As test items are entered, the correct answer is marked, and hints and feedback can be entered. This program provides hints when students ask for them and gives feedback after an incorrect answer. Options available with the program include setting a time limit for each item on the test, randomizing the order of the test items, specifying the number of hints, providing feedback after answers, and supplying the correct answer after errors. *Educatabase* prints tests as well as answer sheets and administers the tests online. Limitations of this program include only being able to create multiple choice questions, not being able to include graphics, and not being able to change font styles and sizes. As with any software package, it is important to know the limitations and capabilities to determine if it will suit the needs of the users.

SUMMARY

An ever increasing array of technology is available to support teachers' lessons and organize the paperwork that is an integral part of their job. Electronic gradebooks and portfolios provide well-organized ways to track student progress and print customized reports. Gradebooks can save time by accurately and efficiently averaging grades. Electronic portfolios can compress stacks of papers, tapes, and videos into a neat, easy to store package.

Integrated programs offer teachers a wide variety of programs at a reasonable price. These integrated packages of word processing, draw, paint, database, spreadsheet, and communications modules have endless uses in the classroom for both teachers and students.

Lesson planners, presentation programs, and authoring systems allow teachers to create and store customized lessons for their students. Many of these programs support nonlinear presentations that incorporate sound, graphics, and video. Additionally, they can be used by students to create presentations to share with their classmates.

Teachers tailor curricula to meet the needs of their students. To enhance and supplement their lessons, they design bingo games, crossword puzzles, word searches, and flash cards. A variety of software programs help them produce attractive support materials. Students also enjoy using these programs to design their own learning materials.

Test generators are invaluable tools for making different versions of tests for each section of students. Because many of the same novels and books are read each year, these tests can easily be saved and revised each year. The ability to import graphics and to use multiple question formats enhances the use ability of this software.

Technology helps teachers organize and control the paperwork that can easily overwhelm them. Technology helps teachers create multimedia presentations to capture students' attention and enhance their learning.

MICROTEACHING ACTIVITIES

1. Select one of the test creation and test administration packages available to you and create a test-item bank based on one of the chapters in this book. Then create two different versions of the test that can be distributed to other students in your course. Distribute those two forms to the other students in your class along with a 1–2 page evaluation of the package you selected. What are its most powerful features? What are its weaknesses? What features would you like to see added to the program? Would it be suitable for a high school teacher, a middle grades teacher, an elementary teacher? Then microteach a staff development activity in which you are the trainer responsible for introducing test creation and test administration programs to a group of teachers. Cover reasons for using such a program and walk your colleagues through the process of loading and using a test creation/administration program.

2. Produce a presentation using one of the programs discussed in this chapter (*HyperCard*, *HyperStudio*, *Authorware Star*, *PowerPoint*) or another presentation program familiar to you. Use the presentation to support a 5-minute microteaching session on a topic covered in this book.

3. Select a topic in the subject you plan to teach that would be suitable for some form of direct instruction that involves a teacher demonstration or lecture. Then create a short presentation using presentation software for that direct instruction and microteach the lesson using the presentation you created.

REFERENCES

Barrett, H. C. (1994). Technology-supported assessment portfolios. *The Computing Teacher, 21*(6), 9–11.

Hofstetter, F. (1989). PODIUM: Presentation Overlay Display for Interactive Uses of Media. *Academic Computing, 4*(3), 10–13, 48–50.

Hofstetter, F. (1994). *Multimedia Presentation Technology.* Belmont, CA: Wadsworth.

SOFTWARE DISCUSSED IN THIS CHAPTER

Authorware Star. Macromedia, 600 Townsend, San Francisco, CA 94103.

Calendar Maker. CE Software, Inc., PO Box 65580, West Des Moines, IA 50265. Phone: 515-224-1995.

ClassMaster. Techbyte International, Inc., N. Tonawanda, NY. Phone: 800-535-3487.

Crossword Wizard. Cogix, 419 Redwood Road, San Anselmo, CA 94960. Phone: 800-455-3388.

Educatabase. This program is available in many collections of educational shareware.

Educator's HomeCard. Intellimation, PO Box 1922, Santa Barbara, CA 93116-1922. Phone: 800-346-8355.

Excelsior Grade2. Excelsior Software, Inc., PO Box 3416, Greely, CO 80633. Phone: 800-473-4572.

Friday Afternoon. Available from Educational Resources, 1550 Executive Drive, Elgin, IL 60123. Phone: 800-624-2926.

Grady Profile. Available from Educational Resources, 1550 Executive Drive, Elgin, IL 60123. Phone: 800-624-2926.

HyperStudio. Available from Educational Resources, 1550 Executive Drive, Elgin, IL 60123. Phone: 800-624-2926.

LTC Classmate. Learning Technology Center, Peabody College, Vanderbilt University, Nashville, TN 37203. Phone: 615-322-8070.

Learner Profile. Sunburst Communications, 101 Castleton Street, Pleasantville, NY 10570-0100. Phone: 800-321-7511.

Lesson Planner. Available from Educational Resources, 1550 Executive Drive, Elgin, IL 60123. Phone: 800-624-2926.

MakeTest. Mountain Lake Software, 298 Fourth Avenue, San Francisco, CA 94118. Phone: 800-669-6574.

Planalyst: The Lesson Plan Generator. Available from Educational Resources. 1550 Executive Drive, Elgin, IL 60123. Phone: 800-624-2926.

PODIUM. The Instructional Technology Center, 305 Willard Hall, Education Building, University of Delaware, Newark, DE 19716. Phone: 302-831-8164.

PowerPoint. Microsoft Corporation, Available from Educational Resources, 1550 Executive Drive, Elgin, IL 60123. Phone: 800-624-2926.

SuperPrint. Scholastic Software, 2931 East McCarty Street, PO Box 7502, Jefferson City, MO 65102. Phone: 800-541-5513.

Print Shop Deluxe. Brøderbund. Available from Educational Resources, 1550 Executive Drive, Elgin, IL 60123. Phone: 800-624-2926.

The Multimedia Workshop. Davidson and Associates, PO Box 2961, Torrance, CA 90509. Phone: 800-545-7677.

CHAPTER EIGHT

Electronic Resources, Publications, and Organizations

Case 1: Jean's Dilemma

Note: the following is an edited version of an exchange that took place in the Elementary Education section of the Prodigy Education Bulletin Board. The messages, from February 1995, illustrate one type of sharing and debate that can take place on bulletin boards, special electronic meeting places where people from all over the world who have similar interests can communicate. Names of schools and respondents have been changed, but the messages are reproduced here much as they appeared on the Prodigy bulletin board.

```
From: Jean
Subject: BASAL VS WHOLE LAN
Have any of you had negative reactions from parents about
using Whole Language methods? I feel I was a real victim and
scapegoat in my building. I was labeled as a Whole Language
teacher and I have never been questioned as much in my 23
years of teaching as I was this year! I love literature and
use it a lot. I have always used writing as a major impetus
in my room, but I also teach phonics and spelling.
    One of the things I have discovered is that anti-Whole
Language sentiment seems to be a strong platform in much
larger movements. If you are going to use this method, you
may be taking on more than you bargain for if you live in a
fundamentalist area. My entire program was undermined. I
will be changing schools. I have had to leave my friends
```

171

and colleagues of more than 10 years. How do I start over in another location, yet still use the methods I believe are right?
Jean

From: Caroline
I think Whole Language is not so much the problem as the "look-say" way of teaching reading. When parents receive papers home with wrong spelling, no corrections, and a great big smiley face at the top, they are concerned that teachers are reinforcing wrong habits, which will be much harder to break later on than if you were to lovingly correct the child immediately. When parents listen to their children read wrong words, taking clues from context, then saying that their teacher said it was okay to do it that way, parents become concerned. When my children began in public school 3 years ago, they were just discovering that the total Whole Language approach wasn't working. My children were in on the "pilot" to reintroduce phonics into the curriculum. This was done because the test scores were falling dramatically. I think, too, that if there were A LOT more communication between home and school, there would be a lot fewer problems. We get something from the teachers MAYBE once a quarter about what the kids are learning. If they could see on a weekly basis what is being accomplished in a "Whole Language" classroom, then it may not be so scary.

You're right, for many people Whole Language is a platform for bigger issues. Classical Whole Language discarded phonics, the need for accuracy, and generally produced less able readers. It is a big red flag for some of the educational woes in America today. If this is being fundamentalist, so be it. I am one, and proud of it!!!

Personally, I love the literature-based approach. It makes learning for my children much more fun. We home school, and use literature for learning history, science, and reading. Yes, we also use phonics and teaching spelling and writing. I think it is necessary (even vital) to be able to integrate subject matter, which literature-based education does.

When you move to your new school, start at the beginning with good communication to the parents. You are teaching THEIR children, and they have a right to know what and how they are learning!!!
Good luck,
Caroline

From: Jean
Dear Caroline
Thank you for replying. I did not mean to offend by using
the term fundamentalist. I felt I became embroiled in something far more complicated than my teaching style. I had
been looked at favorably for many years as a teacher and I
have taught this way since 1971. I have tried to keep current with the research on the best ways to teach children
and incorporate the best of any method. Not all teachers
send home work that is accepting of inaccuracies. That is a
result of inadequate training. I think it has been important for me to learn that there was a growing controversy
going on right outside my classroom door. I just wish I
could have learned it at less cost to me professionally and
personally. By the time the parents were done with me I
lost all confidence in myself as a teacher. I have taken an
educational sabbatical for a whole year to retool myself
for my remaining years as a teacher. After reading replies
from many parents on Prodigy, the first thing I will do when
I return to teaching is get to know what the parents think
about education and what their expectations are. I will
still use many Whole Language methods, but I will not label
methods as anything but my own.

From: Mary
Jean, I think you are absolutely right about not labeling
what you are doing in terms of Whole Language. Call it
something else, because a red flag is raised at the mere
term WL. Maybe "phonics in literature" <g> would keep
everyone quiet. [Note: <g> is short for "grin."] I'm sorry
you had a bad situation escalate. I know how defeating it
can be to be teaching your heart out and believe in what
you're doing only to have half informed people undermine
what you do. I guess it comes down to playing a game. Try
to use vocabulary that appeases them. Good luck at your new
school.
Mary

From: Carl
Jean, at the Post Spring Elementary School, in Baltimore
County, Maryland, a parent group did a study comparing the
reading comprehension scores correlated with the introduction of a Whole Language program. In the majority of cases,
these scores have been seen to drop after the introduction
of WL. Research on this subject indicates that the most

effective approach to reading instruction is a combination of the best of WL (integrated subjects, rich literature, and emphasis on critical thinking), and intensive, systematic phonics. From my perspective as a parent I do not see the word-attack skills from kids who have had WL. DO NOT de-emphasize the phonics component.
Carl

From: Mike
Jean. The same thing happened to me two years ago. I was given a self-contained chapter I class and I used real literature and no worksheets, and the students and parents loved it. After Xmas a child that had been home schooled moved into my class, because his mom decided that she (the mother) was not cut out for home schooling. (Disclaimer: this is not a knock at home schoolers; this was what she told me.) He was only in my class for a week when she asked for a parent conference. She said that she noticed that I did not use workbooks or worksheets, and then she asked me if I was a Whole Language teacher. I, of course, told her yes; she then started sending me Eagle Forum and Christians for Excellence in Education materials. She also started the phone chain, and she had all of the parents upset. She called the principal, the curriculum coordinator, the superintendent, and the State Board of Education. She tried to say that I was trying to invade her family's privacy by using journals, and that I was trying to brainwash students. She said that I was helping to brainwash them because I told them to add more detail to their stories. I told them to close their eyes and pretend that their story was a movie, then write down all of the details that they saw. BIG MISTAKE! Well, around April we had to take the Stanford Test, and after that, all you know what broke loose. By the first of May three students had withdrawn from my class and their parents started home schooling. I had mothers coming into my class during the middle of the day and cussing me out.

I pleaded for this Eagle Forum woman to come to my class to observe, but she never would. She absolutely refused to come into my class. I then invited other parents to come and several did. There was even an altercation at the softball field when one of the fathers that liked me said for the Eagle Forum woman to shut up. I finally made it through the year.

The last week of school, I had an appointment with the Eagle Forum lady and a few people in administration at the county board of education. The lady brought up all of these accusations about me teaching witchcraft (I did a fairy tale unit), and that I was New Age. My curriculum supervisor then asked her if she knew that in addition to being a teacher I was also the Minister of Music at a Southern Baptist Church in another city. The woman's jaw dropped, and she was speechless. I then lit into her. She let me alone. When she sees me in the Wal-Mart store she goes through the back to avoid me.

The ending of the story is that my class that year made higher scores on their Sanford Achievement Test than any other class at my school, and outscored all the chapter I students county wide. When the classes were announced that summer, I had a lot of flack again, but I had a parents' night and we talked about it. I gave them very good explanations of my teaching philosophy, and I explained to them how I taught reading. There were some who came to do battle, but I talked all about their misgivings. I had but one parent problem the whole year last year, and it was not over Whole Language.

As for calling it something that it is not, I don't think you should do that. I think you need to be as up front about what you are doing in your classroom as you can possibly be. Parents will look on this bulletin board and see notes telling you to call it something else, and that just perpetuates this myth that Whole Language is this secret plot. I would also like to suggest that you should read as much literature as you can on Whole Language. I try to read negative and positive articles, because this helps me prepare for when my teaching is questioned. I also keep those books in my classroom library. If there is a question, I will let parents see that I have a basis for my teaching. Mike

From: Jean
Dear Mike and Mary
Thanks for the support. If only parents understood how devastating it is for the children in a classroom that become part of the controversy. I really feel that I am teaching according to the syllabus provided by New York State. I think parents should direct some of their energy in that direction instead of trying to actually get rid of someone.

I respect Caroline's opinions and feel she probably does an outstanding job with her children. Home schooling is a wonderful privilege for some families.
Jean

From: Michie
Dear Jean
I too am a WL teacher in central Massachusetts. Don't be
overly discouraged yet. Change takes time, and parents as
well as teachers need time to adjust to a very successful-
enjoyable approach to teaching reading. I thus worked in
Australia for years and it can work here as well. Industry
is asking for people who can use strategies and think for
themselves. WL allows this to happen through the use of
rich children's literature. Parents are uncomfortable
because this is all new to them. Read Marie Clay for some
ideas on supporting your program. This beats See Spot Run.
Good effort!
Michie

Case 2: Larry's Leap to the Past

Note: Although this case is fictional, it is based on several reports of how teachers are using Virginia's Public Education Network (PEN) in their classrooms.

Larry Keller teaches 5th grade in a small Virginia town and heard about some of the activities on Virginia's Public Education Network (PEN) at a regional computer confer- ence. At the time he was interested in two things: doing some interdisciplinary lessons that cut across several of the subjects he teaches, and encouraging some of his stu- dents to write more. He was looking for authentic activities. A vague idea of how to accomplish both goals formed as he heard one of the conference presenters discuss service on PEN that puts students in contact with famous people from the past. In essence, the service worked this way. A faculty member or graduate student at the University of Virginia who was very familiar with the life and times of a famous person would play the role of that person. Students, using PEN, would send e-mail to that per- son, and the expert would reply as if he or she were the famous person from history. Larry realized that to get this up and running in his classroom he needed a modem to add to his classroom computer and a phone line. The parent teacher organization paid the $75 for the modem after Larry talked with the chair of the parent advisory commit- tee on technology. He was able to convince the district technology coordinator to foot the bill for installing a telephone line in his room (after pointing out that a nearby dis- trict was in the middle of adding phone and computer data lines to all classrooms).

With his new modem and phone line in place, Larry did a few trial runs on the equipment and, with the help of the computer coordinator, was able to establish reli- able connections to PEN. Larry had problems at first. Sometimes he was disconnect- ed in the middle of a session. Larry discovered the principal had decided to save a little money by having the phone company run an extension from a phone in the business manager's office down to his classroom. That saved the cost of adding another line, and the business manager's phone would now be paid for by the district computer coordinator. The principal thought this would work well because the business manag- er used the phone usually for less than 30 minutes a day, and many of his calls lasted *less than 30 seconds. Each time the business manager picked up the phone and heard the burble of computer modems communicating back and forth, he said "Excuse me" and hung up the phone. The modem, however, was not impressed with his politeness. It immediately disconnected and sent a CARRIER LOST message to the computer screen. After some detective work the phone sharing scheme was discovered by the computer coordinator, who patiently explained to the principal that modems do not work on party lines. The principal then asked the business manager to stop using that phone line and added a second line to the business manager's office because it was cheaper to run a new one to the office than to the classroom. Larry eventually switched off the ringer on the phone in his room because the calls were always from people wanting to talk to the business manager, who now had a new number.*

The PEN connections still did not work well. Disconnections in the middle of sessions, though less frequent, were still happening. More troubleshooting led to the discovery that the business manager's phone had a call waiting feature, which produced a buzz in the background when someone called the number. The modem took just as much offense at the buzz as it did the business manager's "Excuse me." The problem was solved by turning off the call waiting feature. Finally, after two months of frustration and struggle, Larry had a reliable connection to PEN in his classroom.

Larry used the PEN connection for a multidisciplinary lesson on Thomas Jefferson. The lesson, which lasted four weeks, covered many aspects of Jefferson's life and times. Collaborative groups of students were required to select a topic and, after doing some research, make a multimedia report to the class using HyperStudio, a program for the Macintosh computer that lets you combine text, graphics, video, and photographs. Several groups had questions that were not answered by the reference materials at the school. They created short e-mail messages to Thomas Jefferson at the University of Virginia and sent them via PEN. The replies were eagerly awaited. When they came, they were printed out on the classroom printer and copied for distribution to all the students in the group. Frequently the reply generated additional questions, and the interaction between students in Larry Keller's class and Thomas Jefferson continued over several weeks. Even after all the groups had made their multimedia presentations, several groups continued to send and receive e-mail from Mr. Jefferson.

Case 3: Joan's International Connections

Joan Reese is a 7th-grade teacher in a coastal school district. Although a literacy educator, Joan team teaches with several others in her middle school who have other specialties, and the team is always looking for interdisciplinary projects that can meet curricular objectives in more than one subject area. With two clusters of computers in the classroom area, Joan's team has already used computer-based collaborative writing in several projects. In one, students created a series of reports on the ecology of the region, with a focus on wetlands and bays. Each team had to create a response paper from the point of view of a particular group. For example, the four students in the Chemical Industry Environmental Group wrote their paper from the perspective of the chemical industry, which had many plants in the area. The students in the Agribusiness Coalition wrote from the perspective of farmers who were being criticized for the phosphates that flow into the bay from fertilized fields. Other groups gathered position papers, reports, and newspaper coverage from environmental groups, city, state, and county government agencies, the Environmental Protection Agency, and other sources. Group reports were created using the collaborative writing software on the cluster computers. Then, after each group had a chance to respond at a hearing held by a simulated legislative committee, the students in the legislature tried to hammer out a bill that advanced the cause of improved environmental conditions and that could be passed in a legislature where many special interests had strong support.

Their experience with collaborative writing led Joan's team of teachers to try an even more complicated project that involved collaborative writing and telecommunications. Using a service on the Internet, they announced a plan to complete an international project on cost of living in different parts of the world, and they asked students in other parts of the world to join the project. Classes in Japan, Canada, England, Finland, New Zealand, Germany, and Russia joined the project, and students at Joan's school created a survey form that asked about the price of certain items such as hamburgers, music CDs, movies, gasoline, and many other "necessities of life." The survey also asked about the typical salaries of different jobs—teacher, physician, engineer, factory worker, farmer, and so on. As the data began arriving via e-mail, students organized the information into a database and began writing a report on what the data meant. As they worked on the final report, which was a collaborative effort by students at all eight sites, they discovered that the data, which in this case were numbers, didn't tell the whole story. Students participating in the project began to discuss their lives, what they did after school, how they earned money for extras, and where they lived.

Joan's students learned as much, if not more, from these informal discussions as they did from the numbers. One student at a Russian school, for example, talked about going to the McDonald's restaurant in Moscow. For students in Joan's class, McDonalds was a fast food restaurant where you could buy a Big Mac for pocket change. For the Russian student, the visit was to an exotic and expensive place where a Big Mac cost more than a week's pay for the average Russian. Even for professionals, the Russian student pointed out, if a family of four ate at McDonald's each day for a month, they would wipe out a parent's entire salary. The final report produced by the collaborative group was as much about feelings, experiences, and perspectives as it was prices and products.

DATA, DATA EVERYWHERE, AND NOT THE KNOWLEDGE WE NEED

We are often overwhelmed with data and just as frequently starved for information. It is easy to drown in a sea of data that comes to us in many forms—books, magazines, journals, friends, colleagues, experience, conferences, television, newspapers, and electronics. Within that sea of data, finding precisely the information we need can be difficult. The day is gone when a dedicated literacy teacher could subscribe to all the magazines, attend all the conferences, and buy all the books relevant to his or her area of teaching. Knowing how to find information when it is needed has become more important than amassing a large collection of reference materials.

In this chapter we will introduce you to several sources of information, with an emphasis on electronic resources. The resources include databases of lesson plans, repositories for special types of information, discussion groups and special interest groups, or SIGs, where you can communicate with others who have similar interests, and the electronic homes of several organizations of interest to literacy educators.

We believe that in the immediate future electronic forms of communication, especially computer-based systems, will become critical conduits for the dissemination of information. Hundreds of electronic resources are already available on the Internet (a collection of interconnected computer networks that many educators have free access to) and on commercial services such as Prodigy, America Online, and CompuServe, which charge a monthly fee (usually about $10 to $15) and an hourly access fee (about $2 to $8) if you use more hours than are included in the basic monthly fee. We will explore some of those resources in this chapter.

As computer-based sources of information become important resources for the general public, literacy curricula will change. Twenty years ago literacy skills included using print reference materials such as encyclopedias and critically reading publications such as newspapers. As they completed writing assignments and projects, students used encyclopedias and newspapers as information resources. In the 1990s, basic literacy skills include the ability to use electronic information resources such as electronic databases available over the Internet, the largest component of the information highway. Classroom use of telecommunications will be addressed in this chapter.

GETTING CONNECTED

Someday, perhaps in the near future, using your computer to connect to electronic information services will be simple and straightforward—like buying a car. When you buy a car, you can be confident that, regardless of the model and brand you buy—Ford, Chevrolet, Toyota, KIA, BMW, or Volvo—you will be able to drive on the roads in your area and use the fuel available at the local Chevron, Texaco, Exxon, or Shell station. Although cars differ in terms of appearance and features, they all meet certain standard conditions. None, for example, are too wide to be driven on ordinary highways.

Standardization has not yet come to computer-based information resources. The three major families of computers (Macintosh, Windows-based PCs, and Unix systems) connect to electronic services in widely different ways, and the several hundred different communications programs—the software required to connect your computer to a service—all work in different ways. In addition, the hundreds of telecommunications services vary in the way you connect to the service and navigate to the different resources. Because of such variations, we will not include any detailed how-to information in this chapter. When you decide to connect to the Internet or begin using a commercial service such as America Online, CompuServe, or Prodigy, the easiest way to get started is to ask for help from someone who is already connected. The commercial services provide information and assistance for new subscribers. In many school districts, computer coordinators regularly help teachers connect classroom computers to telecommunications resources. Also, several types of computer systems sold in discount electronics stores such as Best Buy and Circuit City come with the hardware and software needed to telecommunicate already installed. All you have to do is connect the computer to the phone line.

One general issue you must consider is the way you will connect to information services. Today there are two ways of telecommunicating: modems and direct connections. Most schools, and most teachers who connect to services from home, use a modem, which connects your computer to the phone line. If you want to use an electronic service such as Prodigy in your classroom, you need a computer, a telephone line, a modem, and cables to connect the modem to the computer and the phone line.

The three general factors to consider when shopping for modems are compatibility, speed, and price. Some modems work only with certain computer models; others work with most models if you have the correct cables. Speeds vary from as slow as 2400 bits per second to 28,800 bps or higher (a "bit" is the electronic equivalent of a 1 or 0, but you don't really need to know such technical details). Slower modems are, of course, cheaper, but most of the modern services you will be using work best if your modem speed is at least 9,600 bps. In fact, speeds of 14,400 and higher are becoming standard. You can find 14,400 bps modems for under $100, and faster modems for less than $175. Generally, the faster the modem the better.

If you are fortunate, you may work in a school district that has a direct connection to the information highway (the current term for all the interconnected networks available for "net cruising"). Direct connections generally involve attaching your computer to a local area network (LAN) that may interconnect all the computers in your building. The district may have a wide area network (WAN) that connects computers throughout the district so you can exchange files with teachers and administrators at other locations. If the LAN or WAN has a connection to the Internet, you can use special software to connect your computer to the Internet via the school district's LAN. The Internet is the largest component of the information highway. It is really a collection of large WANs that serve regions. In Georgia, for example, the colleges and universities are connected through a WAN called PEACHNet. PEACHNet is part of the Internet. In Texas, higher education institutions are interconnected via THEnet (Texas Higher Education Network) and K–12 schools are connected via TENET (Texas Educator's Network).

When teachers connect to services like TENET in Texas, Virginia's PEN (Public Education Network), or similar services, they usually do so via a modem. In 1996 less than 2 percent of schools had direct connections, but that percentage will increase rapidly over this decade. For a direct connection, your district must have a LAN or WAN installed that is connected to the Internet. The cabling for the LAN must provide a connection in your classroom or office. Many new schools include network connections as a basic utility service along with electrical power, but most older schools do not. If you have a network connection in your classroom, three other items are required for a connection: a network card for your computer that is compatible with the school's LAN, networking software compatible with your computer, and a cable to connect the network card to the LAN.

SOME MOVEMENT TOWARD STANDARDIZATION

If all this talk of modem speeds, telecommunications software, and network cards gives you the impression that this use of computers is still evolving, you are correct. Getting connected is, for many, still a process of trial and error until all the glitches and incompatibilities in equipment and software have been worked out. However, several signs indicate that we are moving quickly toward easy-to-install, easy-to-use telecommunications resources. For example, commercial services such as America Online (AOL) and Prodigy come with their own software. To install AOL on your computer, you insert a disk and click the mouse pointer on a small icon named Install. Then the software installs itself on your computer, determines what brand of modem you are using, dials an 800 number, and asks you to indicate where you are located. Then it picks a local access number for you (so that no long distance charges are required to use the service), places the number in your computer software, hangs up, and redials the local number. After that, connecting to AOL is simple—just click on the America Online icon on your computer screen, type your AOL membership name, and enter your password. The other commercial services are just as easy to install on your computer and begin using.

Once you're connected to a service, most of the decisions you make are from menus. Figure 8-1 shows the main menu from America Online. AOL has organized the resources on this service into 14 general categories—including Education and Kids Only. To move to the Education section, you move the cursor to the icon labeled Education and click the mouse twice (called "double clicking"). AOL then presents the Education menu, which is shown in Figure 8-2. You can click on one of the three options at the bottom of the screen for routine tasks, such as returning to the main menu. Another section of the Education menu lists featured services. For example, you can access the

FIGURE 8-1   The America Online Main Menu.

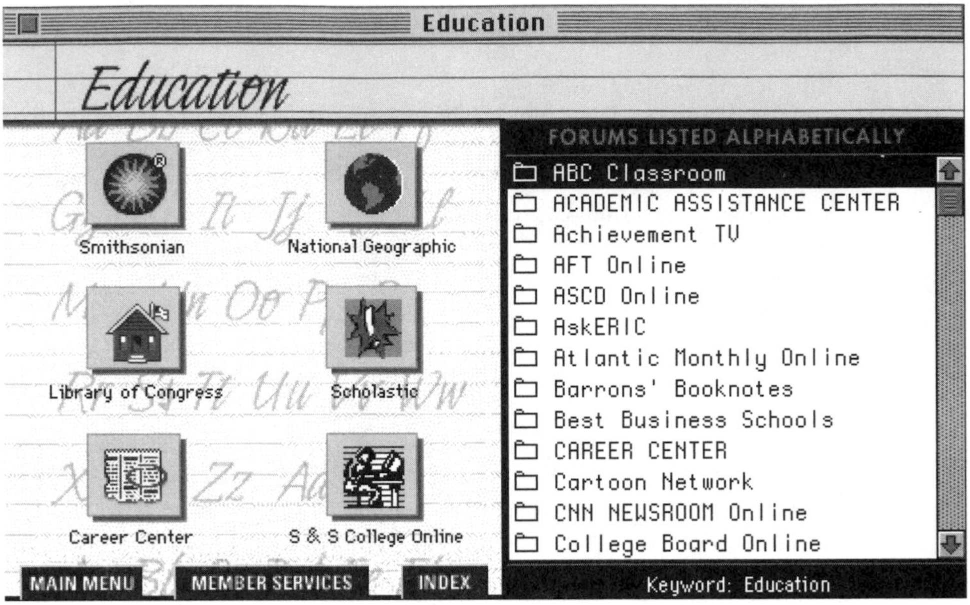

FIGURE 8-2   The America Online Education Menu.

Smithsonian Institution and the Library of Congress. The six featured services you see in Figure 8-2 are just a sample of the hundreds of resources in the Education menu. The list on the right is scrollable. Click on the arrow pointing down at the bottom right of the screen and the list scrolls up to show you the names of over a hundred different companies, organizations, and services. Access to services like AskERIC involves no more than clicking on the name of the service.

Space limitations don't allow us to properly review all the resources available to educators, but two will be explored in more detail later in this chapter. One resources of interest on AOL is the lesson plan library. Figure 8-3 shows some of the language arts lesson plans available.

USER-FRIENDLY ELECTRONIC RESOURCES

America Online, Prodigy, CompuServe, Apple Computer's E-World, and Microsoft's new telecommunications service are some of the leaders in ease of use. Until recently, arcane commands, complex patterns of use, and services that had all the organizational structure of a bowl of spaghetti were the *sine qua non* of the Internet, that semi-organized collection of regional LANS and WANS that now interconnects the world. Before the arrival of some easy-to-use services like World Wide Web and software like *Mosaic* and *NetScape* that take some of the burden of remembering commands off the shoulders of the users, the Internet was not for the faint of heart or the easily discouraged. Learning to use it well

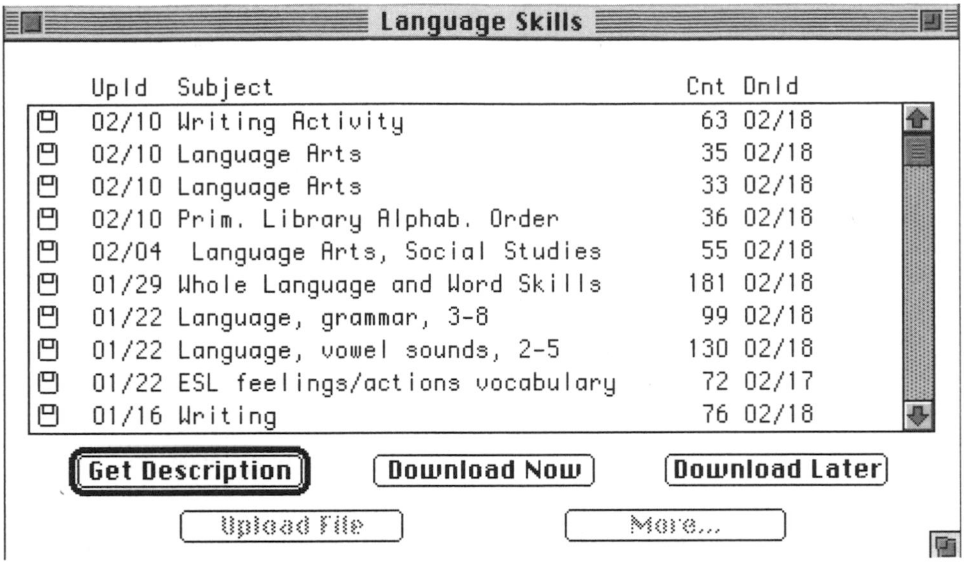

```
┌─────────────────────────────────────────────────────────┐
│▒▒█░══════════════ Language Skills ══════════════░█▒▒     │
│                                                           │
│    UpId  Subject                        Cnt  DnId         │
│  ┌─────────────────────────────────────────────────┐ ▲  │
│  │🗐 02/10 Writing Activity              63 02/18  │    │
│  │🗐 02/10 Language Arts                  35 02/18  │ ▒  │
│  │🗐 02/10 Language Arts                  33 02/18  │    │
│  │🗐 02/10 Prim. Library Alphab. Order    36 02/18  │    │
│  │🗐 02/04  Language Arts, Social Studies 55 02/18  │    │
│  │🗐 01/29 Whole Language and Word Skills 181 02/18 │    │
│  │🗐 01/22 Language, grammar, 3-8         99 02/18  │    │
│  │🗐 01/22 Language, vowel sounds, 2-5   130 02/18  │    │
│  │🗐 01/22 ESL feelings/actions vocabulary 72 02/17 │    │
│  │🗐 01/16 Writing                        76 02/18  │ ▼  │
│  └─────────────────────────────────────────────────┘    │
│   ┌─────────────────┐  ┌──────────────┐ ┌──────────────┐ │
│   │ Get Description │  │ Download Now │ │Download Later│ │
│   └─────────────────┘  └──────────────┘ └──────────────┘ │
│       ┌──────────────┐      ┌──────────────┐             │
│       │ Upload File  │      │   More...    │         🗐  │
│       └──────────────┘      └──────────────┘             │
└─────────────────────────────────────────────────────────┘
```

FIGURE 8-3   The Language Skills menu on AOL.

could take as much time and effort as learning to play the piano or fly a plane. Fortunately, in an era when most people don't have the time or the masochistic tendencies needed to master the raw Internet, a large collection of programs and services have been developed for Internet users. Today there are probably ten million computers or more connected to the Internet, in part because new software and services are so much easier to use. A few of those user-friendly resources are described in the sections that follow.

WORLD WIDE WEB

World Wide Web (WWW, or "the Web") is a standardized system of creating electronic pages on the Internet. Web pages are multimedia and hypermedia. They are multimedia because they can contain high-resolution color graphics, voice, and video as well as text. The home pages (the first or welcome pages) of some Web sites are beautiful! The pages of Web sites are hypermedia because you can jump from one location to another. For example, you might go to a Web site that contains many of the classics of literature. The titles available might be listed on the home page. You could click "Tale of Two Cities," for example, and jump to that document. That same site might mention other sites around the world that contain related material. Often you can click the name of another location and jump to that site.

To access World Wide Web sites you must have special software such as *Mosaic* (which is free) and either a direct connection to the Internet or a fast modem and access to a dial-up service that is either a SLIP or PPP connection. We won't offer a detailed explanation of SLIP or PPP because you don't need all the technical details to use either. You do need access to this type of connection, however, to use World Wide Web.

Below are the addresses and brief descriptions of a few Web sites you might find interesting.

http://browe.ncsa.uiuc.edu

This is the Web home page of the Champaign Centennial High School. It includes photos of the school and staff as well as a section where students can download homework assignments they forgot or missed.

http://web.cal.msu.edu/JSRI/GR/BradClass.thumb.html

Brad Marshall and his 5th-grade students at Grand River Elementary School in Lansing, Michigan, created this Web site, which has pictures of the students and a message from each.

http://c3.lanl.gov/!cjhamil/SolarSystem/homepage.html

This site at the Los Alamos National Laboratory in New Mexico has many subsections on various aspects of space exploration and astronomy. Many images are available for downloading, including quite a few from NASA and the European Space Agency.

http://ednews2.asa.utk.edu/papers.html

Interested in college newspapers? This site lets you read a number of papers, both U.S. and foreign, online.

http://www.cc.columbia.edu/!emj5/yourmom/ymhome.html

While at Evanston Township High School in Illinois, several students edited the school humor magazine, *Your Mom.* Now in college, they have continued the magazine on the Internet as a Web site.

http://metaverse.com/vibe/misc/favlinks.html

Adam Curry, a former MTV videojockey, created this site, which is really a gateway to many other Web sites that carry information on all types of music, from Frank Sinatra to Nine Inch Nails and the stars of tomorrow. You can click a link in Curry's web and jump to Web sites all over the country.

http://www-lips.ece.utexas.edu/~delayman/solar.html

Solar-powered vehicles are the focus of this site, which includes graphics and photographs.

- NCSA's <u>What's new</u> with the web.

- The On-Line Yellow Pages of the net are finally here! Look for yourself in the <u>The Global On-Line Directory Services</u>

- <u>SUN releases it's new VOYAGER I love it! Check it out for yourself.</u>
- <u>Tori Amos</u>
- <u>Led Zeppelin</u>
- <u>Beastie Boys</u>
- <u>Bjork</u>
- <u>Blues Brothers</u>
- <u>Jimmy Buffett</u>
- <u>Eric Clapton</u>
- <u>Deep Purple</u>
- <u>Devo</u>

FIGURE 8-4   A screen from Adam Curry's World Wide Web site.

http://reptor/-dalewis/frisbee.html

David Lewis at Swarthmore College, a member of the college's "swarming earthworms" frisbee team, created this frisbee information site.

http://web.msu.edu/vincent/index-html

This is Vincent Voice Library at Michigan State University, from which you can download an unbelievable number of voice recordings. Available here are speeches such as John Kennedy's inaugural address and Richard Nixon's resignation speech. Also available is a reading of Othello.

http://www.pathfinder.com/twi

The Web site of Time Warner's record and interactive video game divisions. You and your students will find demos of video games, video and audio clips from popular performers on Time Warner's label, graphics, and information about Time Warner products.

http://www.hcc.hawaii.edu/dinos/dinos.1.html

The Honolulu Community College created this interesting and useful site devoted to dinosaurs. It has images, many easy to understand papers on the topic, and some audio narration of exhibits.

http://www.macom.co.il/museum

The Israel Museum site, which contains electronic versions, including photographs, of exhibits at the museum. You can, for example, view photographs of Jerusalem in the 19th century.

http://mistral.enst.fr/~pioch/louvre/

This is Le WebLouvre, from the Louvre museum in Paris, and one of the busier sites on the Internet. Le WebLouvre contains text and outstanding graphics and photographs related to Louvre exhibits.

http://faldo.atmos.uiuc.edu/weather/weather.html

This University of Illinois site contains many types of information on weather-related topics, for example, how weather topics can be included in writing and reading instruction, and games about weather topics that students can play.

http://rs560.cl.msu.edu/weather/

This popular site contains images from the weather satellites scattered around the globe. They are updated several times a day. If you do not have access to Web sites, the same images are available on an ftp site (explained later in this chapter). The address of the ftp site is wuarchive.wustl.edu and the weather images are in the multimedia/images/wx subdirectory.

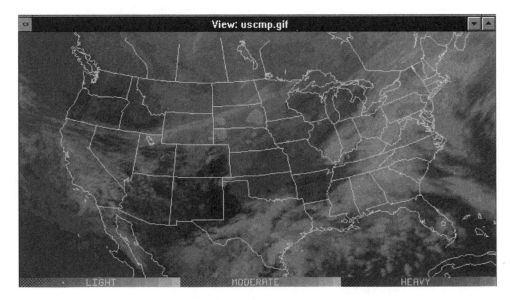

FIGURE 8-5   A satellite weather photo from the Internet.

http://www.teleport.com/-vincer/starter.html

Elementary school teacher Vince Ruggiano created this site, which contains information about his school, including pictures of students and administrators. It also describes many other Web sites Vince thinks would interest elementary and secondary teachers. When you click the name of a Web site, Vince recommends the web software that will transfer you to that location.

http://www.whitehouse.gov

Yes, the White House. In 1995 this site contained many different types of information, from press releases and policy papers to pictures of Socks, the cat.

GOPHER

Developed at the University of Minnesota, gopher software lets you visit thousands of gopher sites around the world. Gopher does not do anything that could not be done before it was invented. It just allows you to do it without having to learn many confusing and complicated commands. Through gopher (which is available on most services) you can access documents, pictures, sounds, music, and graphics from all over the world. With Gopher most of the decisions are options from menus. Below are the addresses of a few gopher sites around the world that contain educational material. Note: on some systems you have to add Gopher. to the beginning of the addresses listed below:

chico.rice.edu

The Texas Studies Gopher at Rice University has a wealth of information about Texas, especially the social and natural history of the state. Although it can be used by anyone, it is designed for use by middle grades teachers and students.

Copernicus.bbn.com

This gopher has a number of resources related to education and contains some lesson plans under the national School Network Testbed option.

cosn.org

The Consortium for School Networking (CoSN) gopher is a rich source of information on the use of telecommunications in education. It has tutorials on the basics of educational telecommunications, projects you can collaborate on with other schools, and connections to hundreds of other resources on the Internet, such as the Center for Children and Technology gopher, NASA's Spacelink gopher site, AskERIC, and the BBN National School Network Testbed.

dewey.lib.ncsu.edu

This site at North Carolina State University has thousands of historic government documents in files that can be downloaded. Look in the Library Without Walls, Study Carrels, and History directories.

ericir.syr.edu

This is one of the most useful gopher sites for educators. You have probably used the ERIC microfiche collection of documents in your college library or the ERIC database on CD-ROM to search for papers on an education topic. (ERIC is short for Educational Resources Information Center.) This site, maintained by ERIC's Clearinghouse on Information and Technology at Syracuse University, has many types of resources, including a database of lesson plans, guides to the Internet, short papers on many different education topics, and services that let you do an ERIC search on the Internet if you don't have the ERIC CD-ROM database at your schools. If you have difficulty finding relevant material, the AskERIC service will take your request, do a search, and e-mail the results to you in a day or two.

ernest.ccs.carleton.ca

The Kindergarten to Grade 6 Corner on this gopher is for young children. It includes a section listing students looking for electronic penpals (called keypals).

AskERIC: Key Areas

    `Lesson Plans`   `AskERIC's Collectio`

FIGURE 8-6   A screen from the ERIC gopher site.

io.org/pub/human-rights

This Amnesty International site includes information on the organization and human rights abuses around the world.

niaid.nih.gov

This National Institutes of Health site has a large collection of databases and documents on AIDS, including the full text of articles from the *AIDS Treatment News* magazine.

nyork1.undp.org

The United Nations gopher contains important UN documents such as the charter, plus a large number of databases on educational, commercial, political, and social topics.

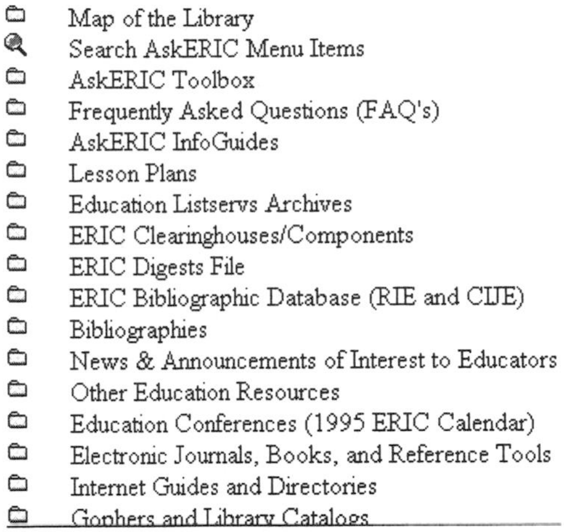

Map of the Library
Search AskERIC Menu Items
AskERIC Toolbox
Frequently Asked Questions (FAQ's)
AskERIC InfoGuides
Lesson Plans
Education Listservs Archives
ERIC Clearinghouses/Components
ERIC Digests File
ERIC Bibliographic Database (RIE and CIJE)
Bibliographies
News & Announcements of Interest to Educators
Other Education Resources
Education Conferences (1995 ERIC Calendar)
Electronic Journals, Books, and Reference Tools
Internet Guides and Directories
Gophers and Library Catalogs

FIGURE 8-7 This screen from the ERIC gopher site illustrates some of the services available.

nysernet.org

The New York state educational network supports this gopher, a resource for K–12 teachers interested in using telecommunications in the classroom.

riceinfo.rice.edu

Interested in census data? This gopher site at Rice University contains data from the current U.S. Census as well as from earlier ones.

stolaf.edu

This site has data on earthquakes. Look in the Internet Resources and Weather & Geography directories.

tiesnet.ties.k12.mn.us

Select the Best of K–12 Internet Resources at this gopher and you will find a wealth of resources for K–12 students and teachers.

wiretap.spies.com

This location has a collection of historical government documents. Look in the Government Documents and the U.S. Historical Documents directories.

FTP

FTP stands for File Transfer Protocol, the process by which you locate files on a remote computer and download them to your computer. The week this chapter was written, for example, one of the authors downloaded the following files:

1. From a computer at a university in London, a program for converting certain types of graphics files to formats that can be used by *PageMaker,* a desktop publishing program.

2. From the Microsoft FTP site (ftp.microsoft.com), a program called Internet Assistant that lets version 6.0 of Microsoft Word create HTML documents. HTML (hypertext markup language) documents are the basis for World Wide Web pages. Many schools have created their own Web sites by creating HTML documents onto a computer connected to the Internet. Programs such as *Mosaic* and *Netscape* contain readers that let you view and browse through HTML documents such as Web pages, but to easily create HTML documents yourself, you need additional software such as Internet Assistant.

3. From a computer in Finland, a program that searches hard disk drives for files that meet certain criteria (e.g., you could type lit* and it would look for all files with names that begin with "lit."

FTP sites contain everything from collections of software for IBM and Macintosh computers to files of historic photographs, copies of documents from the Kremlin, and much more. Until a few years ago getting FTPable files was complex and often unreliable. Now, however, programs like Mosaic and Gopher automate the entire process. FTP features are built into most easy-to-use telecommunications programs. A few FTP sites are listed below.

ftp.deneva.sdd.trw.com

This is the home of Project Gutenberg, a volunteer effort to make thousands of out-of-copyright books, poetry, and historic documents available over the Internet—from the CIA World Factbook to classics such as *Moby Dick* and *The Night Before Christmas.*

ftp.microsoft.com

Microsoft's site has hundreds of documents on Microsoft products, plus over a thousand software files that contain everything from upgrades of programs that fix bugs to files·that enhance the operation of Microsoft programs.

ftp.ncsa.uiuc.edu

This site for the National Center for Supercomputing Applications at the University of Illinois has Macintosh and Windows programs (versions of *Mosaic*) for connecting to the Internet.

NEWSGROUPS, LISTS, AND FORUMS

Thousands of groups on the Internet and commercial services were created so that people with similar interests could communicate with each other. You can find a newsgroup for language arts teachers, a discussion list about the works of William Blake, or a forum about shareware. At least 3,000 newsgroups, even more lists, and hundreds of forums are available through the Internet or the commercial services. They differ somewhat in how they work. To read the latest messages on a newsgroup, for example, you must use newsreader software to select the group and begin reading messages. Newsreaders are built into programs for accessing the Internet and the software for many of the commercial services.

Lists work a bit differently. Every time someone posts a message to a list, that message is sent to every member of the list. If you are a member, the next time you read your e-mail, the message will be in your "in box." Newsgroups are like a magazine you buy at the newsstand when you want to read it. You may not read every issue. Lists are like magazines you subscribe to. They regularly arrive in your mailbox, whether you read them or not. Some lists generate only a few messages a week, but others can forward 100 or more messages a day. We recommend subscribing to lists only when the topic is something so important you don't want to miss a single comment. Subscribe to newsgroups when you have an interest in the topic but don't want messages about it clogging up your mailbox every day. Many lists are "echoed" as newsgroups, which means you have the option of subscribing to them as lists or newsgroups.

Finally, each of the popular telecommunications services supports forums that work like newsgroups. The difference is that newsgroups are available to anyone with access to the Internet, whereas forums on the commercial services are available only to subscribers. A few newsgroups and lists are listed below. Anyone with access to the Internet can use newsgroups and lists. The forums available to you will depend on which commercial service you subscribe to.

Newsgroups

Following are the names of several education-related newsgroups and their topics.

K12ed.comp.literacy	Computer literacy
K12.chat.elementary	Elementary student chat
K12.chat.junior	Middle grades student chat
K12.chat.senior	High school student chat
K12.ed.lang.esp-eng	Spanish and English
K12.ed.soc-studies	Teaching social studies
K12.lang.art	Teaching language arts
K12.ed.tag	Teaching gifted and talented students
misc.education.language.english	Teaching English to non-English speakers

The text on the following page, which was posted on the K12.lang.art newsgroup in February 1995, describes a children's literature Web site.

The Children's Literature Web Guide is a World-Wide Web directory to Internet resources for Children's and Young Adult Literature.

It provides access to Children's Literature announcements and awards lists, list of recommended books, topical bibliographies, lesson plans, the full text of out-of-copyright children's "classics," information about a wide variety of children's authors, and more.

It is available at

http://www.ucalgary.ca/~dkbrown/index.html

and can be accessed using a World Wide Web browser such as "lynx" (for text-based Internet connections), or Netscape or Mosaic. If you need advice in how to gain access, e-mail me at dkbrown@acs.ucalgary.ca and I will try to help.

I am also looking for contributors. If you wish to make an announcement about an upcoming children's literature conference or event, or if you have bibliographies, literature-based lesson-plans, or related information that you are willing to share on the Internet, please get in touch with me.
David K. Brown
Doucette Library of Teaching Resources
University of Calgary

Figure 8-8 shows part of the menu from the Children's Literature Web site at the University of Calgary.

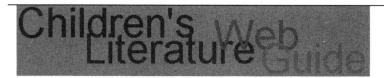

Check out What's New on the Children's Literature Web Guide. Last updated 27 February, 1995.

Table of Contents

- News, Announcements, and Press Releases NEW
- Children's Book Awards NEW
- Recommended Books and Bestsellers NEW
- Information about Authors
- Information about Fictional People and Places
- Electronic Children's Books

FIGURE 8-8   The Children's Literature Web site has many resources.

Lists

Subscribing to a list involves sending a message to the computer where the list is maintained. For details on how to subscribe, see your computer coordinator, copies of current magazines on telecommunications like *Classroom Connect* or *Netguide*, or any of the hundred or more books on using the Internet. One piece of information you need is the exact address of the list you want to join. Many books on using the Internet contain directories of list addresses, or you can get an electronic list of list addresses if you e-mail this message

Get list of lists

to this address

listserv@vm1.nodak.edu

There are thousands of lists, however, so be prepared for a very long e-mail message in return!

Following are the names of some of the lists that might interest language arts teachers. Some would be of interest to students.

AP-L	For teachers of advanced placement courses
ALLMUSIC	For students of all forms of music
APPLIT	The Appalachian Literature Discussion List
ARTIST-L	For student artists
BILINGUE-L	Developmental bilingual elementary education list
BLAKE-ONLINE	Works of William Blake discussion list
BRONTE	Discussion list on the Bronte sisters
CESNEWS	Coalition of Essential Schools News K–12.
CETH	Center for Electronic Texts in the Humanities
CHILDLIT	Children's Literature: Criticism and Theory
CL_NEWS	Teaching with collaborative learning
COGDEVEL	Cognitive Development discussion list
COLT-L	Discussion list on learning technologies
COSN	Discussion list of the Consortium for School Networking (CoSN)
CREWRT-L	Creative Writing in Education for Teachers
CSSWU-L	Chinese students discussion list
ECEOL-L	Early Childhood Online List
EDRES-L	Educational resources on the Internet
EDSTYLE	Learning Styles Theory and Research
EDTECH	Educational technology

EDUCOM-W	Women and information technologies
ELEMUG	Elementary School Users' Group
ENGLISH-TEACHERS	Discussion List for English Teachers
GC-L	Global Classroom Discussion List
GTRTI-L	Research and Teaching with Global Information Technologies
H-AMSTDY	American Studies discussion list
HEMING-L	Hemingway Society Discussion List
HST-L	NASA Classroom of the Future discussion list
HYPEREDU	Hypertext in Education discussion List
ICWP-L	International Center for Women Playwrights
INCLASS	Using the Internet in the classroom
INTER-EU	International Educators discussion list
ITD-JNL	Information and technology for the disabled
JEI-L	Technology in education
K12PALS	To propose telecommunications projects and list requests for keypals
KIDLIT-L	Children and Youth Literature
KIDCAFE	Discussion list for youth
KIDZMAIL	Discussion list for kids
LEARNER	Adults learning to read and write can post messages
MULT-ED	Multicultural Education Discussion List
NASAIP-L	NASA Internet Project
PBL-LIST	Problem-Based Learning in Education
SCOLT	Southern conference on language teaching
SHAKSPER	Student discussion list on Shakespeare
SIGTEL-L	Special Interest Group on Educational Telecommunications
SS435-L	Elementary teacher education
T-AMLIT	Teaching American Literatures
TEACHING	Teaching discussion list
TEACH-L	For the exchange of ideas about classroom dynamics
TEACHEFT	Teaching effectiveness
TEACHNET	For students and teachers
T321-L	Teaching Science in Elementary Schools
WAC-L	Writing Across the Curriculum
WIOLE-L	Writing Intensive Online Learning Environment
WVNK12-L	Internet Access for K–12 Schools list

A NOTE ON THE HALF-LIFE OF LISTS, NEWSGROUPS, WEB, GOPHER, AND FTP SITES

The resources mentioned in this chapter were operating in February 1995, but if they are a typical collection of Internet resources, by the time you read this book, some will be enhanced and look quite different from the way they did in 1995, some will look the same, and some will not exist anymore. Unlike books and journals at the library, which remain essentially the same year after year, electronic resources evolve, change, and sometimes die. Of course, there are thousands of resources not mentioned in this chapter that will interest you—some were not included because there was not enough space, and some have been created and become operational since this chapter was written. Exploring sites such as AskERIC that keep track of new resources is a good way to locate new resources.

USING ELECTRONIC RESOURCES IN THE CLASSROOM

So many resources are available through commercial services and the Internet that it is easy to get lost in the electronic forest and never find your way to the highway. Many teachers look at the complexity of the Internet and decide they just don't want to take the time to explore all that is there. A wise choice. Exploring the Internet can become a full-time preoccupation. Other teachers may become familiar with one aspect of the Internet, such as electronic mail, and become experts on that feature while ignoring everything else. That may be a wise choice at least in the beginning. Get comfortable with one thing before exploring others. For most teachers our advice is to select one or two things that interest you and explore them in depth. However, if you are just beginning, we suggest you also become aware of what is out there before selecting your primary targets for exploration.

To help you think about uses that might interest you, some of the services most relevant to literacy education are briefly described in this section. The organization of this section is an adaptation of the format proposed by Harris (1994), who divided educational telecomputing activities into categories according to the underlying instructional model used. Three general categories are *interpersonal exchanges*, *information gathering*, and *problem solving projects*. Case 1 at the beginning of this chapter is an example of a teacher using telecommunications resources for interpersonal exchanges. Jean heard from teachers and parents all over the country with regard to whole language instruction. Larry's use of Virginia's PEN to put students in contact with Thomas Jefferson is another example of interpersonal exchanges, but because students had a specific purpose in mind, Case 2 has some aspects of problem solving as well. Joan's project is in the general category of information gathering because data were collected from many different sites, but Case 3 is also a problem solving project because it included collaborative writing across the sites. Harris subdivides the three general types of uses into several subtypes. Each of those will be discussed below with examples along with some additional categories we have added.

Interpersonal Exchanges

Most education uses of telecommunications involve talking to others. One person may talk to one other person using standard e-mail, or to many others through participation in one of the thousands of special newsgroups, forums, or lists. Or the talking may be group to group, as described in Joan's classroom in Case 3. Her class communicated with classes of students in several other countries. Six different types of interpersonal exchanges are popular today: keypals, global classrooms, electronic appearances, electronic mentoring, impersonations, and special interest groups (SIGs).

KeyPals.   Thousands of students each year communicate via e-mail with students in other schools, states, and countries. Stan Smith, a 7th-grade teacher in Missouri, says students like e-mail "because part of what drives the kids' enthusiasm for going online is their desire to communicate with other students. They think that it's great to make a new friend in a distant state or country—especially a friend of the opposite sex" (Crim, 1995, p. 76). Below are a few samples of messages asking for keypals. The addresses of the teachers are not included because these requests were made in early 1995 and may not be active today.

```
I teach Spanish at North Medford High School in Medford,
OR. My students would like to communicate with young people
from Spanish-speaking countries to foster friendships and
cultural awareness/understanding.

I am looking for keypals to communicate with my fifth and
sixth grade gifted students in Lee's Summit, MO. We're
seeking English speakers from countries outside the U.S. to
develop friendships and greater understanding. This will be
our first experience.

I teach world literature to eleventh graders in a Chat-
tanooga high school. We'd love some keypals in Nigeria,
Japan, China, and/or India.

I teach English as a foreign language in a kibbutz regional
jr./sr. high school in Upper Galilee in Israel. I have a top
level eighth grade class and eleventh grade class, with a bit
less than 30 students. I would like to link each class to one
of similar size and grade outside of Israel. I am looking for
native English speakers or good ESL/EFL students.

Sergey Rulenko, the headmaster of a junior technology school
in Siberia, Russia, requests keypals for his students. They
are 15 and are learning English and technical subjects.

I teach first grade in Beaumont, Texas. I want to encour-
age my new first grades to read by corresponding with
other students. If you're interested we'll begin as soon
as possible!
```

Global Classrooms.   Many telecommunications projects involve group to group interactions. For example, Harris (1994) described how American literature classes at two schools read *The Glass Menagerie* together and discussed the play via e-mail. Telecommunications can take students beyond the classroom walls and make the world their classroom. For details on how one teacher used class-to-class telecommunications, see Montoya (1992). Below are a few examples of the type of messages teachers post to establish links between classes. We have not included the teacher's e-mail addresses since these posts were made in early 1995 and may not be active now.

I am a teacher/librarian at Wanniasa Hills Primary School in a suburb of Canberra. I am working with grades five and six on the effects of drought on people, the land, and animals. We are applying de Bono's Six Thinking Hats and Gwen Gawaith's Action Learning steps in our investigation. We would like to contact people living in drought areas who would like to assist us in learning about this topic. We welcome drought-related information from anyone.

I am a sixth grade teacher in Mendocino, California, seeking to telecommunicate with a class outside the U.S. to arrange an Environmental Box exchange. The purpose is to gain a deeper understanding of each local environment and how it affects and is affected by lifestyles of the people who live there. Students will plan and discuss the exchange by e-mail. Each will contribute at least one item for the box with museum catalog cards telling about the item. Items might include samples of flora and fauna, audio or video tapes, postcards, photos, newspaper articles, and so on. Students will discuss the environment after the exchange. I would like to begin this project the end of October.

Our fourth graders at Audubon Elementary School, Baton Rouge, LA, would like to correspond with others studying threatened and endangered species. We're also learning to use CD-ROMs, scanners, translation software, and telecommunications. Also, our fifth grade gifted classes are planning a "trip" around the French-speaking world. We'd like to learn about the customs and habits of the countries we might visit. We'd like to hear your ideas for other activities and any information about Francophone countries.

I teach three tenth grade English classes of 30 students each in Eugene, OR. I'd like to match my classes with three other classes for a cultural exchange project. We can be flexible with scheduling and content.

```
I teach English to eleventh grade honors students and
twelfth grade U.S. government students at Hawthorne High
School in Hawthorne, California. We have a multi-ethnic
student body of 3000 with Hispanics comprising the majori-
ty. I seek advice on helping my students connect to others
for writing projects.
```

Electronic Appearances.   Guest appearances by community leaders, authors, and other interesting people are often highlights of a school year, especially if the students are reading about them or reading works by them. However, the limitations of geography and time mean that most of the people you would like your students to meet won't be able to come to your classroom. One alternative is to make contact electronically. Many authors, for example, have electronic mail accounts, and quite a few are willing to correspond with students who are reading their works.

Electronic Mentoring.   Sam Houston State University is one of several that has created an electronic support network for new teachers. Graduates of SHSU can use their e-mail accounts to communicate with each other and with faculty at SHSU after they begin their teaching careers. Many find this service an excellent way to get advice, help, and support. Lists and newsgroups sponsored by special interest groups are another source of support and advice for teachers.

Electronic mentoring also is used with students. At the University of Houston, for example, teacher education students in a reading methods course taught by Lee Mountain worked with elementary children who were writing papers. The teacher education students were an audience for the children's writing and helped them edit and enhance their compositions.

Telecommunications may provide a way for writers, journalists, scientists, and business people to participate more fully in the education process via mentoring activities supported by e-mail.

Impersonations.   Case 2 at the beginning of this chapter described the use of telecommunications to put students in contact with a Thomas Jefferson impersonator. This use, which was pioneered at the University of Virginia, is becoming more popular.

Special Interest Groups (SIGs).   Teachers and students are sure to find interesting opportunities for interpersonal exchanges among the many special interest groups (SIGs) available through the Internet or the commercial services. See this chapter's section on newsgroups, lists, and forums.

Information Gathering

A second type of telecomputing activity involves gathering information via the Internet. Some of the global classroom requests listed earlier fall into this category. Projects usually involve collaboration between at least two classrooms, and the focus of information gathering can be anything from the water quality of local streams to the games and folk tales of the regions where participating students live. Although some information gathering projects simply exchange information between classes, many involve pooled data analysis, such as comparing the water quality of different regions and the environmental regulations in place. Often a report will be produced and electronically published on the Internet. A few collaborative projects have created databases that other schools can access via the Internet.

Another information gathering use of the Internet is tele-fieldtrips. Students can take electronic field trips to local sites such as zoos or museums, or distant locations such as the Louvre and outer space. Tele-fieldtrips also can involve receiving messages from students who are on real trips. For information on current fieldtrips involving students who correspond with classes, contact Nancy Sutherland at fieldtrip@bonita.cerf.fred.org.

Problem Solving Projects

The Internet can be used for projects that involve the solution of a problem. Some teachers set up Internet scavenger hunts that put students to work searching the Internet for information. A few of the thousands of databases available on the Internet and commercial services were discussed earlier in this chapter, and any of the many Internet guides will list more.

In most cases, however, problem-based projects are more than straightforward information searches. Students look for information because it will help them deal with a more authentic or realistic problem they or their teachers have posed. This might be termed *problem-based learning.* Harris (1994) describes five other types of problem-solving projects: *electronic process writing,* which involves students publishing their work on the Internet and receiving feedback from others; *parallel problem solving,* in which the same problem is posed to students in more than one class who then communicate over the Internet; *sequential creations,* in which papers, poems, and reports are written collaboratively by students in several classrooms; *simulations,* which are played by students at more than one school; and *social action projects,* which involve students at various locations in meaningful social action.

THE NATIONAL COUNCIL OF
TEACHERS OF ENGLISH NET

One of the many electronic resources for teachers is NCTENet, which is available on America Online or through a gopher. You will find NCTENet in the Education menu of AOL. When you select it, the menu in Figure 8-9 will be displayed, through which you can access information on upcoming conferences, job openings, and NCTE position statements. The push pin icon on the left takes you to Talk About Language Arts, a discussion section where you can take part in conversations about a number of topics, some of which are shown in Figure 8-10. Figures 8-11 and 8-12 display a message asking for information on Reading Recovery.

Online conversations in NCTENet's talk section are threaded, which means someone can start a subject such as Reading Recovery and, as people respond, other messages are added to that thread. Over a few weeks, several hundred messages might be added to the

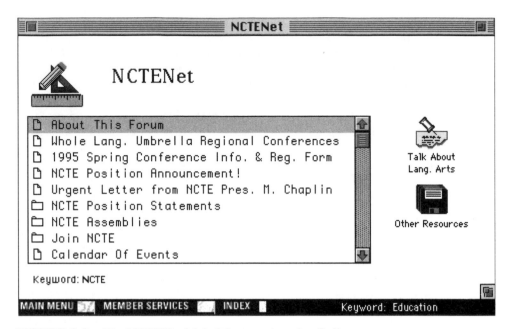

FIGURE 8-9 The NCTENet Main Menu on America Online.

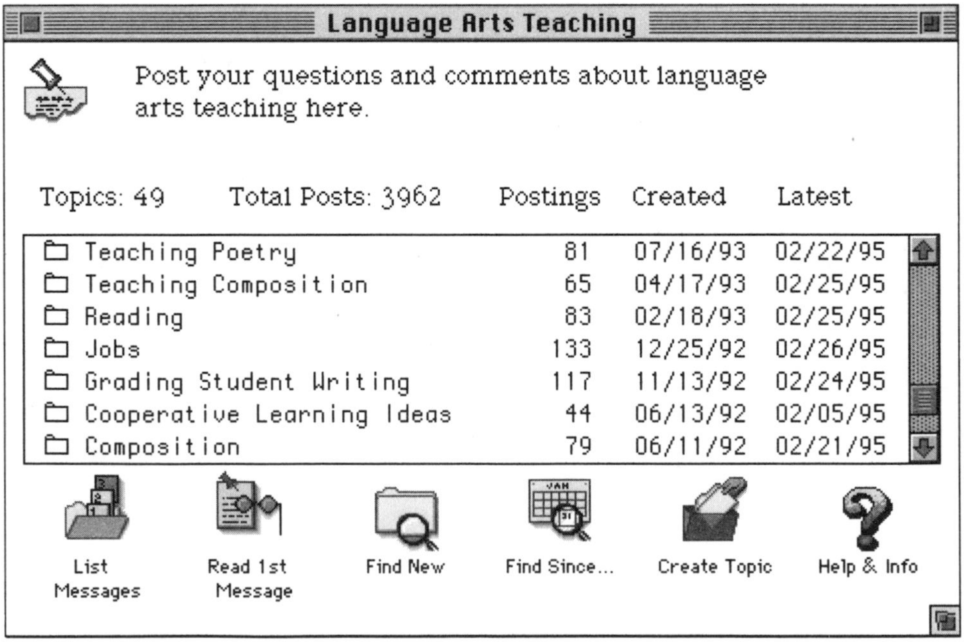

FIGURE 8-10 Topics in NCTENet's talk section.

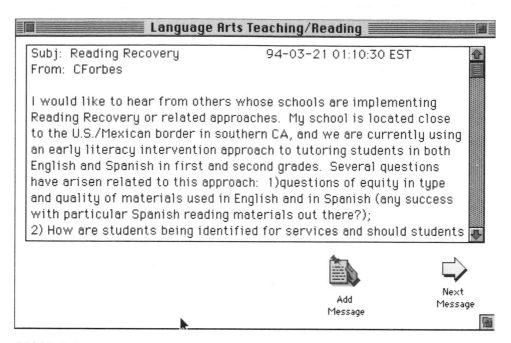

FIGURE 8-11   The first half of a message asking for information on Reading Recovery.

talk section of NCTENet, but only 10 of those related to the Reading Recovery topic will be threaded with the original message. To follow the thread, you can click the Next Message arrow and go to the next Reading Recovery message without having to read all the other messages that have been posted on other topics. To add a message to this thread, you would click the Add Message icon and then type your comments.

In NCTENet's main menu (see Figure 8-9), you will see a diskette icon labeled Other Resources. Click it and a scrollable list of materials you can download is displayed. As shown in Figure 8-13, several types of documents can be downloaded—for example, enrollment forms for a conference, an English glossary, a list of best-selling children's books, an index of NCTE publications, and a bibliography of publications on a certain topic. Often the brief descriptions on this screen are not enough to let you decide whether you want the document or not. You can click the Get Description button at the bottom of the screen and learn more about the document or program. If you decide you want it, you can click Download Now and a copy will be transferred to your computer and stored on your hard drive.

NCTENet on America Online is one example of several hundred resources of interest to literacy teachers currently available on commercial services. The drawback, of course, to access through services like America Online is the monthly fee you must pay. Fortunately, many of the resources on AOL and other commercial services are available through the Internet. For example, NCTE's electronic resources can be accessed via an Internet gopher. If you gopher to marvin.clemson.edu, one of the options will be NCTE. The mar-

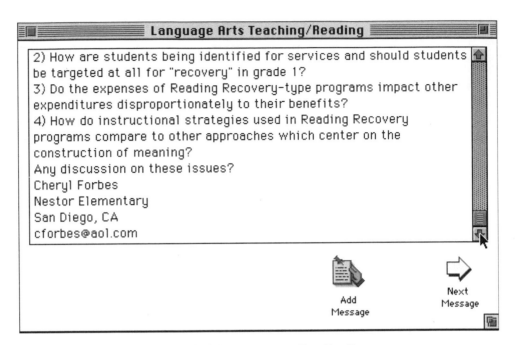

FIGURE 8-12   The second half of the message on Reading Recovery.

vin.clemson.edu gopher site is maintained by the Document Design Lab at Clemson University in South Carolina and is also the home of the Carolina Alliance for Computers and Writing. Using the Internet gopher is not as convenient as using the service on AOL, but the price for connect time, if you have a free Internet connection, is $0.

THE NEW YORK EDUCATION GOPHER SITE

One of the most useful gopher sites on the Internet is the one maintained by the New York State Education Department. The address is unix5.nysed.gov. The following message, which was downloaded from this site, explains the roles this site plays.

```
This gopher is run by the Office of Telecommunications Poli-
cy Analysis and Development, at the New York State Educa-
tion Department in Albany NY.

OTPAD is an office created from people of various other
parts of the department. The gopher administrator, for
example, is officially a member of the Office of Elementary,
Middle and Secondary Education. The machine on which this
gopher runs is owned by the Office of Higher and Profession-
```

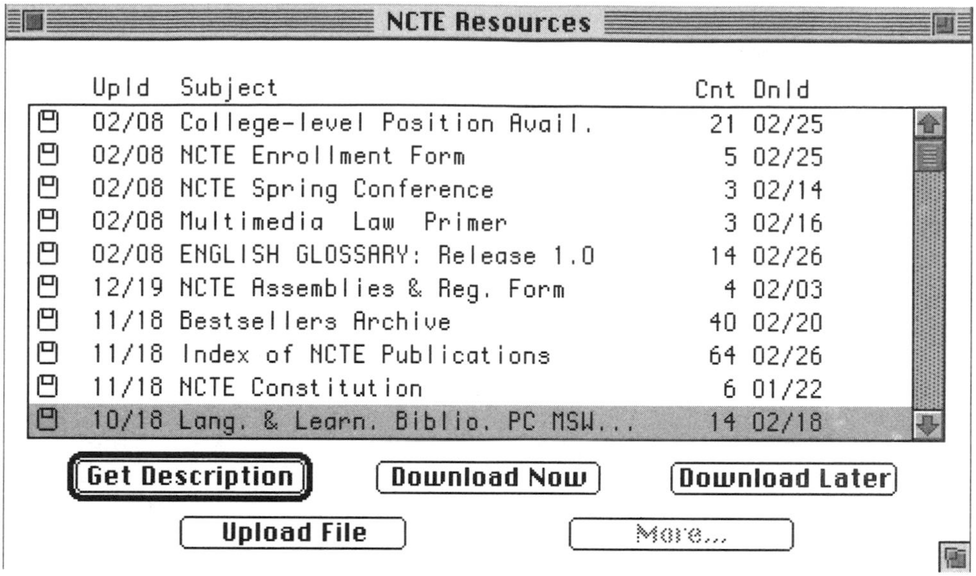

FIGURE 8-13   Some of the documents you can download from NCTENet.

al Education. The deputy commissioner responsible for this office, however, is the Deputy Commissioner for Cultural Education.

What we have set out to do here is serve two purposes: to collect and distribute information relating to telecommunications and telecommunications policy, so our advisory committee (ACT—Advisory Committee on Telecommunications) can look at one place and collect a great deal of information easily; and also to provide a gathering and organizing place for resources which may be of use to the classroom teacher.

The menu items which contain items which change most frequently are:

• Conferences, Calls for Papers—pretty self-explanatory, eh? We make an effort to ensure than no item in this folder is more than one month old and that few of the items in it are "stale." If you find one which is stale, please email gcasler@unix5.nysed.gov to alert him to the fact and he will remove it. Please put the word "feedback" in the subject line; he'll get to it more quickly that way.

• Internet Resources—this folder contains links to lists of 'Net resources, training materials and guides to using the 'Net.

• K-12 News—this holds news items of interest to the K-12 education community, although others may find the items useful also. We make an effort to ensure that no item in this folder is more than one month old.

• K-12 Resources—this folder holds other folders. The folders in this one are curriculum areas grouped according to the method used by the Curriculum and Assessment Council of New York State. In the curriculum folders are resources from the 'Net which may be of use to classroom teachers. This part of the project was started in response to the recognition that, although there are valuable teaching resources available on the 'Net, very few teachers have the luxury of being able to spend hours surfing in search of them.

• Requests for Comment—this folder includes not only requests for comment but also requests for collaboration on various telecomm projects from around the world. An effort is make to ensure that no item in this folder is more than one week old.

• TelecommInfo—this folder contains news from the world of telecomm policy and two folders: Reference Desk (archives of documents and speeches relating to telecomm policy) and Reading Room (articles and essays relating to telecomm policy—OPINIONATED ARTICLES occur in this area).

Finally, this gopher is constantly changing. To help folks keep up with the changes without having to log in each day and go through several levels of menus trying to remember what wasn't there yesterday, we have established a mailing list. This list sends at most one piece of mail per day (and at least one piece of mail per week), detailing the changes which have been made to the gopher since that last piece of mail. To subscribe to this mailing list, send email to gcasler@unix5.nysed.gov with the word subscribe in the SUBJECT field.

A Call for Participation

We would like you to join us in the growth of this gopher. There are two ways you can do this, at present:

• you can provide feedback. If you would like to comment on the products and services offered on this gopher, please email the gopher administrator, gcasler@unix5.nysed.gov with the word "feedback" in the subject field. All pieces of email will be read, but we have decided to keep replies to a minimum. This will allow staff to continue feeding the gopher.

• you can work with us as a scout. If your favorite information source does not show up on this gopher, drop a line to gcasler@unix5.nysed.gov with the word "scout" in the subject line. We do not plan on competing with The InterNIC Internet Scout, Gopher Jewels, Net-Happenings or any of the other "What's Out There" services. What we do want to do is make this gopher as organized and complete as possible, given available human and financial resources.

As you can see, the New York Education gopher has a number of resources for literacy educators. Figure 8-14 shows the first menu you see on this service. It contains several lists of resources available at other sites on the Internet. Figure 8-15 shows the K–12 Resources menu, and Figure 8-16 is part of the English–Language Arts menu.

NON-ELECTRONIC SOURCES OF INFORMATION

Although the information highway is a major source of information, we do not think that all information will be distributed electronically anytime in the near future. Other resources are relevant for the use of information technology in literacy education. We cover some of these below.

Journals and Magazines

The major journals and magazines on reading and language arts publish papers on the use of technology, including telecommunications. In addition, journals

About This Gopher
Conferences, Calls for Papers
Education News
GovernmentInfo
Higher Education
Internet Resources
K-12 Resources
Requests for Comment or Collaboration
TelecommInfo
TelecommNews
NYSERNet's ftp site (test only)
Search the Internet
State Library's ftp site (test only)

FIGURE 8-14   Resources on the New York Education gopher.

and magazines like *Computers in the Schools*, *The Computing Teacher*, and *Technology and Learning* regularly publish papers on the use of technology for literacy instruction. Two publications of special interest are described below.

Classroom Connect. First published in 1994, *Classroom Connect* focuses on the use of the Internet by teachers and librarians. Based on the first two issues, we highly recommend this publication for teachers interested in using telecommunications in the classroom. It is available from Wentworth Worldwide Media, 800-638-1639.

- Arts & Humanities
- Disability Resources & Information
- English-Language Arts
- General
- Health, PhysEd & Home Ec
- Languages Other than English
- Math, Science & Technology
- Occupational and Technical
- Other Educational Gophers
- Social Studies
- Zip (Get There Faster)

FIGURE 8-15 The K–12 Resources menu on the New York Education gopher.

- Bibliography Styles (from Writer's Workshop, UIUC)
- Book Discussions and Reviews
- Cause and Effect - Expository Writing -- Lesson Plan
- Collection of Mini-Lesson Plans from AskEric (all grade levels)
- Communications and Mass Communications Resources
- Creative Writing in a Global Classroom -- Lesson Plan
- Database of Student Research in Language Arts
- Drama (from CMU's English-Server - often busy)
- Egyptian Literature: Classroom Activity Plan
- English Instructor's Source Book for Running a Discussion
- English Server at Carnegie-Mellon (often busy, always slow)
- Essay Starters in Science (from Nat'l Inst. of Science & Tech.)
- Essay Starters in Social Studies
- Flight: Confluence of Technology and Dreams -- Lesson Plan
- Index of Poetry magazine
- Palindrome Collection

FIGURE 8-16 Part of the English-Language Arts menu on the New York Education gopher.

The Writing Notebook.   This established journal has been published for over 10 years. *The Writing Notebook* carries articles on the use of telecommunications and other types of information technology in the classroom. The focus is on writing although the context may be reading/language arts, science, social studies, or any other aspect of the curriculum. It covers both elementary and high school and is available from Visions for Learning, PO Box 1268, Eugene, Oregon 97440-1268, 503-344-7125.

Organizations and Conferences

Large organizations such as the International Reading Association (IRA) and the National Council of Teachers of English (NCTE) hold annual meetings that usually include many sessions on how to integrate technology into literacy instruction at every level. However, the expense of attending a national or international conference can be considerable if you teach in Southern California and the conference is in Boston. In such cases the cost of registration, airfare, and hotel can easily exceed $1500 per person. There are, however, many regional and state organizations affiliated with IRA, NCTE, and other groups. They generally hold annual conferences as well. Registration fees and hotel expenses are often lower for regional and state conferences, and you generally will be able to drive to these meetings. Like the national meetings of IRA and NCTE, these conferences include many opportunities to hear other teachers talk about the way they are using technology in their classrooms. When the national IRA and NCTE conferences are near enough to be affordable, consider attending these excellent meetings. Others you may find useful are described below.

Technology, Reading, and Learning Difficulties Conference.   This international conference, held annually for 15 years, is the only meeting we know of that concentrates specifically on technology and literacy. The conference program is generally a mix of workshops, presentations, and demonstrations. The emphasis here tends to be on practical "I can use this in my classroom" topics and is highly recommended. The conference has strands for virtually every type of literacy education, from early childhood to adult literacy, and it has strands for different types of technology, including telecommunications, multimedia, and hypermedia. The conference is held in January each year in San Francisco. For more information contact Diane Frost, TRLD Conference, 1070 Crows Nest Way, Richmond, CA 94803, 800-255-2218 or 510- 222-1249.

International Society for Technology in Education (ISTE).   One of the largest groups dedicated to the topic of technology use in education, ISTE publishes a number of journals, newsletters, and books and also distributes materials from other publishers as well. *The Computing Teacher* is the organization's flagship journal. Others published by ISTE include the *Journal of Research on Computing in Education, Microsoft Works in Education, Telecommunications in Education,* and the *Computer-Assisted English Language Learning Journal.* Many of ISTE's publications are about practical issues of interest to teachers.

The National Educational Computing Conference, which is managed by ISTE, is the largest annual conference on technology in education. It is held in June each year. Each November ISTE sponsors Ed-Tel, a conference on the use of telecommunications in education. ISTE's comprehensive catalog of resources for technology-using educators lists regional and state affiliates. Current contact information is provided for a variety of groups—from the Alaska Society for Technology in Education to the Israeli Association for Computers in Education. You can get a copy of the current ISTE catalog from: ISTE, 1787 Agate Street, Eugene, OR 97403-1923. ISTE has a gopher site on the Internet (iste-gopher.uoregon.edu.) and a forum on America Online.

Association for the Advancement of Computing in Education (AACE).   This organization publishes journals on the use of technology in education and holds conferences. AACE's journals are *Educational Technology Review*, *International Journal of Educational Telecommunications*, *Journal of Artificial Intelligence in Education*, *Journal of Computers in Mathematics and Science Teaching*, *Journal of Educational Multimedia and Hypermedia*, *Journal of Technology and Teacher Education*. AACE's conferences are Ed-Media: World Conference on Educational Multimedia and Hypermedia; AI-ED: World conference on Artificial Intelligence in Education; SITE: Society for Information Technology and Teacher Education Conference. For additional information on this organization contact AACE, PO Box 2966, Charlottesville, VA 22902, 804-973-3987. Fax: 804-978-7449. E-mail: AACE@Virginia.edu.

State and Regional Organizations.   In virtually every state there are organizations of teachers who use technology. These groups can be an important source of support for beginning teachers who are interested in using technology. Some of the larger groups, like California's CUE (Computer Using Educators), publish a newsletter or journal. Many hold at least one annual conference, and several have both state and regional meetings. California's CUE (saarmst@ctp.org) and the Texas Computer Education Association (kathyk@tenet.edu), for example, hold at least one statewide conference a year as well as regional meetings. Two other states, Florida and Michigan, have large conferences that draw attendees from several states. Contact information for many regional and state organizations can be found in the ISTE catalog mentioned earlier. To contact the Texas Computer Education Association, you can write to Anne Meyen, 4011 Milton, Houston, TX 77005. For information about the Florida Educational Technology Conference, contact Peter Lenkway, Technology Center, 120 Lowery Place, S.W., Fort Walton Beach, FL 32548.

SUMMARY

Educational telecommunications is a large and growing enterprise. It provides the literacy teacher with access to the Internet or commercial services like America Online with a rich collection of resources that can be used in many ways in the classroom. It also changes the role of the literacy teacher as the world becomes less print based and much more dependent on information displayed on the screen of a computer. The ability to effectively use e-mail, electronic databases, newsgroups, and forums will be important, even critical, for many jobs in the future.

MICROTEACHING ACTIVITIES

1. Explore some of the newsgroups, lists, or forums mentioned in this chapter. Select two that seem particularly useful for teachers or students at the level you plan to teach. Make a presentation in your class that illustrates how to access one of the services and demonstrates the type of materials available.
2. Use the ERIC gopher mentioned in the chapter to search for information on a particular topic such as "process writing using computers" or "Whole language instruction and computer support." Do an ERIC search, look for ERIC Digests on the topic, and submit an AskERIC request. Summarize the results of your search in a 1- to 4-page paper that highlights the sources of relevant information, the new information you learned, and the implications of that information for your teaching plans. Include a lesson plan from the ERIC lesson plan database if a plan appropriate to your topic is available.
3. Select one of the World Wide Web sites listed in this chapter (or another one you are familiar with) and demonstrate it in class. Produce a 1- to 3-page handout on the Web site that describes the resources available and how they might be used in the classroom.

REFERENCES

Crim, E. (1995, February). Connected classrooms. *Online Access,* 74–78.

Harris, J. (1994). A Model for integration of telecomputing in precollege curricula. In J. Willis, B. Robin, & D. Willis (Eds.), *Technology and Teacher Education Annual— 1994* (pp. 637–642). Boston: Allyn & Bacon.

Montoya, I. (1992). Put a star in your classroom. *The Computing Teacher, 20*(4), 18–19.

An Introduction to Microteaching

One of the major problems of attempting to explore how to be a professional teacher by reading a textbook is the theory-practice gap. That gap is the difference between reading about something and actually trying to do it. The theory-practice gap is something every profession must grapple with when considering how the next generation should be prepared. In medicine, students first take many "theory" courses that provide background knowledge. Then they proceed through several years of education that involve both classroom "theory" courses and a wide range of "on the job" experiences—clerkships, internships, and other types of experiences that involve the student in actual practice under the tutelage of an experienced professional. In other professional fields the theory-practice gap may be spanned by apprenticeships. In teacher education, students typically complete a series of theory courses such as foundations of education, educational psychology, and child development before embarking on courses that deal specifically with professional practice. This second set of courses generally includes several methods courses and a course on classroom management. Then, the final component of preservice education is usually some sort of student teaching experience or internship. Preservice teacher education thus tends to progress along a continuum that begins with basic or theoretical courses such as foundations of education, which is generally taught in a traditional lecture/discussion format, and ends with the teacher education student in charge of a classroom under the mentorship of an experienced teacher.

The general progression described above of course has many variations. Methods courses, for example, are sometimes taught in the same lecture/discussion format as the foundations and educational psychology courses. Or they may include many experiences in which students practice teaching lessons. If a teacher education program is based on a professional development school (PDS) model, the practice may occur in real classrooms with real children. Unfortunately, few colleges and universities fund teacher education programs at the level required to use a full PDS model, which is similar to the internship experience in medicine. A more affordable model that many teacher education programs use includes observing classrooms (via video or school visits) and practice in the university classroom before completing a semester of student teaching. For example, when aspects of the whole language approach are discussed in a reading/language arts methods class, students might view a video of a teacher using that approach and then develop their own whole language lessons. In some classes, where time permits, they may teach those lessons to other students in the class. One or two students, for example, might take the role of teacher and teacher aide while some or all the other students take the role of 4th-grade students. This approach, which is sometimes called role playing, is better known as microteaching. Whatever the name, the goal is to give students some experience, in the relatively safe environment of the college classroom, with professional practice. Although not the same as working in a real classroom, it does help bridge the gap between textbook theory and classroom practice. Many students, when they microteach for the first time, find that things that seemed clear when they read about them in the textbook are actually quite complex and unclear. It is much better to have that particular insight in a methods class than in front of a group of eager 4th-grade students.

DEFINITION OF MICROTEACHING

Although many variations on the concept of microteaching are found in preservice teacher education, all involve delivering a short, usually 5–20 minutes, mini-lesson to a group. Typically, the person who takes the role of teacher is a student in a methods class, and the people who take the roles of pupils are other students in that class. Sometimes each student prepares and teaches the lesson, but in many classes students are organized into groups of two to four for microteaching.

TYPICAL MICROTEACHING FORMATS

Microteaching can be organized in several different formats. Cruickshank and Metcalf (1990), for example, take a technical-skills approach that emphasizes specific skills thought to be important to teaching. The approach they describe has seven steps:

1. Students are given or select a particular technical skill—such as waiting the appropriate time after asking a question.
2. They read about the skill in books, articles, or material prepared especially for the class.
3. They observe a master teacher demonstrate the skill. The demonstration may be via a video link to classrooms in a cooperating school, or via videotape, videodisk, or CD-ROM digital video.
4. The student prepares a lesson of 3–5 minutes to demonstrate the skill.

5. The student teaches the mini-lesson to a group of peers who play the roles of pupils. The lesson is videotaped.
6. The student who taught the lesson, the instructor, and some or all of the class critique the lesson using the videotape.
7. The student, with the help of the instructor, comes to a decision about whether the skill was demonstrated adequately or the lesson should be retaught.

If you have read the chapters in this book, you may notice that the microteaching procedure described above is quite behavioral. It breaks down teaching into technical skills, has the student practice those skills, provides feedback on performance, and requires additional practice if the skill has not been mastered. The seven-step procedure described above does not reflect the spirit of this text, which is based on constructivist approaches to teaching and learning rather than behavioral approaches. Alternative ways of approaching microteaching are based on the reflective practice model, which is a constructivist approach to preparing professionals.

In their review of microteaching, Freiberg and Waxman (1990, p. 626) differentiate behavioral microteaching from reflective microteaching:

> The microteaching format includes a process in which a preservice student learns and then employs a series of teaching behaviors (e.g., nonverbal cues; wait time for questioning . . .). These skills are usually demonstrated to preservice teachers during methods-related coursework. Later the students are asked to teach a group of five to six other preservice students for 10 to 20 minutes. The minilesson was videotaped, and the student received feedback from the instructor or a graduate student. The feedback was provided while the student and the instructor watched the videotape of the minilesson . . ., using a checklist in many instances. . . . Students were then graded on their ability to perform a specific teaching behavior during the microteaching lesson. Both students and educators, however, questioned the appropriateness of this summative use of microteaching. . . . The opportunity for reflection was not part of the simulated learning experience. . . . The summative environment of many microteaching situations provided minimal opportunities for either exploration or reflection. Recent modifications of the microteaching process, however, have provided opportunities to use a reflective tool. Rather than simulating teaching's being a summative occurrence, the opportunity exists for formative feedback, peer-feedback, and self-assessment during microteaching experiences. Building in the opportunities and providing the opportunity and climate for reflection both individually and collectively in cohort groups increases the chance of professional growth. The combination of experiences and reflection equals growth.

Freiberg and Waxman (1988) as well as others, including MacLeod and McIntyre (1977) and MacLeod (1987), have developed microteaching strategies that emphasize reflective teaching rather than technical skills. They emphasize a more global approach and argue that self-analysis of the videotaped microteaching activities is critical. Peterson and Peterson (1985) use the term "microteaching" for technical skills training and "reflective teaching" for experiences based on the reflective practice model. We have decided to use "microteaching" for both because the term is already in use and has many different variations.

VARIATIONS

As noted in the previous section, microteaching experiences can be based on different theories of teaching and learning. Behavioral approaches generally emphasize specific, technical skills that are to be mastered by the student. Reflective or constructivist approaches emphasize helping students develop the ability to think about the teaching environment, construct an understanding of what it means to teach in a particular way, make on-the-fly decisions about what to do, and reflect on their performance with an eye toward deciding what they might do differently in future teaching activities.

Use of Videotape

Variations in the microteaching process can depend on the time available, the purpose, and whether microteaching is a primary instructional approach or supportive of other approaches. The use of videotape is a good example. In situations where time is short, videotaping may be eliminated and discussion of the microtaught mini-lesson may begin immediately after the lesson ends. On the other hand, if time is available, the lesson may be videotaped and then played back in the next class period during an extended exploration of the lesson. We generally recommend that you videotape microteaching if it will be a major focus of the course and there are no more than 10–12 students in the course. If there are 20 or more students in the class, extended analysis of videotaped microteaching episodes is difficult unless it is done individually or in small groups outside the class period. In another common format, which reduces the amount of class time required for microteaching, the student does a self-evaluation of the videotaped microteaching and has a peer-evaluation from two to three other students in the class. The self- and peer-evaluations are completed outside of class.

Use of Classroom Video

Another variation involves the use of video from classrooms as a precursor to microteaching. Behavioral approaches often use video of expert teachers in action to demonstrate the "right" way to perform a particular skill. Constructivist approaches often use video of typical teachers in action as a focal point for reflective discussions of teaching. In either case, the time available and the availability of appropriate video often determine whether video is used.

Format and Style of Feedback and Debriefing

The type of feedback or debriefing (often a group discussion of the lesson led by the instructor) that follows teaching the mini-lesson varies considerably. When time is limited, the temptation is to eliminate feedback and debriefing or to restrict them to a few instructor comments. However, some of the available research suggests the post–mini-lesson activities may be quite important. In a study of microteaching in a methods course, Yeaney (1978) found that the procedure was much more effective when the student who did the microteaching either did a self-evaluation or received feedback from the instructor.

Summative Evaluation, Formative Evaluation, or Reflection?

Some systems treat microteaching as the last step in a sequence of instruction. The microteaching exercise is where the preservice teacher education students demonstrate that they have mastered the targeted teaching skills. Failure to demonstrate those skills is an indication that the student needs more work. Another way to look at microteaching is to consider it one of many experiences a student will have that provides an opportunity for feedback. Much more polished performance, for example, is expected of a student who is about to enter student teaching than is expected of students who are just beginning their professional program. Using this formative approach, students still receive feedback, usually from the instructor and often from other students, but the purpose of the feedback is to give students information they can use to do their own self-evaluation.

Still others who use microteaching adopt a reflective model that views the experience as a way of helping students focus on the decisions and context of teaching. In this approach the post–mini-lesson session is more of a debriefing in which issues and points are raised by the group (the instructor and the class), rather than an evaluation session in which students learn if they have met the criteria to pass that activity or not.

Although some teacher educators treat the three alternatives discussed here—summative evaluation, formative evaluation, and reflection–as either/or options, others believe each has its place in teacher education. Summative evaluation, with detailed guidelines and specific expectations, might be used with students just beginning their teacher education program; formative evaluation might be used later; and near the end of the program a reflective model might be most appropriate.

Targeted Skill or Act of Teaching

As noted above, behavioral microteaching tends to concentrate on a specific skill—such as appropriate wait time after asking a question. Constructivists argue that teaching subskills out of context is inappropriate and does not lead to professional growth. They suggest a more holistic approach that allows students to practice teaching in context rather than practicing specific subskills of teaching. This is much like the whole language versus discrete skills argument in reading instruction, and there are just as many perspectives on the issue. In this book we have generally proposed microteaching activities that are more holistic, but a case can be made, especially with beginning teacher education students, for including some subskill microteaching as well.

Use of Checklists and Other Instruments

Microteaching based on behavioral models often includes evaluative components that rely on checklists or observation forms to evaluate a student's performance. More constructivist approaches often eliminate these instruments, but they may include handouts or guidesheets that provide an overview of the activity as well as some explanation of what is expected of participants at each point. For example, without some verbal or written explanation of the format for debriefing activities, students may be reluctant to ask questions about another student's mini-lesson.

SUGGESTED MICROTEACHING FORMAT

The format we suggest for microteaching is summarized below. It is an adaptation and combination of several formats for microteaching (Freiberg & Waxman, 1990) role playing (Joyce & Weil, 1986), and simulation (Freiberg & Driscoll, 1992; Willis, Hovey, & Hovey, 1987).

Keep a Journal

As you work on the various phases of microteaching outlined below, keep a journal that describes your experiences, your perspectives, and your analysis of the work. A journal is a running account of the important events and activities related to the microteaching activity. It should tell the story of your work, but it should be more than a "factual" account of the process. Include your views and opinions, concerns and issues, and your assessment of your performance and progress. Be sure, also, to include tips on the most useful sources of relevant information you found (include their location) as well as any problems or frustrations you had. If you found ways around the problems or frustrations, include them so other students can profit from your experience. End the journal for each microteaching activity with a reflective analysis of your work-to-date and aspects you plan to change the next time.

Phase 1: Search and Selection

The microteaching activities at the end of the chapters in this textbook are relatively general assignments. They specify an area of work and a general approach, but they are not specific enough to serve as all the guidelines you will need to complete the assignment. After you have selected one of the microteaching activities, you probably will have to do some homework before beginning to plan the mini-lesson you want to teach. Use telecommunications resources (see Chapter 8) to locate sources of lesson plans that might provide detailed guidelines. Use electronic databases such as ERIC on CD-ROM to search for articles and papers relevant to your topic. ERIC on CD-ROM is probably in the reference room of your college or university library. The learning resources center or educational computing center at your college also may be excellent sources of information.

Phase 2: Creating or Adapting a Lesson Plan

Some microteaching may involve using a lesson plan that is already available. The plan may have been included in the manual for the software you will use, or you may have selected it from a collection of lesson plans available online, in the library, or in the learning resource center. However, virtually any lesson you select will require some adaptation to fit your context. It may be necessary, for example, to use fewer computers because the number called for in the original lesson plan is not available. Issues such as the time available and the resources needed may force you to make many changes in the lesson plan. Adaptations may be made because your objectives are somewhat different from those of the teacher who created the lesson plan (or you will be using it with students of a different age or with different experiences). In any case, you should develop your own lesson plan, word processed of course. There are hundreds, if not thousands, of lesson plan formats. Use one of the formats supported and used in your teacher education program.

If the microteaching assignment you are doing does not involve adapting an existing lesson plan, you will have to write a plan from scratch. Again, you should use a format supported by your teacher education program. If you do not have experience writing lesson plans, before beginning your plan you may want to look at plans that have been developed by others.

Phase 3: Selecting the Mini-Lesson

A lesson plan can cover several hours, but the time available for a microteaching activity is generally too short to allow you to teach the entire lesson. Instead, you should select a portion of the lesson plan and teach that as a mini-lesson. In general, mini-lessons should be between 5–13 minutes in length. They should cover an important aspect of the lesson and illustrate some of the more important roles teachers and students play in this particular lesson.

Phase 4: Preparation

Lessons involving the use of technology can be tricky to pull off without some difficulties with the equipment, the software, or the student-technology interaction. In your lesson plan, be sure to include details of what is needed (software, hardware, room arrangements, printed materials including directions, consumables such as diskettes).

This is also the time to select participants. Although you may be creating a lesson plan for use in a 5th-grade classroom with 27 students, microteaching generally involves a smaller number of pupils (other students in the class who take the role of pupil). In general, microteaching seems to work best if you have 3–7 pupils.

If your mini-lesson involves work students must have completed before the lesson, make that assignment the week before the mini-lesson or supply prepared material they can use that takes the place of homework or student-created material.

Do at least one dry run of your lesson. Draft friends to be pupils and teach the lesson just as you plan to do in the class. You may be amazed at the number of things you did not think about that must be handled before the lesson can go smoothly.

If possible, on the day you are to do your mini-lesson, check out all the equipment to be sure it is working and that all the software you need is installed on the computers and works correctly. Do this at least an hour before your mini-lesson so that any problems you find can be corrected. This can be difficult to do in shared computer labs or in centers where many classes use the equipment. However, if it can be done it may save you and your pupils a great deal of frustration.

If your instructor has decided that the mini-lessons will be videotaped, be sure to check the videotaping arrangements. Is the camera available? Do you have a videotape? If microphones in addition to the one on the camera will be used, are they in place? If the camera operator will be one of the other students in the class, is that person familiar with the operation of this particular camera?

Phase 5: Preparing the Observers and the Simulated Pupils

When the time arrives for you to teach your mini-lesson, begin with an overview. Since you will not be delivering the entire lesson, it is important to set the scene by describing briefly the entire lesson and indicating where the mini-lesson fits in. Is it an introductory activity? Is it a capstone or finishing activity? Is it one of the things students will do in the middle of the lesson? What is the purpose of the mini-lesson and how does it relate to other activities in the lesson plan? Also, point out teaching strategies you want the observers to scrutinize carefully or points in the lesson you would like them to pay attention to so they can provide feedback or suggestions. For example, if you are concerned about a transition point from one type of activity to another, ask the observers and pupils to watch for the transition and think of ways it could be improved if it is a problem point. In general, you should always give the observers a task to do—pay attention to a particular skill that concerns you, such as asking questions; critically look at one of the roles you will play, such as coach or mentor; or think about the instructional strategies you will be using relative to the purpose of the lesson.

Phase 6: Teaching the Mini-Lesson

This phase is the heart of the activity. Teach the lesson as you would if your pupils were in the grade called for in the lesson plan. Because technology is required in most of the microteaching activities in this book, be sure to prepare backup options in case problems arise with some of the equipment. Computers and associated equipment are not yet as reliable as the chalkboard, the overhead projector, and the textbook. For example, if you will require students to connect to the Internet and go to a particular World Wide Web site, what will you do if the network is down when you teach your lesson? An option is to download the material from the Web site as a file and then tell students to use the Open Local File option in their Web software should the network connection not be available during the 10 minutes you will need it. The authors of this book will readily admit that they do not always prepare backup options when they depend on technology, but each can tell at least a few horror stories about technology that did not work or was not available at precisely the time we needed it.

Phase 7: Debriefing

Debriefing is an important, though often de-emphasized, aspect of microteaching. We prefer a debriefing phase that is more reflective than evaluative. We also prefer a group debriefing—the entire class if everyone participated as a teacher, pupil, or observer. If the instructor leads the debriefing, he or she may ask the student who taught the mini-lesson to comment on it. Were there rough spots? Were there things that you would do differently the next time? Are there unresolved questions or issues? Are there things about teaching the lesson that became apparent while it was being taught that were not before? Questions like these can prompt comments from the students who were observers and pupils. In addition, any issues the observers were asked to pay particular attention to in the preparation phase should be addressed in debriefing. Debriefing helps participants consolidate the concepts and procedures they learned through the microteaching exercise, and it helps students identify misconceptions or inaccurate assumptions about different teaching strategies.

Phase 8: Reflection on Action

The final phase, reflection on action, may be a continuation of debriefing. This final phase is a thoughtful evaluation of the microteaching activity. This can be done in the debriefing phase with all the students in the group participating. Another option is for this to be a personal activity that shows up in the journal you keep about your microteaching. Reflection on action involves considering your participation in the activity and the potential implications for future work. For many who are unsure of their own abilities, it becomes an affirmation that they can do many things well.

REFERENCES

Cruickshank, D., & Metcalf, K. (1990). Training within teacher preparation. In R. Houston, M. Haberman, & J. Sikula (Eds.), *Handbook of research on teacher education.* New York: Macmillan.

Freiberg, H. J., & Driscoll, A. (1992). Universal teaching strategies. Boston: Allyn & Bacon.

Freiberg, H. J., & Waxman, H. C. (1990). Changing teacher education. In R. Houston, M. Haberman, & J. Sikula (Eds.), *Handbook of research on teacher education.* New York: Macmillan.

Freiberg, H. J., & Waxman, H. C. (1988). Alternative feedback approaches for improving student teachers' classroom instruction. *Journal of Teacher Education, 39*(4), 8–14.

Joyce, B., & Weil, M. (1986). *Models of teaching.* Englewood Cliffs, NJ: Prentice-Hall.

MacLeod, G. R. (1987). Microteaching: Modeling. In M. J. Dunkin (Ed.), *The international encyclopedia of teaching and teacher education* (pp. 720–722). Oxford, UK: Pergamon.

MacLeod, G. R., & McIntyre, G. (1977). Towards a model of microteaching. In D. McIntyre, G. MacLeod, & R. Griffiths (Eds.), *Investigations of microteaching* (pp. 253–263). London: Croom Helm.

Peterson, P., & Peterson, S. (1985, February). *Impromptu teaching model for pre-service teacher preparation.* Paper presented at the annual meeting of the Association of Teacher Educators, Las Vegas, NV.

Willis, J., Hovey, L., & Hovey, K. (1987). *Computer simulations: A source book to learning in an electronic environment.* New York: Garland Publishing.

Yeaney, R. H. (1978). Effects of microteaching with videotaping and strategy analysis on the teaching strategies of preservice science teachers. *Science Education, 62,* 203–207.

Index